To Jones,
my for
good + supportive friend.
Warmly,
Ted

International Political Economy Series

Series Editor
Timothy M. Shaw
Visiting Professor
University of Massachusetts Boston
Boston, MA, USA

Emeritus Professor, University of London, London, UK

The global political economy is in flux as a series of cumulative crises impacts its organization and governance. The IPE series has tracked its development in both analysis and structure over the last three decades. It has always had a concentration on the global South. Now the South increasingly challenges the North as the centre of development, also reflected in a growing number of submissions and publications on indebted Eurozone economies in Southern Europe. An indispensable resource for scholars and researchers, the series examines a variety of capitalisms and connections by focusing on emerging economies, companies and sectors, debates and policies. It informs diverse policy communities as the established trans-Atlantic North declines and 'the rest', especially the BRICS, rise.

More information about this series at
http://www.palgrave.com/gp/series/13996

Anil Hira • Norbert Gaillard
Theodore H. Cohn
Editors

The Failure of Financial Regulation

Why a Major Crisis Could Happen Again

palgrave
macmillan

Editors
Anil Hira
Department of Political Science
Simon Fraser University
Burnaby, BC, Canada

Norbert Gaillard
NG Consulting
Paris, France

Theodore H. Cohn
Department of Political Science
Simon Fraser University
Burnaby, BC, Canada

International Political Economy Series
ISBN 978-3-030-05679-7   ISBN 978-3-030-05680-3   (eBook)
https://doi.org/10.1007/978-3-030-05680-3

Library of Congress Control Number: 2019931019

This Palgrave Macmillan imprint is published by the registered company Springer Nature
Switzerland AG.
The registered company address is: Gewerbestrasse 11, 6330 Cham, Switzerland

Dedicated to Ted (Theodore) Cohn, for his lifetime dedication to the study and teaching of global economy. His tireless work helped provide a strong foundation of knowledge for the next generation of scholars.

Acknowledgements

This volume began with a series of impromptu conversations between Ted Cohn and Anil Hira about how the political economy side of the 2008 crash had generally been neglected in the outpouring of literature and policy papers in its wake. What followed was an effort to find a wide variety of specialists to participate in a project that would help fill this gap. Not all the contributors are reflected in this volume, as we chose to narrow the focus to financial regulation, in order to create more coherence and focus for an academic audience and improve the depth of our analysis. We would like to thank Martin Murillo, Mike Webb, Kathryn Lavelle, Leslie Elliot Armijo, and Michelle Bonner for their valuable contributions to this work. We would also like to thank Simon Fraser University's (SFU) Dean of Arts and Social Sciences, Jane Pulkingham, and the Chair of the Dept. of Political Science, Alexander Moens, for their financial support for a workshop held at SFU in Spring 2017. Thanks are also due to the Western Political Science Association, where we presented our papers in a panel in Vancouver in April 2017. Finally, we would like to thank several anonymous reviewers who helped us improve the overall coherence and introduction to the volume.

Praise for *The Failure of Financial Regulation*

"This book could not be more timely. Little more than a decade after the global financial crisis of 2008, governments are once again loosening the reins over financial markets. The authors of this volume explain why that is a mistake and could invite yet another major crisis. Care is taken to offer meaningful policy recommendations to deal with such looming problems as regulatory capture, moral hazard, and unregulated financial flows."

—Benjamin Cohen, *University of California, Santa Barbara, USA*

"This book examines the fundamental failure of financial regulatory reform efforts since 2008. It is a most prescient and timely work, with the signs of the next potential crisis already appearing in Argentina and Turkey. It mobilises the talents of leading political scientists from several generations, with insights enriched by economists and lawyers. It offers historical depth with a focus on the critical concepts and issues such as moral hazard, banking regulation, the relationship of public and private sector depth, the role of monetary policy, remittances, and offshore finance. It offers sensible suggestions about what reforms are needed now. It speaks poignantly to the contemporary challenges of governing financial instability and anti-globalisation, populist and protectionist pressures."

—John Kirton, *University of Toronto, Canada, and Co-founder of the G7 Research Group*

"One of the major political puzzles of our time is the failure of governments in America and Europe to respond to the global financial crisis with the sort of wholesale regulatory restructuring last seen during the Great Depression of the 1930s. The contributors to this volume show that after the immediate response to the crisis authorities did not address the root causes of the meltdown. What reform there was has been inadequate, and some has been reversed. The authors suggest not having made finance safer risks fostering populism and protectionism when instability strikes again. This book is a valuable antidote to complacency. It should be of great value to policy-makers, scholars and students."

—Timothy J. Sinclair, *University of Warwick, UK*

CONTENTS

1   **Persistent Issues with Financial Regulation**   1
Anil Hira, Norbert Gaillard, and Theodore H. Cohn

2   **Financial Regulation and Monetary Policy: The Spectre of Government Failure**   37
Laurent Dobuzinskis

3   **The Effects of Regulatory Capture on Banking Regulations: A Level-of-Analysis Approach**   71
Theodore H. Cohn

4   **How and Why Moral Hazard Has Distorted Financial Regulation**   111
Norbert Gaillard and Richard J. Michalek

5   **Remittances, Regulation, and Financial Development in Sub-Saharan Africa**   153
James Busumtwi-Sam

6   **Regulatory Mayhem in Offshore Finance: What the
    Panama Papers Reveal**   191
    Anil Hira, Brian Murata, and Shea Monson

7   **Concluding Remarks**   233
    Anil Hira, Norbert Gaillard, and Theodore H. Cohn

Index   247

NOTES ON CONTRIBUTORS

James Busumtwi-Sam is an Associate Professor in the Department of Political Science at Simon Fraser University (SFU) in Canada. His research interests are in international political economy and international organisation with a regional specialisation in the political economy of development and security in sub-Saharan Africa. His publications have examined development assistance and the role of international financial institutions, macroeconomic policy reform and financial liberalisation, global governance and sustainable development, and the political economy of human security and peacebuilding in Africa. He was founding Director of the SFU Institute for Diaspora Research and Engagement (2013–2015). His most recent research examines the conditions affecting diaspora formation and the impact of migrant/diaspora on development and security in Africa.

Theodore H. Cohn is a Professor Emeritus of Political Science at Simon Fraser University (SFU). He received his PhD in Political Science at the University of Michigan. He was a visiting scholar at El Colegio de México and was Chair of the SFU Political Science Department from 1982 to 1987. He has authored and co-edited a number of books, smaller monographs, and articles on international political economy, international trade, global food and agricultural issues, and Canada-US-Mexico relations. The seventh edition of his book *Global Political Economy: Theory and Practice* was published by Routledge in 2016. His other authored books include *Governing Global Trade: International Institutions in Conflict and Convergence* (Ashgate, 2002; paperback ed. published by Routledge in 2017), *The International Politics of*

Agricultural Trade: Canadian-American Relations in a Global Agricultural Context (University of British Columbia Press, 1990), and *Canadian Food Aid: Domestic and Foreign Policy Implications* (University of Denver, 1979). He continues to do research and writing on trade, financial, and monetary relations, and he regularly teaches courses on global political economy to senior adults at SFU.

Laurent Dobuzinskis teaches political science at Simon Fraser University in Burnaby, Canada. His areas of specialisation include public policy, political economy, and the philosophy of social science. His research interests concern the history of ideas and theoretical debates within these areas, with a particular emphasis on classical liberal and libertarian perspectives. He has written extensively and co-edited several books on these issues.

Norbert Gaillard is a French economist and independent consultant (www.norbertgaillard.com). He studied at Sciences Po Paris and Princeton University. He has served as consultant to the International Finance Corporation, the World Bank, the State of Sonora (Mexico), the Organisation for Economic Co-operation and Development (OECD), the European Parliament, and various financial institutions (including a credit rating agency). He has taught at the University of Geneva and the Graduate Institute (Geneva). He is a Euromoney Country Risk expert. His main areas of expertise are public debt and sovereign risk, local government debt and subnational risk, country risk, and credit rating agencies. Norbert has written more than 20 research articles and published three books since 2010.

Anil Hira is a Professor of Political Science at Simon Fraser University in Burnaby, Canada. He is a political economist specialising in industrial, technology, and energy policies for development. He is the editor of the special edition, *Culture and Corruption in Developing States,* published in the *Journal of Developing Societies* in 2016; several chapters and articles on structural adjustment, Latin American finance, and dollarisation; and the article "Irrational Exuberance: An Evolutionary Perspective on the Underlying Causes of the Financial Crisis", published in *Intereconomics: Review of European Economic Policy,* in March/April 2013. He has written extensively about industrial, technology, and energy policy in developing countries. His interests are on climate change strategies for the developing world. Anil is a frequent contributor to media outlets in Canada.

Richard J. Michalek is a New York-based independent legal and financial consultant. He graduated from Columbia University with both a JD and an MBA. Rick is a former senior credit officer at the rating agency Moody's Investors Service in the structured derivatives group. He worked abroad as a securitisation consultant to the New Zealand law firm Chapman Tripp and as an associate attorney in the New York office of Skadden Arps. He has consulted on a number of complex structured derivative litigation matters and continues to consult hedge funds, private equity investors, and government agencies on matters relating to the rating agencies and their processes.

Shea Monson received his master's degree in Political Science from Simon Fraser University and is studying Philosophy at SFU. His research interests include public policy, research methodology, finance, gaming studies, and the philosophy of science. He works as poker player and a consultant in the gaming and entertainment industries.

Brian Murata is a recent graduate of Simon Fraser University's Master in Political Science programme. Brian's research during his MA focused on assessing the economic impact and political interests influencing financial regulation in the post-2007/08 Global Financial Crisis environment, such as the proposed Tobin/Financial Transactions Tax and the Dodd-Frank Act. He is working as a financial policy analyst.

ACRONYMS

ABC	Austrian Business Cycle
ABS	Asset-Backed Securities
AfDB	African Development Bank
AHPIFF	African High-Level Panel on Illicit Financial Flows
AIR	African Institute for Remittances
ARRA	American Recovery and Reinvestment Act
AU	African Union
AUC	African Union Commission
BCBS	Basel Committee on Banking Supervision
BEA	Bureau of Economic Analysis
BEPS	Base Erosion and Profit Shifting Package
BIS	Bank for International Settlements
BVI	British Virgin Islands
CBO	Collateralized Bond Obligation
CDO	Collateralized Debt Obligation
CEO	Chief Executive Officer
CFPB	Consumer Financial Protection Bureau
CFTC	Commodity Futures Trading Commission
CHOICE	Creating Hope and Opportunity for Investors, Consumers and Entrepreneurs
CINB	Continental Illinois National Bank and Trust Company
CMBS	Commercial Mortgage-Backed Securities
CPI	Consumer Price Index
CRA	Credit Rating Agency
CRS	Common Reporting Standard
CSE	Consolidated Supervised Entity
DC	Determination Committee

ECA	Economic Commission for Africa
ECB	European Central Bank
EU	European Union
FASB	Financial Accounting Standards Board
FATCA	Foreign Account Tax Compliance Act
FATF	Financial Action Task Force
FDI	Foreign Direct Investment
FDIC	Federal Deposit Insurance Corporation
FINRA	Financial Industry Regulatory Authority
FIU	Financial Intelligence Unit
FOMC	Federal Open Market Committee
FRB	Federal Reserve Board
FSB	Financial Stability Board
G20	Group of 20
GAO	Government Accountability Office
GDP	Gross Domestic Product
GLBA	Gramm-Leach-Bliley Act
GNP	Gross National Product
GSE	Government-Sponsored Enterprise
ICIJ	International Consortium of Investigative Journalists
IEP	Integrated Estate Plan
IFAD	International Fund for Agricultural Development
IFF	Illicit Financial Flows
IIF	Institute for International Finance
IMF	International Monetary Fund
IPE	International Political Economy
IRB	Internal Ratings-Based
IRR	Internal Rate of Return
IRS	Internal Revenue Service
ISDA	International Swaps and Derivatives Association
LLP	Limited Liability Partnership
LTV	Loan-To-Value
MAP	Mutual Agreement Procedure
MBS	Mortgage-Backed Securities
MNC	Multinational Corporation
MNE	Multinational Enterprise
MTO	Money Transfer Operator
MVT	Money or Value Transfer
NRSRO	Nationally Recognized Statistical Rating Organization
OCC	Office of the Comptroller of the Currency
ODA	Official Development Assistance
ODI	Overseas Development Institute

OECD	Organisation for Economic Co-operation and Development
OPEC	Organization of the Petroleum Exporting Countries
OTC	Over-The-Counter
OTS	Office of Thrift Supervision
PAC	Political Action Committee
PCA	Prompt Corrective Action
PCC	Protected Cell Company
PCF	Private Capital Flows
PM	Prime Minister
QE	Quantitative Easing
REIT	Real Estate Investment Trust
RMBS	Residential Mortgage-Backed Securities
RSP	Remittance Service Provider
S&P	Standard & Poor's
SARS	Suspicious Activity Reports
SBN	Solidarity-Based Network
SDG	Sustainable Development Goals
SEC	Securities and Exchange Commission
SF	Structured Finance
SFAS	Statement of Financial Accounting Standards
SIFI	Systemically Important Financial Institution
SIFMA	Securities Industry and Financial Markets Association
SIV	Structured Investment Vehicle
SMS	Short Message Service
SPV	Special Purpose Vehicle
SWIFT	Society for Worldwide Interbank Financial Telecommunication
TARP	Troubled Asset Relief Program
TBTF	Too Big To Fail
TFTP	Terrorist Finance Tracking Program
TIC	Transparency International Canada
TIEA	Tax Information Exchange Agreement
TJN	Tax Justice Network
UN	United Nations
UNCTAD	United Nations Conference on Trade and Development
VAT	Value-Added Tax
WB	World Bank

LIST OF FIGURES

Fig. 1.1   DJIA, October 1989–November 2017   12
Fig. 1.2   DJIA and US GDP, 1989–2015. Note: 1989 = 100   13
Fig. 4.1   Public and private debts, 1975–2015. Note: Quarterly data   112
Fig. 4.2   Prices of different types of assets, 1975–2015. Note: Index 100
            for 1975. Annual data   138
Fig. 5.1   Remittance channels to and within sub-Saharan Africa   178
Fig. 6.1   FDI stocks, top 9 countries in 2014 (in % of GDP)   199
Fig. 7.1   CDS for Brazil and Russia, July 2007–December 2009   240

CHAPTER 1

Persistent Issues with Financial Regulation

Anil Hira, Norbert Gaillard, and Theodore H. Cohn

INTRODUCTION

The central contention of this collection is that the literature focusing on the 2008 financial crisis and the reforms in its wake miss large, fundamental trends in finance that *preceded and have continued* after the crisis itself. We examine financial regulation in a broader context to make this point. We try to demonstrate that financial regulation at the global and domestic levels remains inadequate on a number of fronts, with each chapter providing a different angle to prove this central point. Most of our chapters focus on US (United States) examples, but we argue that the same issues remain unaddressed at the global level. While we do not claim that the regulatory gaps we discuss are the sole causes of financial crises, we contend that failure to address them inevitably raises the probability that they will occur again, thus exacerbating middle and working classes' anger against finance, capitalism, liberalism, and even democracy (Foroohar 2016).

A. Hira (✉) • T. H. Cohn
Department of Political Science, Simon Fraser University, Burnaby, BC, Canada
e-mail: ahira@sfu.ca; cohn@sfu.ca

N. Gaillard
NG Consulting, Paris, France
e-mail: gaillard@alumni.princeton.edu

© The Author(s) 2019   1
A. Hira et al. (eds.), *The Failure of Financial Regulation*,
International Political Economy Series,
https://doi.org/10.1007/978-3-030-05680-3_1

The failure of regulatory reform at the domestic and global levels can help to explain the political backlash to finance around the world. While the Occupy Wall Street movement has ended, politicians such as New Yorker Donald Trump and UK (United Kingdom) Labour leader Jeremy Corbyn have railed against finance. Although President Trump later brought Wall Street into his administration, claims about corruption on Wall Street were an important part of his election campaign. Reports regarding the evasion of taxes through offshore finance such as those concerning technology giants Apple and Microsoft only add fuel to the tensions evoked by lower wages in the labour market. Furthermore, technology-based leaks such as the Panama and the Paradise Papers have reinforced the perception that financial regulations favour elites to the detriment of middle classes. In the developing world, such leaks have revealed massive corruption through capital outflows from the public sector, with elites investing in a wide range of Western and other offshore assets. These revelations only deepened the ire of Western electorates that no one was held criminally accountable for the questionable and at times fraudulent acts that led to the 2008 crash.

Though the chapters in our volume use different departure points, we organise our analysis of the global financial system in each chapter around four principles. First, we trace the long-term roots of the 2008 financial crisis to regulatory problems in the financial sector dating back decades. Second, we examine the nature of proposed reforms for the financial sector since 2008 and expose their strengths and shortcomings. Third, we focus on the challenges that prevent the building of long-term stability and trust in the US and international financial systems. These challenges include market failure, government failure, regulatory capture, moral hazard, offshore finance, illicit capital flows, fraud, conflicts of interest, and barriers to entry in the financial sector. Fourth, we advance concrete proposals to address these issues. All our chapters are underpinned by the common assertion that the rules of *liberal* capitalism have long been distorted to the benefit of a small group of firms and individuals.[1] Our recommendations promote fair competition, simple regulatory rules, uncompromising regulatory practices, and greater cooperation among policy makers at the international level.

---

[1] We contrast *liberal* capitalism and *finance* capitalism. The two systems have many features in common (with respect to property rights, free price system, free trade, etc.). However, in *finance* capitalism, the role and the influence of financial institutions are so disproportionate that they tend to affect and even dominate the interests of other economic sectors and taxpayers.

We begin with an illustration to demonstrate that a series of financial reforms have overlooked the fundamental issues of financial regulation for a long period, going back more than a century. We argue that there are deeper issues with financial regulation that have never been adequately considered.

HISTORICAL PRECEDENTS AND NAGGING PROBLEMS FROM FINANCIAL HISTORY

While it is beyond the scope of this collection to review the entire history of financial crises and the factors behind them, a few illustrative notes will help to demonstrate that the regulatory issues we discuss are nothing new. In other words, though the financial system itself is ever evolving, the fundamental weaknesses that we focus on have not changed.

In early US history, banking was largely regulated at the state level. An important regulatory development came naturally, through the establishment of Clearinghouse Associations among banks to provide liquidity in crises. These associations took hold around 1857 and were sometimes matched by deposit insurance at the state level. Hendrickson (2011, 34) considers that they also were conducive to moral hazard, as banks experiencing a run would rely on others to bail them out. Financial crises occurred on a regular basis in the nineteenth century, most notably in 1837 and 1857, and a series of panics from the 1870s through 1907. The post-Civil War turmoil forced policymakers to find a new means of intervention to create stability in finance, a situation that has been repeated throughout history.

This came at the end of the nineteenth century. The conclusion of some was that the US needed an official gold standard to create confidence in the currency, the ability to defend it, and a supposedly automatic adjustment of currency exchange rates in response to deficits or surpluses. The adoption of the Gold Standard in 1879 paved the way for the hegemony of financial institutions—unshakeable "pro-gold" forces—to the detriment of big farmers and, to a lesser extent, of industrialists (Frieden 2015, 49–103). A strong debate around using a mixed currency reserve, including the famous campaign for including silver by Democratic candidate for President William Jennings Bryant in 1896, ensued. However, the gold standard was ultimately adopted in 1900 (Friedman and Schwartz 1963, 111–120).

The 1907 crisis is of particular interest because it has been traced to the attempt by brokerage houses to corner the stock of the United Copper Company (Hendrickson 2011, 94). When banks were linked to stock price manipulation, bank runs ensued, reflecting a collapse of confidence in the system—an early example of regulatory evasion and opportunism in the sense that the trusts involved, like modern day nonbank financial institutions were not covered under banking laws. Here again, the result was an increase in the scope of regulation without examining the underlying causes of the crisis—though clearly identified by the Pujo Committee's investigation on the "money trust" (1912–1913). The Federal Reserve Bank (Fed) was established in 1913 to substitute for the activity of the Clearinghouses. Shortly after, in 1914, the Fed had to bail out New York City which was close to bankruptcy, in what could be regarded as an early illustration of moral hazard, in the guise of "too big to fail" (Silber 2007, 4). By the early 1920s, new deposit and lending requirements promoted a wave of consolidating mergers among banks (Hendrickson 2011, 26). This period of US history (from the 1880s through the 1910s), also known as the "Robber Barons" era, was rife with familiar concerns regarding financial concentration and successful attempts, such as those by John D. Rockefeller's allies James Stillman and Jacob Schiff to bypass regulations—for example, those preventing banks from owning equities and branching across state lines (Rockoff 2000, 681–683).

The 1920s are notorious for the creation of an asset bubble in the New York Stock Exchange. This reflects an early example of under-regulation amidst financial evolution; in this instance, the beginning of the shift of the centre of global financial gravity from the UK to the US. Exhaustion, both material and emotional, in Europe, along with war reparations and wartime market share gains amidst the blooming of manufacturing, gave the US economy a huge boost. Eventually, the irrational expectations discussed by Reinhart and Rogoff (2009) took over, with stock prices soaring well above reasonable levels. Thousands of investors were duped into believing that their savings would multiply forever, without understanding the fundamentally speculative nature of the bubble. The evolution of finance also revealed the limited ability of monetary policy to steady a mass market whose innovative complexity was underestimated by regulators, and an underlying panic that markets alone were unable to resolve. Precursors of "shadow banks" took form in financial institutions that operated outside of the Federal Reserve System, and flooded markets with liquidity, despite efforts by the Fed to tighten credit

(Duca 2017, 50–64). Starting in 1929–1930, the collapse of thousands of banks led to a series of important and equally resounding reforms. Keynesian policies were de facto adopted as the Roosevelt administration became a major source of credit and confidence along with fiscal stimulus and stringent financial regulations. The most famous legislative responses were the Glass-Steagall Act and the creation of the Federal Deposit Insurance Corporation (FDIC). Glass-Steagall, enacted in 1933, was designed to insulate commercial banking activities from investment activities. The FDIC sought to reassure ordinary depositors by guaranteeing deposits even in the event of bank failure. According to Friedman and Schwartz (1963, 442), such insurance schemes would have reduced the severity of the 1929 crash had they been in place before the crisis.

However, every rose has its thorn. Deposit insurance and the expectations of bailouts started cementing moral hazard as a cornerstone of financial regulation (Grossman 1992, 800–821). Moreover, the separation of banking from investment activities indirectly contributed to the financialisation of the economy, where the financial sector became a dominant target as well as a source of investment. Furthermore, the promotion of investment houses created greater concentration in the financial sector, leading to the envy of bankers seeking greater returns, even if at higher risk. In this respect, the rise and fall of Salomon Brothers—well known for its innovative and aggressive strategy in the 1980s—is very telling (Mayer 1993). In addition, the possibility for commercial banks to engage in certain investment businesses from the 1980s erased the traditional line between banking and investment, as transactions between the two sectors became intertwined, even before the repeal of the Glass-Steagall Act in 1999. What is needed is not a blind Glass-Steagall Act or a deposit insurance system, but a regulatory framework where financial institutions are involved in a limited set of business activities tied to reasonable performance. Our thoughts are consistent with Kindleberger ([1978] 2005) who points out that regulation has consistently failed to anticipate irrational, herding behaviour that often leads to runs on commodities and asset bubbles. Once the bubble bursts, panic ensues.

After a quiescent postwar period, banking crises resurfaced in the 1970s. In 1974, the 20th largest bank in the US, Franklin National, failed. The bank had made a series of bad loans and speculated in the currency markets to try to recoup the losses. The Federal Reserve stepped in and in the process acquired over $700 million of foreign exchange liabilities (Hendrickson 2011, 178). In general, Keynesian spending policies were overused throughout the period, to the point where the inflationary crises of the 1970s and ever-expanding government debt have decreased its capabilities and credibility. In fairness, Keynesian policy was never really followed, as it has proved politically impossible, in general, to accrue surpluses during boom periods. But our main point here is that this bailout reflected a further cementing of moral hazard into the financial system, a vulnerability that Keynesianism did not resolve.

On the global level, financial innovation continued to outpace regulators (Van Zon 2016). The movement towards flexible exchange rates, the gradual freeing of capital controls, and the Organization of the Petroleum Exporting Countries (OPEC) oil crisis accelerated the creation of a global financial system where vast pools of capital flow in and out of economies, notwithstanding the creation of the 1974 Basel Accord on liquidity reserve requirements. As discussed in Hira et al.'s chapter, offshore banks, called Eurobanks, had been set up in the 1960s to help manage foreign exchange for corporations and individuals. They built upon the innovation of new financial instruments, such as commercial paper, interbank reserve transfers, and higher rate "jumbo" certificates of deposit (Guttmann 2009, 51). They were outside of regular state regulatory authority, mostly in islands off the UK, and therefore could offer services, including loans, at more competitive rates. Following OPEC's new strategy, the price of oil quadrupled in 1973, sending a shock wave through Western economies. More importantly, the proceeds of the increase, accruing mostly to Middle Eastern monarchies and dictatorships, created large pools of capital in less developed financial systems. This propelled further the development of offshore banking and large volumes of lending of petrodollars through Western banks to developing countries, most of them oil importers. Ongoing concerns about US inflation and an additional oil price shock in 1979 led to austerity programmes in the West, which raised interest rates precipitously. Such moves cut inflation successfully but triggered severe economic slowdown in industrialised countries and, for many, created a serious public debt that continues to constrain fiscal policy options. Much of the South was wracked by a debt/financial crisis as rates adjusted. As we discuss throughout the volume, while monetary policy was apt to cut inflation, regulatory policy failed to evolve alongside it.

Beginning in the 1980s, the gospel of deregulation spread around the world. In the US, among other changes, depository insurance requirements were loosened, and banking services could be more easily offered across state lines. The development of new financial instruments such as money market accounts, with less insurance but offering higher rates, helped to spur a wave of financial innovation exacerbating leverage strategies. These changes were met by banking failures in the US, culminating in the savings and loan crisis in the 1980s. Opening the era of "too big to fail" (TBTF), the FDIC bailed out 1010 banks from 1980 to 1990, including the massive Continental Illinois failure in 1984. In most cases, neither customers nor bankers experienced any consequences for bad decisions (Hendrickson 2011, 196).

The 1980s witnessed another spread of innovation, as mutual funds and pension funds began to pool household capital for larger investments, and financial institutions began to create hedge funds to lower risk on investment bets. In the 1990s, new innovations in debt instruments led to the securitisation revolution, whereby loans could be repackaged as investment vehicles with varying levels of risk (Hill 1996). Only a few authors presaged the regulatory challenges of the new financial instruments (Coleman 1996, 238). Sovereign debt crises that spilt over in the 1980s were largely solved by the 1990s through a variety of patchwork solutions that contributed to the boom of sovereign bond markets and rendered many governments dependent on credit rating agencies (Gaillard 2011, 9–10). These early crises, while resolved in time through ad hoc vehicles such as Brady bonds in the case of Mexico and other emerging countries, revealed once again that globalisation was outpacing financial regulation. Private actors were not alone in evolving, for example, a widespread proliferation of sovereign wealth funds developed from the 1990s (Yi-chong and Bahgat 2010). Cohen (2009, 714) estimates these at $3.9 trillion as of 2008 and growing fast, with at least 40 countries participating. The funds are tied to governments, including Russia and China, and reinforce our doubts about economists' easy separation of markets and politics.

The development of a capitalist China, the crash of the Japanese real estate bubble, and the fall of the Soviet Union created new challenges for the financial order in the 1990s. The global financial system showed its continuing vulnerability to runs that could be internationally transmitted through financial contagion, such as the Asian financial crisis which began with a massive run on Thailand's *baht* currency in 1997. Several authors note that the Asian financial crisis was marked by regulatory capture of governments and international institutions by firms that expected subsidisation for questionable industrial projects and bailouts in the event of failures, leading to morally hazardous decisions (Calomiris 1998). These were accompanied by a property asset bubble, enabled through easy credit, similar to the run up to the 2008 crisis (Corsetti et al. 1999).

Speculative runs periodically surfaced in the period up to the 2008 crisis, such as the collapse of Long-Term Capital Management (LTCM) hedge fund in 1998, which required the Fed to intervene. LTCM marked the mainstreaming of automated trading based on quantitative models of stock prices, which were shown once again to have a limited ability to deal with extreme events and panics. This was followed by the "dot com bubble" of 2001, whereby emerging tech stocks tumbled from lofty heights. In short, what we see is that the 2008 crisis has deep roots in regard to the continuation of fundamental weaknesses that persist and evolve with changes in technology and financial practices. More importantly, *none of these earlier crises presaging the 2008 meltdown resulted in major changes in regulatory approaches.*

EXACERBATING FACTORS IN THE YEARS PRECEDING THE 2008 CRISIS

Stable US monetary policy under the stewardship of Alan Greenspan (1987–2006) convinced many scholars that the global financial system could absorb such shocks. The rise of the Chinese economy as a vast store of global capital accumulated through trade surpluses and the expansion of large mutual and pension funds gave some hope that global liquidity was sufficient. Moreover, the development of new financial instruments (e.g., derivatives, futures, options, etc.) led to the belief that adequate hedges against any downturn were in place. In fact, during the Greenspan years, US and international investors took advantage not only of such financial sophistication but also of a low volatility of business cycle fluctuations, largely fuelled by low interest rates and more predictable monetary policy decisions. This "Great Moderation" era—a term coined by James Stock and Mark Watson (2003) and used by Greenspan—ended with the 2008 financial crash, revealing the fundamental flaws of the global financial system and, as we argue in this volume, the continuing failure to address the persistent issues facing financial regulation.

Greenspan had faith in markets to self-correct. In a speech to the Futures Industry Association on March 19, 1999, Greenspan lauded the emergence of derivatives markets as a way to spread risks, as bets were taken on both sides of an event. Greenspan eerily pointed out that the derivatives market and the mathematical models on which they were based were sound, but *only if* they included historical data, including "low probability" events such as previous financial panics. In fact, they did not include such events, and the temporary success of the quantitative models may have been due to their creation and use during an asset bubble rather than any underlying breakthrough in modelling company value (Hira 2013). When Brooksley Born famously suggested that her agency, the Commodity Futures Trading Commission, begin to regulate over-the-counter (OTC) derivatives, she was dismissed by Greenspan and a wide array of other economists—including Larry Summers, who would help to direct the Obama administration's recovery plan a decade later.[2] Similarly, the strong possibility of a coming housing crisis was pointed out by Case-Shiller's housing index and by Raghuram Rajan in a prescient 2005 speech to economic leaders that was widely panned at the time. Yet, in a speech to mortgage bankers on September 26 of the same year, this time to the American Bankers Association, Greenspan rejected the dangers of a housing bubble. Clearly, most economists not only ignored the irrationality of markets but also their own irrationality, especially in regard to how markets are interconnected (Hira 2013). This is reflected in the continuing ad hoc and haphazard approach to regulation, from Greenspan's decision to bail out LTCM in 1998 to the movement towards "quantitative easing," generating essentially zero or negative interest rates in the post-crisis period, effectively politicising monetary policy. In none of these cases were the underlying persistent issues we discuss in this volume—namely, the growing issues of moral hazard and regulatory capture, the untrammelled globalisation of finance, and linkage of markets across sectors and geography—seriously addressed. If anything, Greenspan's speeches were particularly notable as they were directed to the interest groups the Fed was designated to regulate.

A primary issue is the failure to manage the financial globalisation process beginning with the breakdown of the Bretton Woods era of fixed exchange rates in the early 1970s.[3] As Benjamin J. Cohen explains (2008), state-centric power has diffused, but global financial regulatory institutions alone are not currently capable of ensuring harmonisation and stability

---

[2] See https://www.cftc.gov/sites/default/files/opa/speeches/opaborn-33.htm and http://www.washingtonpost.com/wp-dyn/content/article/2009/05/25/AR2009052502108.html [accessed Aug. 13, 2018].

[3] In 2016, Jacques De Larosière, Managing Director of the International Monetary Fund (IMF) during 1978–1987, explained that the collapse of the Bretton Woods system had had incalculable negative consequences on the world economy. See https://www.odilejacob.fr/catalogue/sciences-humaines/economie-et-finance/cinquante-ans-de-crises-financieres_9782738134028.php

of the financial system over the long run. Simply put, regulation at the global level has been too limited to deal with the evolution of finance (Goldbach 2015). In the early 1980s, the expectation was that the Bretton Woods institutions, such as the International Monetary Fund (IMF), would continue to set standards through managing a regime including private financial actors—in the case of the IMF, avoiding balance of payments problems (Cohen 1982, 475). However, the notion of international public and private sector harmony is increasingly being questioned (Moschella 2010, 166). The emergence of China as a major surplus holder matched by US deficits has stretched that norm. Moreover, the regulation misses the vast growth of offshore finance where, with little to no scrutiny, trillions of dollars—coming from developed as well as developing countries—are funnelled, areas where international financial organisations have little information and limited influence. Regulations also do not deal with changes in technology, from electronic money transfers that enable corporations to shift money among entities to cryptocurrencies such as Bitcoin or remittances that are under the radar of national regulatory authorities. These flaws in international financial regulation are analysed in two chapters of this volume. Hira et al. focus on the Panama and Paradise Papers scandals, while Busumtwi-Sam examines why an excessive percentage of remittance flows sent by African immigrants are diverted from recipient countries.

At the domestic level, regulation struggles with the politicisation of finance. The unmistakable influence of lobby groups is found throughout the regulatory system, from personnel to regulatory approaches to major campaign donations. The "revolving door" between regulatory bodies and the financial industry also often places bankers in regulatory positions, with similar world views to those they are regulating. This issue, connected to the "regulatory capture" problem, is studied in Cohn's chapter. In a complementary chapter, Gaillard and Michalek explore how de facto and de jure regulators have accelerated the growth of TBTF banks, thus exacerbating moral hazard. As Reinhart and Rogoff (2009, 282) suggest, an entirely new global regulatory institution is needed, one that would be divorced from ubiquitous financial lobby groups at the domestic level. Not only does lobbying impede objective regulation, it also decreases the possibilities that domestic authorities will agree to regulatory harmonisation and enforcement at the global level. Recall that one of the purported motivations of the Brexit vote was the objection of UK firms to new European Union (EU) regulations on banking transparency.

The lack of transparency and harmonisation at the global level has compounding implications for monetary and fiscal policy. Regulatory authorities have moved back somewhat from the largely pro-deregulation perspective in the years leading up to the 2008 crisis to a more regulated model, yet there is evidence that they remain reluctant to act against the wishes of the financial sector. Rather, regulation is often oriented towards the financial sector's interests to the potential detriment of the rest of the economy. Interest rates remain low throughout the West, even amidst blatant signs of asset price bubbles (e.g., major stock market indices and housing markets in the two biggest economies, namely, the US and China). The Dow Jones Industrial Average (DJIA) index has increased, on average, more than 1% a month since the US economy recovered from recession in July 2009 vs. 0.45% during the previous business cycle expansion (i.e., December 2001–November 2007).[4] Fiscal policy reform is increasingly difficult given the limitations that states have in taxing corporations that can move money offshore. Several of our authors show that three of the main issues leading up to the 2008 crisis—regulatory capture, moral hazard, and offshore finance—have not been adequately addressed.

THE CRASH OF 2008

The 2008 crash was the worst financial disaster for industrialised countries since the Great Depression. The events leading up to and after the crisis are all too familiar: the US subprime mortgage crisis erupted in July 2007 and threatened some financial institutions (e.g., Northern Rock and several Icelandic banks). In March 2008, the US administration bailed out New York-based investment bank Bear Stearns and arranged for its purchase by JP Morgan. In September 2008, the US government intervened again to save government-affiliated mortgage behemoths Freddie Mac and Fannie Mae. That same month, the crisis culminated with the collapse of Lehman Brothers. The aftermath was a series of bailouts in the US and the EU, including large companies whose credit was frozen, such as General Motors and Chrysler. The bailouts averted the implosion of the world economic and financial system but left a number of lingering questions. While housing and employment markets have recovered somewhat, there remains great insecurity and uncertainty in Western countries as illustrated by the rise of non-traditional politicians—such as Donald

[4] Authors' calculations based on nber.org and measuringworth.com

Trump, Marine Le Pen, and Matteo Salvini; the persistent economic fragility of most Southern European economies; and the inextricable negotiations around Brexit.

We can graphically observe the scale of the 2008 financial crash in Fig. 1.1 through a look at the evolution of the DJIA since October 1989. After a sharp fall in 2007–2009, the DJIA recovered quickly and exceeded its historical high as early as March 2013. Since then, the index has continued to rise, spectacularly so after the election of Donald Trump in November 2016.

Figure 1.2 compares the evolution of the DJIA and the US gross domestic product (GDP) for 1989–2015. The financial economy and real economy have systematically diverged during boom periods, with the former growing much faster than the latter. This pattern helps explain why the power of finance has been increasingly questioned since the Great Recession of 2007–2009. Criticism has taken various forms. The fiercest ones came from social movements (e.g., Occupy Wall Street) and populist politicians (from Bernie Sanders to Donald Trump), but academics also expressed concern about the excesses of finance. For some scholars, finance capitalism has been exacerbating inequalities (Piketty 2014). For other

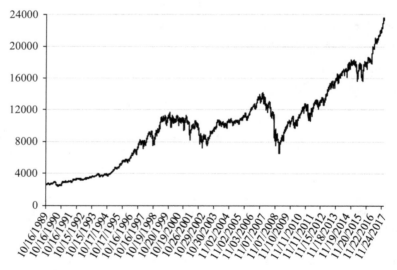

Fig. 1.1 DJIA, October 1989–November 2017. (Source: www.measuringworth. com)

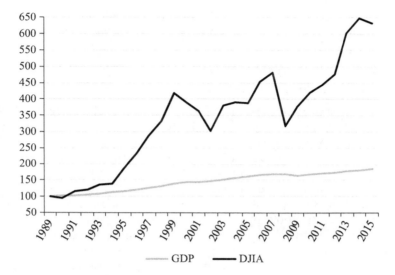

Fig. 1.2 DJIA and US GDP, 1989–2015. Note: 1989 = 100. (Source: Federal Reserve and www.measuringworth.com)

economists, it has contributed to the over-leveraging of Western economies (Mian and Sufi 2014) and harmed R&D-intensive industries (Cecchetti and Kharroubi 2015). Beyond such debates and controversies, it appears that the literature on the Great Recession covers a wider array of issues, much of it overlooking the long-term challenges posed by finance and financial regulation.

What we have seen throughout this review is a failure to confront long-term, persistent problems of financial regulation. From 1907 to the present, insiders have consistently found ways to manipulate markets for their own gains at the expense of economic health. This is not an idiosyncratic feature of the neoliberal paradigm, as some populist politicians and thinkers suggest. Regulators, in turn, have repeatedly missed market signals and used blunt instruments to deal with crises (e.g., bailouts and lax monetary policy that generally fuel the asset bubble that follows). At this point, mounting government debt makes another major Keynesian fiscal stimulus unlikely, and interest rates cannot go much lower, rendering monetary policy ineffective in the event of another economic slowdown. Thus, our intention in this volume is to shed light on the persistent issues that lead up to and fuel financial crises, ones that are more direct causes rather than symptoms underlying the weakness of financial regulation. Only when these weaknesses are addressed can we truly stabilise financial systems.

What the Literature Does and Does Not Tell Us About the Sources and Solutions to the 2008 Crash

The first questions surround the causes of the crisis itself. There is a vigorous "tell all" set of books by those in the eye of the storm, and those critics who point fingers at what they see as a "rigged" system. Such books include *All the Devils are Here* (Penguin Press, 2010) by Bethany McLean and Joe Nocera, and *The Big Short* (Norton, 2010) by Michael Lewis (made into a film); apologetic approaches such as *On the Brink* (Business Plus, 2010) by Henry Paulson, and journalistic stories such as *Too Big to Fail* (Viking Press, 2009) by Andrew Ross Sorkin. Critics such as McLean and Nocera illustrate the voices of the Occupy movement, capturing the sense of grievance by those who suffered the worst consequences of the crisis—often losing their homes and jobs. Such grievances, which have some foundation, have led to a cultural set of sub-narratives about the greed of Wall Street and "the 1%," reflected in media products such as *The Wolf of Wall Street*, *Inside Job*, and *Billions*. The anti-establishment movement generally views the corruption of politics as stemming in good part from the financial sector's growing influence.

Economists have written an important body of literature on policy or regulatory mistakes in regard to the crisis. Regulation is the crucial arena in which policy makers set laws, rules, and enforcement procedures for institutions and markets. The most prominent of these studies is Carmen Reinhart and Kenneth Rogoff's *This Time is Different* (Princeton University Press, 2009), which provides a comparative historical perspective on financial crises. Economists Nouriel Roubini, Raghuram Rajan, Robert Shiller, Joseph Stiglitz, and Alan Blinder also have written important volumes on the causes of the crisis, offering diverse diagnoses ranging from the development of volatile new financial instruments to the inability to recognise asset (housing) bubbles. Many of these books are rather short term in perspective, focused on the events leading up to and in the aftermath of the 2008 meltdown. Reinhart and Rogoff have received acclaim precisely for providing a long-term view including a database on historical financial crises. However, they abstain from advancing solutions designed to prevent future crises beyond greater stopgaps for the system during meltdowns and warning systems around asset bubbles. There is an equally large empirical literature by experts regarding the 2008 financial crisis itself, which covers a range of topics. Many studies deal with the nature of the housing crisis, related to subprime mortgages (Mian and Sufi 2009). Others focus on how to measure and ensure stability in banking liquidity (Cornett et al. 2011); the nature of financial contagion, with crises spreading from one sector or one economy to another (Aloui et al. 2011; Longstaff 2010); and new financial instruments such as those related to securitisation (Keys et al. 2010).

In terms of diagnosis, much of the academic literature is preoccupied with the housing bubble in the US. Some experts have examined the failure of government-backed mortgage lenders and guarantors Freddie Mac and Fannie Mae (Acharya et al. 2011). Other economists have analysed how mortgage debt acted as an "anti-insurance" system, concentrating "the risks on those least able to bear it" (Mian and Sufi 2014, 30). They have also blamed the Federal Housing Finance Agency for its opposition to any restructuring of mortgage debts in the early 2010s (Mian and Sufi 2014, 140). Another set of contentions surrounds financial innovation that amplified the housing bubble. The issue of new instruments, such as residential mortgage-backed securities (RMBS), commercial mortgage-backed securities (CMBS), and collateralised debt obligations (CDOs) mirrored increasing predatory lending and leveraged risk-taking strategies among financial institutions (Bookstaber 2007; Crotty 2009). The common refrain in the literature is that these instruments changed the fundamental nature of finance.[5] In the case of housing, they removed the natural due diligence of the lender through ownership of the collateral to be vigilant in vetting borrowers. As new financial instruments often included a mixture of subprime and prime mortgages, they became increasingly difficult to evaluate (Benmelech and Dlugosz 2009). Moreover, there could be multiple owners of the same mortgage, leaving responsibility for the soundness of the transaction unclear. In this volume, we explore these questions from a different perspective. Our contention, which goes against much of the reactive nature of the literature, is that such problems are long term in nature, preceding and continuing well beyond the 2008 crisis.

A second set of questions concerns the best ways to exit from the crisis and restore economic growth. This, of course, depends upon one's diagnosis

---

[5] It is worth noting that the development of electronic currencies and internet-based trading accelerated financial innovation.

of the causes. For some, the market was not allowed to work, resulting in TBTF financial institutions becoming a source of vulnerability (Dowd 2009). Others see TBTF as a sign of under-regulation, and the capture of the state by financial interests (Wilmarth 2010). In either case, regulation is clearly a centre of discussion, and we therefore highlight it as the core theme for our volume.

In terms of improving recovery, there has been a vigorous debate between neoliberal and Keynesian economists, as reflected in the controversy between austerity and stimulus/debt, reminiscent of that during the Great Depression. While several countries, including the US, created stimulus programmes in the wake of the 2008 crisis, there has also been pressure for austerity, notably in the UK and imposed by the EU on the heavily indebted European countries. Concerns about mounting public debts and doubts about long-term benefits of potential stimulus programmes have paralysed most developed economies. In fact, stimulus programmes are usually oriented towards short-term "shovel-ready" projects, which are unlikely to show long-term repeatable results. These tend to be infrastructure projects, which, once built, will likely be taken for granted, unless they offer completely new services. The latter, such as former President Barack Obama's idea of building high-speed rail corridors, are quite costly and lack a strong existing constituency and so are unlikely to be built. More likely are what will come across as "pork barrel" spending projects for which there are local politician counterparts. The nature of the stimulus is therefore so diffuse that it is difficult to claim or expect visible or measurable long-term benefits. Moreover, the continuing sense of economic insecurity in Western countries, despite positive macroeconomic indicators, suggests that we have not yet fully recovered. There is no appetite for another large stimulus programme; in fact tax cuts are a much easier road to follow, despite their historical record of ineffectiveness. Moreover, the lack of response to continuing low interest rates also puts neoliberals in a more tenuous position. Thus, both sides have ratcheted up their demands. Keynesian-inspired advocates argue that a more progressive rate structure for the personal income tax, more public spending, and more regulation are the solutions (Krugman 2012; Stiglitz 2012). Neoliberals support austerity measures and consider that tax cuts, deregulation, and the reduction of the fiscal role of the state will "free up" the market and business growth for economic recovery (Alesina et al. 2015; Aslund and Djankov 2017). Our perspective in this volume goes beyond these two approaches. We argue that a sustained recovery is contingent upon long-run changes in the nature of finance by curtailing the power of financial institutions and reforming the practices followed by regulatory bodies.

A third set of questions addresses political issues and relates to critical charges about the role of finance in creating a sense of unfairness around growing inequality. In this area, there is a large literature involving campaign finance reform in the US (see Hasen 2016). One of the Achilles' heels of Hillary Clinton's 2016 presidential campaign was her acceptance of large speaking fees from Wall Street. It is clear that the "financialisation" of society at large has become a controversial issue. Whereas finance has traditionally been viewed as a vehicle to enable consumers and businesses to thrive, it is now a vehicle for making profits through bets on the future of everything, from traditional markets to elections (see Foroohar 2016). While we do not engage directly in political discussion, much of our volume attempts to deal with such issues in a more careful and analytical way than the political discourse. We argue from a variety of perspectives that the financial sector is inherently political in its allocation of capital throughout the economy. Both interventionist and laissez-faire approaches create major issues for the direction in which capital is invested, and at what rates. Thus, an important part of our concern is around the *governance* of finance. Our main focus is on the fundamental role played by regulation, avoiding largely values-driven questions on the "macro level" that require political discourse and elections for resolution, as well as "micro-level" questions at the industry or firm level that require access to financial decision-making at the company level (typically major financial institutions), which is closed off to researchers.

The paradox is that the "micro-level" approach has led to various studies and proposals aimed to enhance national as well as international financial regulations. For example, in 2009, G20 leaders agreed that: "All standardised OTC [over-the-counter] derivative contracts should be traded on exchanges or electronic trading platforms, where appropriate, and cleared through central counterparties by the end of 2012 at the latest. OTC derivative contracts should be reported to trade repositories. Non-centrally cleared contracts should be subject to higher capital requirements." The Financial Stability Board (FSB) was asked to regularly assess implementation and whether it was sufficient to improve transparency in the derivatives markets, mitigate systemic risk, and protect against market abuse (FSB 2017, 1).[6] In the US, the Volcker rule—which was advanced

---

[6] The FSB is a reformed version of the Financial Stability Forum, but with a more formal charter and a small staff, to organise basic transparency and liquidity standards.

in 2010 and came into effect in 2014—prohibited banks from conducting certain investment activities with their own accounts (ban on proprietary trading). It also limited their ownership of equity funds and hedge funds. In the UK, the Vickers Report (Independent Commission on Banking 2011) recommended higher capital requirements for retail banks, ring-fencing of UK banks' retail banking operations, and measures to increase competition in the banking sector. The Liikanen Report (2012) made a series of similar proposals for the EU banking sector. Proprietary trading and other significant trading activities need to be assigned to a separate legal entity; the use of designated bail-in instruments should be priori-tised; and more robust risk weights in the determination of minimum capital standards and more consistent treatment of risk in internal models are required. Even former regulators have expressed their views about what good regulatory rules should look like (Davies 2015; Turner 2016).[7]

Although we are concerned about all these issues, we remain sceptical about the way they are being addressed. Derivatives markets, banks' capi-tal requirements, and internal risk models are eminently *technical and complex*. Such complexity seems to have outpaced the ability of de facto and de jure regulators to evaluate risk. A striking illustration is the failure of credit rating agencies (CRAs) and the Securities and Exchange Commission (SEC) to rate and supervise, respectively, structured finance deals. However, we do not think that *technical and complex* regulations are the right answers. In this respect, our views are in line with those expressed by Andrew Haldane, Chief Economist at the Bank of England, who explained that "the type of complex regulation developed over recent decades might not just be costly and cumbersome but sub-optimal for crisis control" (Haldane 2012). Our convictions are supported by the facts that: (i) complex regulatory rules inevitably contain loopholes; (ii) regula-tory bodies lack staff and investigatory power to enforce such rules; and (iii) even if these bodies have enough resources, their action is likely to be hindered by regulatory capture and conflicts of interest problems.

While the approach in much of the economic literature tends to ignore long-term persistent causes and effects in pursuit of debates around appro-priate instruments and the like, much of the political science/economy literature tends to be excessively "macro," devoting too little attention to the question of regulation. Very few research works provide a detailed analysis of the financial crisis and the politics behind it. For example,

---

[7] Davies and Turner are both ex-chairman of the UK's Financial Services Authority.

Jonathan Kirshner's *American Power after the Financial Crisis* (Cornell University Press, 2014) is a very interesting study focusing on the long-term decline of US power in international relations terms. However, he does not examine the details of the financial crisis, suggesting that it resulted mainly from "market fundamentalism." Another general work in the critical vein is Philip Mirowski's book *Never Let A Serious Crisis Go to Waste: How Neoliberalism Survived the Financial Meltdown* (Verso, 2013). In *The System Worked: How the World Stopped Another Great Depression* (Oxford University Press, 2014), Daniel Drezner explains that global economic governance worked well, as the worst scenarios of financial collapse were avoided. American leadership and the acceptance of globalisation show the resilience of regulation and ideas above pecuniary interests, according to Drezner. Special editions of *New Political Economy* in 2010 (Vol. 15, Issue 1) and 2015 (Vol. 20, Issue 3) on the political economy of the crisis also take broad views of the crisis, seeing it as symptomatic of a wider crisis in capitalism, including the dysfunctionality of burgeoning debt taken on by Western consumers. The 2010 edition recognises the emergence of financial globalisation in a historical context and the financial innovations around securitisation related to the financial crisis. Several other publications are critical—but at a very "macro level"—of the global financial system and growing inequality.

A smaller number of authors have scrutinised regulation mainly at the "meso level," comparable to our approach. Keynesian economist James Crotty argues that incoherent deregulation and perverse incentives for risk-taking in regulation are some of the causes behind the crash. He also points to financial innovation, including new securitisation vehicles which led to "dangerously" high risk-taking and leverage in the financial system. Crotty (2009) and some of the authors in this volume (e.g., Gaillard and Michalek) share similar diagnoses, but Crotty's perspective is more tightly focused on US regulation than ours. Timothy Sinclair's 2010 *New Political Economy* article as part of the aforementioned collection points to the need to study regulation, including the problem of credit rating agencies. It is in the same vein as our work, though our authors focus more on a detailed analysis of regulation and less on the state of capitalism (see the chapters by Dobuzinskis, Cohn, and Gaillard and Michalek). Robert Guttmann's 2009 article in the *International Journal of Political Economy* examines the role of global deregulation and financial innovation in creating asset bubbles. It provides useful historical context for our work. There are several articles in the *Review of International Political Economy* that take a similar approach to ours. For example, Matthias Thiemann (2014) highlights the problems stemming from the lack of international regulation around shadow banking, a theme picked up from a different angle in two of our chapters (see the chapters by Hira et al. and Busumtwi-Sam). Sharman (2017) looks at Liechtenstein and the Seychelles through a value chain perspective. Golub et al.'s (2015) examination of regulatory approaches in the US Federal Reserve is consistent with our analysis of regulatory capture. Eric Helleiner, Stefano Pagliari, and Hubert Zimmerman's edited volume, *Global Finance in Crisis: The Politics of International Regulatory Change* (Routledge, 2009), takes a similar approach to the one proposed here, though most of the chapters are focused on individual countries and the topics covered are different.

Helleiner's 2014 offering, *The Status Quo Crisis: Global Financial Governance After the 2008 Financial Meltdown* (Oxford University Press, 2014), is an important contribution through its examination of potential organisational designs for achieving global financial cooperation after the crisis, principally US-EU relations. Another significant book is Tony Porter's edited volume, *Transnational Financial Regulation after the Crisis* (Routledge, 2014). The chapters focus on the complexity of financial governance, involving national and international rules, public and private institutions, and the challenges this complexity has posed for reform since the 2008 financial crisis.

A fourth set of research works has focused on ethical issues. Nielsen (2010) argues that the Great Recession was mainly driven by the Schumpeterian high-leverage finance capitalism model. For him, the growing discrepancy between economic performance and moral judgements has led to excessive leverage and "massive destruction of wealth" rather than "creative destruction" (Nielsen 2010, 300). In a complementary article, Graafland and van de Ven (2011) blame top managers in the finance industry for their lack of ethics. Concretely, they consider that bankers should (i) raise transparency in their dealings; (ii) pay more attention to their clients, employees, and the society at large; (iii) reduce their risk-taking and leverage; and (iv) cut the amounts of bonuses and stock options. Roemer (2012) goes even farther in his criticism of laissez-faire capitalism: he fears that, unless there is a significant change in the mindset and the *social ethos* of American politicians as well as citizens, there may be a major economic and political crisis in the US. This shock will likely spread to the rest of the world. Claassen (2015) has a different perspective as he focuses on moral hazard between states and banks. This problem has arisen in a context that should be characterised as governed by an implicit social contract giving rise to moral obligations. The challenge is precisely that top bankers have escaped their moral obligations.

A careful search through Google Scholar reveals that macroeconomists have hardly cited these four remarkable articles, which supports the view that they have neglected one of the fundamental causes of the 2008 crisis. Although our volume does not directly address ethical issues, several of our chapters are tightly related to this hot topic (see the chapters by Theodore H. Cohn, Norbert Gaillard and Rick Michalek, and Anil Hira et al. which analyse regulatory capture, moral hazard, and tax evasion, respectively).

In sum, we see shortcomings both in the nature of the diagnosis and in the recommendations provided so far in much of the literature, especially the economic literature. Furthermore, reforms, ranging from Keynesian stimulus to Dodd-Frank financial reforms, fell short of expectations and seem to have restored a temporary sense of artificial financial stability and confidence. Yet continuing turmoil in politics, the fragile nature of job markets marked by long-term uncertainty, combined with the volatility of commodity prices, signs of a renewed, globally fed housing bubble in certain areas, and the decision of many large companies to sit on piles of cash are all symptoms of weakness. This recovery does not look like a traditional, robust recovery. As of this writing, the Chinese economy also appears to be faltering, a very troubling sign given the fragility of the Chinese financial system and the probability of an asset bubble there.

Shortcomings of the Post-2008 Reforms

The existing literature already explains to a large degree the character of the reforms undertaken by policy makers to restore order to the global financial system. The immediate reaction was to bail out failing financial institutions. The conditions and degree of state intervention varied considerably from one country to another. In the mid to longer term, governments had to decide on some balance between stimulus and austerity measures to promote recovery from the 2008 financial crash and the 2010 debt crisis that erupted in some EU countries. The US put more emphasis on stimulus measures than the EU. Governments also had to decide on taking reform measures that are discussed in our analyses. On the domestic level, public outcry and concern about the sources of the crisis led to efforts to increase regulation and protect consumers. In the US, for example, the Dodd-Frank Act increased bank reporting requirements and a new Consumer Financial Protection Bureau sought to reduce predatory lending.

On the global level, both US and EU regulators instituted a new set of rules, including stress tests to ensure that the major banks could withstand future runs. The role of the FSB seems to have become central to the international financial system. The OTC derivatives market—at the heart of the crisis—is now subject to global regulation for the first time. Provisions include requiring reporting of contracts through centralised trading platforms or repositories. Nevertheless, as we discuss in this volume, such reforms are inadequate to resolve the issues revealed by the 2008 crash. The global financial architecture did not effectively increase regulation on a global level; ultimately, discretion remains with national authorities. Despite the popular outcry, the prevailing approach remains market oriented, and global regulatory authorities lack enforcement capacity. Hence Helleiner (2014, 12–13 and 102–103) dubs the 2008 crash a "status quo crisis." Basel rules have allowed for many loopholes on liquidity requirements, such as permitting major banks to use their own internal models for assessing risk. Thus, financial houses continue to skirt liquidity requirements, reflecting their political power to dilute regulatory reform (Lall 2012). Furthermore, moral hazard issues, driven by the concentration of market power among TBTF financial institutions, continue to pose a threat to financial stability (Wilmarth 2010; Claassen 2015). In addition, new financial instruments, including derivatives and other instruments of securitisation, require considerably more regulation, and the difference between hedging for insulation against future shocks and speculation remains ambiguous. In fact, we need to admit that TBTF financial institutions have long used a variety of innovative financial vehicles to bypass liquidity requirements and take advantage of the latest technological changes to outdistance regulators. This compounds the problem that for regulation to be effective, it must be adopted by all major national regulatory authorities (Thiemann 2014, 1213 and 1230).

Although it is beyond the scope of this volume to fully analyse evolutionary and technological changes, we highlight their importance in creating a serious challenge for financial regulation. For too long, economists have seen regulation in static terms, reflecting their baseline assumptions of individual rational maximising behaviour, ignoring fairly persistent issues ranging from herd-like financial runs to "irrational exuberance" during asset bubbles. As reflected in our offshore finance and remittance chapters (see Hira et al.'s and Busumtwi-Sam's pieces), the increasing pace of globalisation of financial transactions itself constitutes an innovation that regulators have not yet adjusted to, one that will accelerate as the Chinese economy rapidly develops its global financial interactions over time. Moreover, technological developments related to a series of recent crashes from the flash crash to highly complex financial instruments such as CDOs bring to light even more the outdated assumptions of economists and regulators while underscoring the persistence of the issues we discuss, albeit in new forms. Yet, the Panama Papers also reveal that technology can be an important tool for regulators, if embraced and appropriately harnessed by them. Instead of open-minded regulatory approaches appropriate to the evolving complexity of financial instruments, we tend to observe the use of outdated instruments, whether in the form of simply stating a faith argument that markets will "self-correct" or through allegedly stringent laws and regulations that are feebly enforced (see Gaillard and Michalek's chapter). As a result, we are convinced that technological evolution in the financial area demands a new mindset on how regulations ought to be organised. First, regulators should realise that "benevolent" supervision and monitoring *increase* rather than *decrease* the likelihood of technological and market disruptions. Next, they need to build capacity at the national and global levels to monitor and manage the incredibly rapid technological evolution of global financial transactions. Lastly, financial regulatory rules may lack efficiency unless they are adopted by all major national regulatory authorities.

As Charles Kindleberger pointed out in his seminal study of the Great Depression (Kindleberger ([1973] 2013, 292), it was the transition from UK to US leadership that left a vacuum at the global level in terms of financial and monetary leadership, with the US authorities much more prone to serve as the lender of last resort and to accept twin deficits (i.e., trade and fiscal deficits) in order to support economic recovery. In fact, we may now be experiencing what could be the final step of US-style finance capitalism, characterised by untrammelled capital markets and "institutionalised" moral hazard. All this is occurring in a context where the locus of decision-making is partly shifting towards China, even though China is not a central player in the global financial architecture. It has started its own global activities, such as the "one belt, one road" series of infrastructure projects, and offers an alternative financial system through new regional development banks. Beneath the surface is a lack of regulation in many emerging areas of global finance, from bitcoin to remittances. Kindleberger's ([1973] 2013, 308) final words are as relevant to today's situation as they were to the Great Depression: "In these circumstances, the third positive alternative of international institutions with real authority and sovereignty is pressing."

Our Collection and the Theoretical Perspectives of Global Political Economy

In the chapters that follow, we do not promote any "political" or "ideological" agenda. Our empirically based policy study demonstrates the relevance of a variety of global political economy (GPE) theoretical perspectives. (For a detailed discussion of the GPE theoretical perspectives, see Cohn 2016, chs. 3–5.) Central to the study of financial regulation is the ongoing tension between neoliberalism and interventionist or embedded liberalism. Neoliberals, like orthodox liberals before them, promote "negative freedom," or freedom of the market to function with minimal interference from the state. However, the views of orthodox liberal economists such as Adam Smith and David Ricardo were more complex than simply promoting material self-interest and the self-regulating market. Although Smith wrote about self-interested individuals and the "invisible hand" as underlying a well-functioning liberal economic order, he also described people as basically moral and altruistic, and he explained how the concept of justice is expressed through rules for acceptable behaviour. Smith also recognised that some limited government involvement was necessary in certain areas. As for Ricardo, he wrote about conflict between landowners and other classes, and he had social concerns about the poor (Smith [1759] 2002, [1776] 1999; Ricardo [1817] 1996). Neoliberals by contrast tend to focus more unidirectionally on the self-regulating market, material self-interest, and strong private property rights. As some of the chapters in this volume demonstrate, the neoliberal emphasis on financial deregulation was one of the main factors contributing to the 2008 financial crisis.

Interventionist liberals, by contrast, argue that negative freedom is not sufficient, and that some government involvement is essential to promote more equality and justice in a free market economy. Thus, John Maynard Keynes argued that a market-generated equilibrium might occur at a point where labour and capital are underutilised. He therefore supported government policies to lower unemployment, and government investment when necessary in public projects, even when this resulted in temporary public sector deficits (Keynes 1936). Karl Polanyi warned that the orthodox liberal commitment to the self-regulating market led to financial disasters such as the Great Depression, and that society would spontaneously move to protect itself from unregulated market activities (Polanyi 1965). As a result, the reaction to major financial crises has tended to shift from orthodox liberalism or neoliberalism to interventionist liberalism. John Gerard Ruggie's term "embedded liberal compromise," for example, referred to the fact that following the Great Depression, postwar efforts to promote economic liberalisation included government efforts to cushion domestic economies and individuals (Ruggie 1983). As discussed, Keynesian policies such as the creation of the FDIC and 1933 Glass-Steagall Act were designed to protect the commercial bank deposits of individuals from risky investment activities.

However, problems associated with Keynesianism, particularly stagflation in the 1970s related to oil price increases and unemployment, combined with regulatory capture contributed to a gradual emergence of neoliberalism as the dominant paradigm governing financial regulation and to the 1999 repeal of Glass-Steagall. As with the response to the Great Depression, the 2008 financial crisis revived the interest in interventionist liberalism with the passage of the 2010 Dodd-Frank Act. Nonetheless, neoliberalism has re-emerged as the dominant paradigm much more rapidly under the Trump administration, and Congress has already approved measures to weaken Dodd-Frank (Rappeport and Flitter 2018). In his book *Great Transformations*, Mark Blyth traces this evolution of "ideas," first in building interventionist or embedded liberalism, and then in disembedding it and reverting to neoliberalism (Blyth 2002).

Although the main conflicting theoretical perspectives on financial regulation have been within the liberal camp (neoliberalism vs. interventionist liberalism), the neomercantilist (or realist) and critical perspectives also are highly relevant in this area. Neomercantilists see each state as emphasising relative gains and view international relations as a zero-sum game in which one state's gain is another state's loss. Liberals, by contrast, focus on absolute gains and international relations as a variable-sum game, in which states can gain and lose together. Neomercantilists also emphasise the national interest and hegemonic stability theory in which there is a predominant state. President Trump's "America first" policies and his tendency to focus on relative gains are evident today in his highly protectionist trade policies and his severely restrictive views on immigration. Financial deregulation can stem from neomercantilism as well as from neoliberalism. Thus, *competition states* strive to become more competitive by deregulating financial markets, restructuring development, and supporting research and development (R&D) in high technology industries (Cerny 1997). Recent moves to cut US corporate taxes and to deregulate financial markets are clearly designed to increase US competitiveness and to maintain the US hegemonic position in the world. Neomercantilism is also evident in the US and UK as the dominant financial markets. US and UK representatives have had considerable influence in international fora such as the Basel Committee on Banking Supervision (BCBS) because of their proximity to the Wall Street and London banking centres; and the major US and UK banks have in turn been able to influence their representatives. The US and UK have focused in priority on domestic reforms and overlooked potential global standards. One can project strong possibilities for further mercantilist leanings, stemming from China's growing weight in the world economy. China offers a different model of financial control for the South, one based on controlling financial flows within and outside of its economy, and manipulating its currency to engage in devaluation in order to increase export surpluses. Moreover, its protectionism around strategic sectors, particularly manufacturing and high value-added technology, is designed to leverage its enormous emerging market for the promotion of its own companies. As those companies are increasingly able to compete in global markets, the example will spread. While its state-dominated financial system is fragile, its very success over the long term threatens global principles of free financial markets based on reciprocity and welcoming co-ownership.

Critical theorists, in turn, view economic relations as basically conflictual, with a non-producing ownership class exploiting a class of producers and/or developed countries in the North exploiting developing countries in the South. Under capitalism, the state will always be an instrument of exploitation in the long term. In fact, growing concerns about the fluidity of capital and automation reflect the previously discussed challenges of state-based regulation, from bitcoin currency movements to shadow banking. These are linked to growing manifestations of concern around the capitalist system's ability and willingness to contain inequality as suggested by Polanyi and Ruggie through welfare systems and "shock absorbers" built into trade agreements. This helps to explain the growing sense of insecurity among Western middle classes, even while macro indicators are positive, that has led to extremist/novel political movements, such as Syriza in Greece, the 5 Star Movement in Italy, and not only Trump but a previously unviable socialist candidate, Bernie Sanders, becoming viable political leaders (Hira 2019). Inequality on the global level, in turn, feeds into additional issues around "failing states" and migration crises that are beyond the scope of this volume. Several chapters in this book point to the fact that bankers on "Wall Street" contributed greatly to the 2008 financial crisis, but that consumers and ordinary individuals on "Main Street" bore most of the costs. The US government did much more to bail out financial institutions than they did to assist the ordinary citizen. Regarding North-South relations, Busumtwi-Sam's chapter in this volume shows that money transfer operators (MTOs) such as Western Union and MoneyGram charge much more for sending remittances to and within Africa than the average global levels. These higher charges have posed a significant hindrance to development in a number of African countries. Hira et al.'s chapter on offshore finance, in turn, reflects the growing sense that the financial rules do not apply to everyone as evidence of massive tax evasion mounts.

Our study is basically empirical, and we do not take a position in favour of any particular theoretical perspective. However, we implicitly draw on a variety of GPE theoretical perspectives in our examination of the shortcomings with financial regulation. These in turn inform our recommendations in the concluding chapter.

DISTINCTIVE FEATURES OF OUR COLLECTION AND A BRIEF OVERVIEW OF THE CHAPTERS

In the chapters that follow, we contend that the main challenges posed by international finance are human and involve the way regulators regard their own role as capital market gatekeepers. Since the 1980s, several waves of deregulation and ill-conceived regulations have combined with lack of enforcement and lax behaviours among regulators to distort liberal capitalism and undermine democratic societies.

On the one hand, "inadequate regulatory frameworks" have encouraged regulatory and business capture, and conflicts of interest, enabling a minority of powerful individuals and firms to abuse their influence and distort capitalism. De facto oligopolies have developed, and rent-seeking strategies have spread among an increasing array of economic sectors—the most emblematic one being the financial sector.

On the other hand, "inadequate regulatory frameworks" have facilitated fraud, illicit financial flows, and offshore finance, exacerbated inequalities, and nurtured populist and anti-globalisation sentiments.[8]

---

[8] Müller (2016) describes populists as being critical of elites, "anti-pluralist," and advocating identity politics. See http://www.upenn.edu/pennpress/book/15615.html

Some firms (essentially located in industrialised countries) and wealthy individuals have exploited regulatory loopholes to evade taxes and send part of their cash to tax havens. Not surprisingly, these delinquent behaviours have sparked anger among the middle and working classes. In the meantime, middle- and lower-income populations in the developing world are obliged to accept high transaction costs when sending or receiving remittances, thus losing billions of dollars every year. The persistent issues identified here are tackled in turn. Each chapter provides a brief background to the nature of the issue and its origins, outlines its contribution to the financial crisis and/or to instability in global finance, and advances suggestions about avenues for reform. Our collection is composed of five chapters.

Chapters 2, 3, and 4 analyse the interactions between *market* and *policy* makers and find that market rules have not functioned efficiently, while regulators have not played their watchdog role adequately. What some experts, notably Alan Greenspan, called the "Great Moderation" was in fact the "Great Paradox." The relative stability of financial markets during the 1987–2007 period was misleading and proved to be very costly in terms of economic and political sustainability. The latent shortcomings of this paradigm were revealed with the 2007 crisis, in what can be described as a pure Minsky moment. In the three chapters, greater emphasis is placed on the US because the issues identified have been magnified there.

Going against the grain of the predominant discourse about the origins of the Great Recession, Dobuzinskis' chapter supports the view that the crisis was primarily the outcome of "malinvestment," that is, overinvestment in the housing sector in response to ill-considered political choices and regulatory measures by the US government. In other words, it was less a case of a "market failure" than of a "government failure," warning us that not only a lack of regulation but mis-regulation can distort markets. These observations are but one example of the more far-reaching "knowledge problems" first analysed by Hayek as the risks inherent in interventionist policies are attributable to a lack of deep appreciation of the complexity of market processes by policy makers and regulators. However, renouncing intervention in the future so as not to repeat the errors of the past is politically unfeasible. As discussed above, the US and most liberal democracies have gone through a cycle of conflicting policy goals and contested regulatory reforms that continue to produce uncertainty, especially in the current context of growing populist stances. Dobuzinskis identifies two major priorities: (i) convince political economists and regulators to pay far more attention to the complexity of the incentives motivating the behaviour of all the actors involved and (ii) admit that second-best solutions—based on realism, cooperation, and multilateralism—are better options than allegedly "optimal solutions."

Cohn's chapter focuses on the effects of regulatory capture on banking regulations at the domestic (US) and global levels. Regulatory capture occurs when regulators and politicians consistently give preference to regulated banking interests over the public interest; that is, they are "captured" by the regulated. This chapter assesses the validity of a hypothesis closely associated with regulatory capture theory—that capture resulted in banking deregulation which was a major factor contributing to the 2008 financial crisis. The worst financial crises usually involve banks, because they are often highly leveraged, and there is a mismatch between their borrowing and lending behaviour. Cohn contends that capture remains an issue since the 2008 financial crisis. Whereas most research focuses on regulatory capture through two levels of analysis—the national and global levels—this chapter fills a gap in the literature by also examining capture at the individual level. Regulatory capture has enabled banks and other financial institutions ("Wall Street") to add to their own wealth at the expense of the "Main Street" and has contributed to the populist and anti-globalisation sentiments we have discussed. The conclusion includes recommendations for limiting regulatory capture in banking.

In their chapter, Gaillard and Michalek argue that since the 1980s, moral hazard has, within the constraints and mandates of finance capitalism, encouraged excessive global levels of indebtedness, amplified conflicts of interest, and contributed to greater leniency from regulators and financial gatekeepers towards systemic banks. Examining the rise of the TBTF banking behemoths, Gaillard and Michalek question how moral hazard came to dominate banking culture, and how the developing financial innovation in and after the 1980s combined with that culture to accelerate the growth and pre-eminence of the mega-banks. They then provide an assessment of the dismantling of Glass-Steagall and how the new publicly owned money centre banks leveraged their size to establish themselves as systemically important. They explore how financial gatekeepers—US regulators, CRAs, and the Federal Reserve—became "lenient partners" (or "sweeteners") that enabled and accelerated the growth of the financial services sector. The authors propose a variety of possible reforms, including modifications to existing measures related to the TBTF banks, the indebtedness of American citizens, the CRAs, and the US regulators.

Chapters 5 and 6 illustrate major flaws in the efficiency and enforcement of global financial regulation. While there are many gaps in the coverage and regulation of global finance, we focus on the well-publicised Panama and Paradise Papers revelations about offshore tax evasion and remittance flows. The regulatory failures in these two crucial areas—which have received little coverage in most edited volumes on financial regulation—have led to huge losses for governments and taxpayers. Every year, tax evasion results in losses exceeding $100 billion for developed and developing countries, and high remittance charges would cost around $2 billion to Africa.

Busumtwi-Sam's chapter critically examines the financial regulations needed to leverage remittances into positive sustainable development outcomes in sub-Saharan Africa. In the wake of the 2008 financial crisis, remittances have been the fastest growing financial sources and have been more stable, resilient, and reliable than other private capital flows to the region. The regulation of these sources of finance domestically and internationally, however, has not kept pace with their increased importance. Noting the context-dependent nature of the development impacts of remittances, this chapter focuses on the relationship between remittances and financial development entailing the deepening and broadening of financial services, as a key prerequisite for the attainment of desired development goals. Busumtwi-Sam argues that effective leveraging of remittances into positive development outcomes in sub-Saharan Africa through financial development can only occur if an adequate financial regulatory system is in place that enhances complementarities among the components or phases of the remittance transfer chain. Regulations are needed to enhance market access and competition and reduce financial exclusion, including facilitating mobile and electronic financial services. Regulations are also needed to reduce the high transaction costs of sending and receiving remittances; cut the high proportion of informal transfers; enhance the accuracy of and oversight over remittance reporting; and curb illicit financial flows. It is evident that such reforms require a strong multilateral framework to be implemented adequately.

The final chapter by Hira, Murata, and Monson on the Panama and Paradise Papers discusses the role of leaked documents in revealing how wealthy individuals and multinational firms around the world use offshore financial centres to hide wealth and evade taxes. The issue gained momentum from the 1980s when major offshore centres were established, and the OECD has devoted some attention to dealing with the problem. The failure of governments to harmonise taxes and share information has inflicted an increasingly disproportionate burden on individual taxpayers, exacerbating inequalities and increasing resort to debt by governments. This chapter deals with the challenges around global tax coordination and suggests possible paths forward.

Concluding Remarks

Our volume devotes considerable attention to persistent regulatory issues before and after the 2008 financial crisis. Our primary concern is to shed light on longer-term regulatory problems that contribute to financial crises. We focus on regulatory problems at both the domestic and international levels and identify obstacles to regulatory reform in a political economy that has become increasingly globalised and dominated by finance. *Finance* capitalism has exacerbated moral hazard, distorted market rules, fed shadow finance, and paralysed regulators. Consequently, we consider it is time to restore the fundamental rules of *liberal* capitalism by promoting (i) fair competition, (ii) simple and uncompromising regulatory rules and practices, and (iii) international cooperation among policy makers and regulators.

We note that the post-2008 crisis reforms implemented so far have been primarily focused on restoring GDP growth and boosting stock market prices. The solutions we formulate in our different chapters, by contrast, seek to address long-term persistent flaws of the financial system. These persistent flaws are complex and will require tenacity to resolve. During boom periods, they are systematically overlooked. When there is a severe economic downturn, policy makers recognise their toxicity but turn to other priorities (fighting against unemployment, controlling of public finance, etc.). This is very frustrating. We hope that our discussions will contribute further to the understanding of financial regulatory problems and convince policy makers to move in the right direction. Only by understanding fundamental regulatory failures over the long term can we hope to deliver a more appropriate regulation that will fight populism and restore economic and financial stability on a lasting basis.

References

Acharya, Viral V., Matthew Richardson, Stijn Van Nieuwerburgh, and Lawrence J. White. 2011. *Guaranteed to Fail: Fannie Mae, Freddie Mac and the Debacle of Mortgage Finance*. Princeton: Princeton University Press.

Alesina, Alberto, Omar Barbiero, Carlo Favero, Francesco Giavazzi, and Matteo Paradisi. 2015. Austerity in 2009–2013. *Economic Policy*. 30(83): 383–437.

Aloui, Riadh, Mohamed Safoune Ben Aïssa, and Duc Khuong Nguyen. 2011. Global Financial Crisis, Extreme Interdependences, and Contagion Effects: The Role of Economic Structure?, *Journal of Banking & Finance*. 35(1): 130–141.

Aslund, Anders and Simeon Djankov. 2017. *Europe's Growth Challenge*. Oxford and New York City: Oxford University Press.

Benmelech, Efraim, and Jennifer Dlugosz, 2009. The Credit Rating Crisis. *NBER Working Paper No. 15045*. Washington: NBER.

Blyth, Mark. 2002. *Great Transformations*. Cambridge and New York City: Cambridge University Press.

Bookstaber, Richard. 2007. *A Demon of Our Own Design: Markets, Hedge Funds, and the Perils of Financial Innovation*. New York City: Wiley.

Calomiris, Charles. 1998. The IMF's Imprudent Role as Lender of Last Resort. *Cato Journal*. 17(3): 275–294.

Cecchetti, Stephen G. and Enisse Kharroubi, 2015. Why Does Financial Sector Growth Crowd Out Real Economic Growth? *BIS Working Paper No. 490*. February.

Cerny, Philip G. 1997. Paradoxes of the Competition State: The Dynamics of Political Globalization. *Government and Opposition*. 32(2): 251–274.

Claassen, Rutger. 2015. Financial Crisis and the Ethics of Moral Hazard. *Social Theory and Practice*. 41(3): 527–551.

Cohen, Benjamin J. 1982. Balance-of-Payments Financing: Evolution of a Regime. *International Organization*. 36(2): 457–478.

Cohen, Benjamin J. 2008. The International Monetary System: Diffusion and Ambiguity. *International Affairs*. 84(3): 455–470.

Cohen, Benjamin J. 2009. Sovereign Wealth Funds and National Security: The Great Tradeoff. *International Affairs*. 85(4): 713–731.

Cohn, Theodore H. 2016. *Global Political Economy: Theory and Practice*, 7th ed. New York: Routledge.

Coleman, William D. 1996. *Financial Services, Globalization and Domestic Policy Change*. International Political Economy Series. New York: Palgrave Macmillan.

Cornett, Marcia Millon, Jamie John McNutt, Philip E. Strahan, and Hassan Tehranian. 2011. Liquidity Risk Management and Credit Supply in the Financial Crisis. *Journal of Financial Economics*. 101(2): 297–312.

Corsetti, Giancarlo, Paolo Pesenti, and Nouriel Roubini. 1999. What Caused the Asian Currency and Financial Crisis? *Japan and the World Economy*. 11(3): 305–373.

Crotty, James. 2009. Structural Causes of the Global Financial Crisis: A Critical Assessment of the 'New Financial Architecture'. *Cambridge Journal of Economics*. 33(4): 563–580.

Davies, Howard. 2015. *Can Financial Markets Be Controlled?* New York City: Polity.

De Larosière, Jacques. 2016. *Cinquante ans de crises financières.* Paris: Odile Jacob.

Dowd, Kevin. 2009. Moral Hazard and the Financial Crisis. *Cato Journal.* 29(1):141–166.

Duca, John V. 2017. The Great Depression versus the Great Recession in the U.S.: How Fiscal, Monetary, and Financial Policies Compare. *Journal of Economic Dynamics and Control.* 81: 50–64.

Financial Stability Board. 2017. *OTC Derivatives Market Reforms Twelfth Progress Report on Implementation.*

Foroohar, Rana. 2016. *Makers and Takers: The Rise of Finance and the Fall of American Business.* New York: Crown Business.

Frieden, Jeffry A. 2015. *Currency Politics: The Political Economy of Exchange Rate Policy.* Princeton and Oxford: Princeton University Press.

Friedman, Milton and Anna Jacobson Schwartz. 1963. *A Monetary History of the United States,* Princeton: Princeton University Press.

Gaillard, Norbert J. 2011. *A Century of Sovereign Ratings.* New York: Springer.

Goldbach, Roman. 2015. *Global Governance and Regulatory Failure: The Political Economy of Banking.* International Political Economy Series. Basingstoke (UK): Palgrave Macmillan.

Golub, Stephen, Ayse Kaya, and Michael Reay. 2015. What Were They Thinking? The Federal Reserve in the Run-up to the 2008 Financial Crisis. *Review of International Political Economy.* 22(4): 657–692.

Graafland, Johan J. and Bert W. van de Ven. 2011. The Credit Crisis and the Moral Responsibility of Professionals in Finance. *Journal of Business Ethics.* 103(4): 605–619.

Grossman, Richard S. 1992. Deposit Insurance, Regulation, and Moral Hazard in the Thrift Industry: Evidence from the 1930's. *American Economic Review.* 82(4): 800–821.

Guttmann, Robert. 2009. Asset Bubbles, Debt Deflation, and Global Imbalances. *International Journal of Political Economy.* 38(2): 46–69.

Haldane, Andrew G. 2012. The Dog and the Frisbee. Speech delivered at the Federal Reserve Bank of Kansas City's 366th Economic Policy Symposium, "The Changing Policy Landscape". Jackson Hole, Wyoming, August 31.

Hasen, Richard. 2016. *Plutocrats United: Campaign Money, the Supreme Court, and the Distortion of American Elections.* Yale: Yale University Press.

Helleiner, Eric. 2014. *The Status Quo Crisis.* Oxford and New York City: Oxford University Press.

Hendrickson, J.M. 2011. *Regulation and Instability in US Commercial Banking: A History of Crises.* New York City: Palgrave Macmillan.

Hill, Claire. 1996. Securitization: A Low-Cost Sweetener for Lemons. *Washington University Law Quarterly.* 74(4): 1061–1120.

Hira, Anil. 2019. *The Great Disruption: Explaining the Forces Behind Trump, Brexit and Le Pen* (tentative title).

Hira, Anil. 2013. Irrational Exuberance: An Evolutionary Perspective on the Underlying Causes of the Financial Crisis. *Intereconomics: Review of European Economic Policy.* 48(2): 116–123.

Independent Commission on Banking. 2011. *Final Report – Recommendations.* UK Banking Commission.

Keynes, John M. 1936. *The General Theory of Employment, Interest, and Money.* New York: Harcourt, Brace & World.

Keys, Benjamin J., Tanmoy Mukherjee, Amit Seru, and Vikrant Vig. 2010. Did Securitization Lead to Lax Screening? Evidence from Subprime Loans. *Quarterly Journal of Economics.* 125(1): 307–362.

Kindleberger, Charles P. [1978] 2005. *Manias, Panics and Crashes: A History of Financial Crises.* New York City: Palgrave Macmillan.

Kindleberger, Charles P. [1973] 2013. *The World in Depression 1929–1939.* Berkeley: University of California Press.

Krugman, Paul. 2012. *End This Depression Now!* New York City: W. W. Norton.

Lall, Ranjit. 2012. From Failure to Failure: The Politics of International Banking Regulation. *Review of International Political Economy.* 19(4): 609–638.

Liikanen, Erkki. 2012. *High-level Expert Group on Reforming the Structure of the EU Banking Sector, Chaired by Erkki Liikanen.* Final Report. Brussels, October 2.

Longstaff, Francis A. 2010. The Subprime Credit Crisis and Contagion in Financial Markets. *Journal of Financial Economics.* 97(3): 436–450.

Mayer, Martin. 1993. *Nightmare on Wall Street: Salomon Brothers and the Corruption of the Marketplace.* New York City: Simon & Schuster.

Mian, Atif and Amir Sufi. 2009. The Consequences of Mortgage Credit Expansion: Evidence from the U.S. Mortgage Default Crisis. *Quarterly Journal of Economics.* 124(4): 1449–1496.

Mian, Atif and Amir Sufi, 2014. *House of Debt: How They (and You) Caused the Great Recession, and How We Can Prevent It from Happening Again.* Chicago: University of Chicago Press.

Moschella, Manuela. 2010. *Governing Risk: The IMF and Global Financial Crises.* International Political Economy Series. Basingstoke (UK): Palgrave Macmillan.

Müller, Jan-Werner. 2016. *What Is Populism?* Philadelphia: University of Pennsylvania Press.

Nielsen, Richard P. 2010. High-Leverage Finance Capitalism, the Economic Crisis, Structurally Related Ethics Issues, and Potential Reforms. *Business Ethics Quarterly.* 20(2): 299–330.

Piketty, Thomas. 2014. *Capital in the Twenty-First Century.* Cambridge, MA: Belknap Press.

Polanyi, Karl. 1965. *The Great Transformation.* Boston, MA: Beacon Press.

Rappeport, Alan and Emily Flitter. 2018. Congress Approves First Big Dodd-Frank Rollback. *New York Times.* May 22.

Reinhart, Carmen, and Kenneth Rogoff. 2009. *This Time is Different: Eight Centuries of Financial Folly.* Princeton: Princeton University Press.

Ricardo, David. [1817] 1996. *Principles of Political Economy and Taxation.* Amherst, NY: Prometheus Books.

Rockoff, Hugh. 2000. Banking and Finance, 1789–1914, 643–684. In Stanley Engerman. *The Cambridge Economic History of the United States, Vol. II.* New York City: Cambridge University Press.

Roemer, John E. 2012. Ideology, Social Ethos, and the Financial Crisis. *Journal of Ethics.* 16(3): 273–303.

Ruggie, John G. 1983. International Regimes, Transactions, and Change: Embedded Liberalism in the Postwar Economic Order, 195–231. In Stephen D. Krasner (Ed.). *International Regimes.* Ithaca, NY: Cornell University Press.

Sharman, J.C. 2017. Illicit Global Wealth Chains after the Financial Crisis: Micro-States and an Unusual Suspect. *Review of International Political Economy.* 24(1): 30–55.

Silber, William J. 2007. *When Washington Shut Down Wall Street: The Great Financial Crisis of 1914 and the Origins of America's Monetary Supremacy.* Princeton: Princeton University Press.

Sinclair, Timothy J. 2010. Round Up the Usual Suspects: Blame and the Subprime Crisis. *New Political Economy.* 15(1): 91–107.

Smith, Adam. [1759] 2002. *The Theory of Moral Sentiments.* Cambridge and New York City: Cambridge University Press.

Smith, Adam. [1776] 1999. *The Wealth of Nations.* London: Penguin.

Stiglitz, Joseph. 2012. *The Price of Inequality.* New York City and London: W. W. Norton.

Stock, James H. and Mark W. Watson. 2003. Has the Business Cycle Changed and Why?, in *NBER Macroeconomics Annual 2002.* Cambridge, MA: MIT Press. Vol. 17: 159–218.

Thiemann, Matthias. 2014. In the Shadow of Basel: How Competitive Politics Bred the Crisis. *Review of International Political Economy.* 21(6): 1203–1239.

Turner, Adair. 2016. *Between Debt and the Devil – Money, Credit, and Fixing Global Finance.* Princeton: Princeton University Press.

Van Zon, Hans. 2016. *Globalized Finance and Varieties of Capitalism.* New York: Palgrave Macmillan.

Wilmarth, Jr., Arthur E. 2010. Reforming Financial Regulation to Address the Too-Big-to-Fail Problem. *Brooklyn Journal of International Law.* 35(3): 707–783.

Yi-chong, Xu, and Gawdat Bahgat (Eds.). 2010. *The Political Economy of Sovereign Wealth Funds.* International Political Economy Series. Basingstoke (UK): Palgrave Macmillan.

CHAPTER 2

Financial Regulation and Monetary Policy: The Spectre of Government Failure

Laurent Dobuzinskis

INTRODUCTION

The global economy has recovered from the Great Recession of 2008, but there still are lingering effects, and the lessons that should have been drawn have not been fully acted upon. There is a vast literature on these questions but, as the introduction to this volume makes clear, the crisis has deep-rooted causes and multiple and complex implications. It is precisely the complexity of the financial system that this chapter is concerned with. I argue, siding with the Austrian economics and public choice schools,[1]

---

[1] "Austrian economics" describes a research tradition that can be traced back to the works of Carl Menger and his immediate successors at the University of Vienna; these ideas were then further developed by Ludwig von Mises, Friedrich A. Hayek, and Mises' student Israel Kirzner. Although constituting a heterodox and, therefore, minority current within contemporary economics, there are today many economists working within this frame of reference to name them all here. Two ideas form the pillars of this school of thought: (i) the impossibility governments face in gathering sufficient and reliable information with which they could

---

L. Dobuzinskis (✉)
Department of Political Science, Simon Fraser University, Burnaby, BC, Canada
e-mail: dobuzins@sfu.ca

© The Author(s) 2019
A. Hira et al. (eds.), *The Failure of Financial Regulation*,
International Political Economy Series,
https://doi.org/10.1007/978-3-030-05680-3_2

that the complexity of the financial system creates a "knowledge problem" that persistently prevents monetary authorities and economic policy makers from (i) understanding adequately the nature of the problems they attempt to remedy and (ii) anticipating all the consequences of their actions. The introduction to this volume has already presented several examples of the harm that the unexpected consequences of well-intended reforms can cause. While many analysts concede that this was true of attempts to deregulate banks and financial markets (especially in the US), the literature usually assumes that the crisis resulted primarily from the risky decisions made by corporate actors and that deregulation—or simply lack of enthusiasm for using regulatory instruments when needed—only aggravated the dysfunctions of the market. In other words, it was a classic "market failure" which policy makers failed to prevent. Austrian economists argue that far from having been passive or obsessively preoccupied with deregulating financial transactions, US monetary authorities and policy makers were also actively pursuing interventionist strategies that proved to be even more deleterious than the errors made by bankers. In fact, such errors were merely the consequences of operating in an environment that was shaped by powerful public institutions, which Roger Koppl (2002) calls "Big Players." In other words, it is more accurate to speak of a massive "government failure."

While I provide a supportive account of this thesis, I part company with the Austrian and public choice schools when it comes to the question of how best to restructure the financial regulatory system. I consider that these economists, who are keenly aware of the complexity of market processes, fail to fully appreciate the complexity of the *political* system. The ideologically coherent solutions they propose were never implemented because they are largely unfeasible. To borrow a phrase from the current debate about the introduction of new technologies, these proposals would be more "disruptive" than the public and elected officials are probably willing to accept. This is not to say, however, that their neo-Keynesian or merely pragmatic opponents won the day. For several years now—but especially since the emergence of powerful populist forces in the US,

---

steer the economy towards desirable macro-economic goals; and (ii) the creative and highly beneficial role played by entrepreneurs in "discovering" opportunities for investment is disruptive in the sense that it generally prevents the economy from settling at an equilibrium point.

Britain, and much of Europe—monetary and fiscal priorities have been in a state of flux, and a great deal of uncertainty prevails about where the global economy is heading. "Austrian economists" might well be right about *theoretical* explanations of what has happened and what is needed, but the tug of war between different political and economic interests creates a situation that is ripe with uncertainty and in which policy recommendations based strictly on economic reasoning are not likely to go very far.

To understand the notion of "government failure" it is best to start with a definition of the converse idea of "market failure." Historically, the concept of market failure came first.[2] The phrase "government failure" was coined as a rhetorical device to suggest that policies designed to counter market failures are prone to fail. Ever since the emergence of the Cambridge school of neoclassical economics founded by Alfred Marshall, most economists have insisted that perfect competition results in socially optimal outcomes. Suboptimal outcomes are due to the presence of monopolies or oligopolies in some markets, or to the occurrence of negative "externalities," or to asymmetries of information among the relevant economic agents.[3] In such instances, welfare economics recommends a variety of remedies intended to pull the final outcomes towards something resembling what perfect competition would have produced. They may include taxes (e.g., "a carbon tax"), the creation of new markets (e.g., "cap-and-trade"), or outright government regulations. But critics argue that such interventions are costly, often missing their mark, and that typically market failures are themselves the predictable response of economic agents to perverse incentives created by previous policies. Indeed, when transaction costs are negligible and property rights are well defined, governments should not rush in with taxes or tort law remedies because the participants in the market may themselves hit upon efficient solutions to

---

[2] It is usually traced back to Francis Bator's (1958) famous article on the subject. But the idea itself goes back much further to the very beginnings of welfare economics in the early twentieth century. It suggests that when the conditions under which a perfectly competitive economy is supposed to operate are not met, suboptimal results ensue. Government intervention aimed at rectifying these imperfections are typically advocated by some economists, even if they typically differ on the choice of the most appropriate measures.

[3] Negative externalities are said to arise when not all costs are internalized in prices, e.g., in the case of environmental pollution.

the suboptimal situation in which they find themselves, as argued by Coase (1960).

Yet, regulatory issues are only part of the story of government failure: monetary policy is also an important factor (see Cohn's chapter in this volume). The Austrian school has much to say about the dangers associated with monetary interventionism by central banks, as I explain further in this chapter, but the government failure hypothesis is not strictly coterminous with Austrian economics. What is more unique to the Austrian perspective is its advocacy of radical reforms of the monetary and financial systems that would take most powers away from legislators and government agencies.

In the next section, I examine the case for finding the root causes of the 2007–2008 crisis in the policies and decisions of the US regulatory and political system—including the Federal Reserve which operates at arm's length from politicians—rather than in the behaviour of strictly private firms. Those who argue that there was a government failure also claim that the way forward ought to point in the direction of much less intervention and more competition. I discuss policy options that are consistent with this view in the following section. However, the political feasibility of such libertarian reform proposals was nil in the immediate aftermath of the crisis. Today, some officials in the Trump Administration and a few members of the Republican majority in Congress have expressed interest in some of them. But no clear consensus has emerged, and these signals add to the confusion surrounding the direction of economic policy in the US. A brief survey of the situation outside of the US reveals an even more complicated situation characterized by hesitation and temporizing measures. Although there is no need for a rigid international consensus, the constantly evolving reform priorities that have been discussed or implemented are a cause for concern.

LOOKING BACK AT THE CRISIS: WAS IT CAUSED BY THE UNINTENDED CONSEQUENCES OF INTERVENTIONIST POLICIES?

The Great Recession has given rise to a cottage industry of critiques of the economics profession. The failure to predict the crisis and the clueless satisfaction displayed before the crisis by many economists in academia and central banks has often been lambasted (see Colander et al. 2009).

One of the outcomes of this trend is that the proverbial (neoclassical) "mainstream" has indeed been weakened quite significantly. The first alternative to yesterday's mainstream has come from behavioural economics and its many variants (e.g., neuroeconomics, evolutionary game theory, etc.). But another consequence of this upheaval has been the re-emergence of heterodox currents. Two such heterodox—but widely divergent—schools have recently regained considerable visibility and are arguably more influential than they were in the decade preceding the Great Recession: Austrian economics, on the one hand, and post-Keynesianism, on the other. At the risk of oversimplifying complex arguments, both schools blamed (for different yet partially overlapping reasons) the "mainstream," for having been too complacent about pre-2007 monetary policy and too unconcerned about rising debt levels as a consequence of run-away credit expansion.[4] Whereas the neoclassical general equilibrium model is based on the postulate that money is neutral (i.e., does not prevent the economy from trending towards market-clearing prices), both the Austrian and post-Keynesian schools reject the hypothesis of the neutrality of money. From the perspective of these heterodox schools, shocks are due to *endogenous* monetary factors; neoclassical models can explain crises only by invoking exogenous shocks resulting from presumably *unpredictable* events. The fact that these heterodox schools were proven right about the economic consequences of credit expansion and rising debt levels goes a long way towards explaining the curiosity they elicit inside as well as outside of academia. But these two schools diverge with respect to their respective diagnoses of the origins of these trends. The Austrians blame interventionism and overregulation; post-Keynesians are more likely to indict deregulation and the inability or unwillingness of policy makers to set limits to the continuous push towards the use of riskier and riskier financial instruments. Not surprisingly, they also recommend different policies and strategies for reforming the financial system. I examine these opposing policy recommendations in the next section of this chapter. For now, I focus on the Austrian approach and the explanation

---

[4] In this chapter, I am primarily concerned with the US, in large measure because the financial crisis originated in the US but also because economics and controversies among economists continue to be dominated by works produced in leading US universities and think tanks. This being said, what is going on in the European Union and other countries obviously cannot be ignored.

of the crisis in terms of a massive government failure because it has arguably received less attention than it deserves in the political economy
literature.

The Government Failure Hypothesis

Most Austrian economists argue that *any* government intervention in
monetary and financial affairs is bound to result in failure. This is a corol-
lary of their explanation of business cycles. The Austrian business cycle
(ABC) theory rests on premises first articulated by Carl Menger in his
analysis of the role of capital in the production process (Oppers 2002). For
Menger, there is a "roundabout" connection between savings, investments, and the final production of consumer goods; this connection slowly
unfolds *over time*. It takes longer to produce capital goods than it takes to
produce final goods with existing capital goods. But the ABC theory itself
was first proposed by Ludwig von Mises in his *Theory of Money and Credit*
(1912). The interest rate for loanable funds acts as a regulating mechanism for controlling the amount of investments. In a well-functioning
market economy, when savings increase, the interest rate goes down, thus
making it possible for entrepreneurs to fund new equipment out of these
savings in order to meet anticipated future demand for goods (the purchase of which was delayed by savers). No boom or bust occurs under
these conditions. But things can go awry when interest rates come down
not because of increased savings but as a result of *arbitrary* decisions by a
central bank.[5] Such *arbitrary* decisions have been taken in past years,
reflecting the belief among US central bankers (i.e., Alan Greenspan, Ben
Bernanke, and Janet Yellen at the Federal Reserve) that low interest rates
best support economic growth in the medium term. Any interest rate hike
should be underpinned by the conviction that inflationary pressures are
very likely to materialize in the short term. In fact, this monetary policy—
which was initiated by Alan Greenspan and theorized by Bernanke and
Mishkin (1997) through the concept of "inflation targeting"—is flawed
because it overlooks booms on financial markets and encourages risk-
taking and speculation (see Gaillard and Michalek in this volume). Why?

---

[5] By "arbitrary", I mean decisions and actions that are "based on discretion rather than any
set of rules" (see Koppl 2002, 120).

When the cost of borrowing decreases or remains excessively low, businesses are more inclined to invest in new equipment to produce goods that will not come on the market for quite some time, and for which there may not actually be much demand. This is what the Austrians call "malinvestment", that is, investment that was undertaken on the basis of distorted signals in financial markets—signals that do not reflect *market conditions* but *policy decisions.*

The ABC theory is not universally accepted by economists. Keynesians and post-Keynesian economists have for decades dismissed it. Keynes strongly argued that there are circumstances where savings are not productively invested ("the paradox of thrift") so that less money circulates and demand for goods and services is below what it should be to generate full employment. But in its own terms, the ABC theory has some weaknesses, such as the fact that it assumes a great deal of naïveté on the part of employers, banks, and so on. Austrians, however, would retort that even perspicacious entrepreneurs would not be able to accurately estimate the effects of more or less wide swings in the level of interest rates resulting from central banks' decisions. As Carmen Reinhart and Kenneth Rogoff (2009, xxv) note, "excessive debt accumulation, whether it be by the government, banks, corporations, or consumers, often poses greater systemic risks than it seems during a boom."

What sort of insights does the ABC theory contribute to an explanation of the financial crisis and its aftermath? I argue that, in conjunction with other versions of the government failure thesis, it provides a rather compelling explanation. The crisis is best understood as the combined outcome of questionable policy decisions by the Federal Reserve and of well-intentioned but disastrous regulations of the mortgage lending sector.

The years from the 1990s to 2007—known as the "Great Stability" era (King 2016, 6)—were characterized by low interest rates, no inflationary pressure, and moderate growth. In fact, this period proved to have exacerbated leverage and fed asset bubbles. Accommodative monetary policy—driven by "inflation targeting" strategy—was amplified by regulatory measures intended to help low-income families to enter the housing market. While this is a laudable goal, the result was that too many mortgages were approved for people who were not able to afford them (see Mian and Sufi 2014). The centrepiece of this programme was the *Community Reinvestment Act*; first passed in 1977 as an instrument to prevent discrimination in mortgage lending practices, it was amended several times since then. These amendments and, more importantly, the regulations put in place to guide their implementation aimed at ensuring that all mortgage lending banks were making sufficient efforts to expand homeownership (Wallison 2009). In a similar vein, Congress in the 1990s repeatedly mandated the "government-sponsored enterprises" (GSEs) known as Fannie Mae (Federal National Mortgage Association) and Freddie Mac (Federal Home Loan Mortgage Corporation) to repurchase mortgages. Beginning in 1997, these agencies were under pressure to purchase subprime (riskier) mortgages, thereby encouraging lending institutions to create even more mortgages with very low loan-to-value (LTV) ratios.[6]

> When President George W. Bush came into office in 2001, he went further, advocating that everyone should own a home as part of his vaunted "Ownership Society" initiative. In response, [the US Department of Housing and Urban Development] HUD increased its pressure on Fannie Mae and Freddie Mac to finance an even greater number of mortgages to people with modest incomes and to borrowers of color. The Bush administration embraced subprime loans as the key to growth in homeownership (Engel and McCoy 2011, 21).

The construction industry responded eagerly, as evidenced by the spread of "exurban developments" far away from urban centres and traditional suburbs where land value was rising (the "exurbs" were not surprisingly the hardest hit communities when the housing bubble burst). In and by themselves, these circumstances already appear to constitute an illustration of "malinvestment."

Superimposed on these already alarming patterns was the practice of "securitizing" contractual debt, which occurred as an unintended effect of the Basel I accord of 1988 (Jablecki 2009, 19). Mortgages of varying quality were pooled together and sold as mortgage-backed securities on the secondary mortgage market. This was marketed as a means to average risk but without paying due regard to the fact that it is difficult for buyers to know what they are purchasing. In principle, the ratings issued by the rating agencies Moody's, Standard & Poor's, or Fitch's enabled purchasers to discriminate between safe and speculative securities. Unfortunately, these agencies did a poor job of warning banks against the risks of what

---

[6] "By 2007, Fannie and Freddie were required to show that 55% of their mortgage purchases were [held by low- and moderate-income home owners]" (Wallison 2009, 370).

turned out to be "toxic" products (see Gaillard and Harrington 2016 and the chapter by Gaillard and Michalek in this volume). Here, we encounter yet another government failure, albeit one whose effects resulted from regulations not directly linked to the securitization of mortgage loans. The lack of competition in the credit rating business was not a market failure. As Jeffrey Friedman (2009, 133) explains:

> [a] welter of regulations, going back to 1936 had, by the end of the twentieth century, conferred immense privileges on these firms, effectively making them unofficial arms of the U.S. government. A growing number of institutional investors, such as pension funds, insurance companies, and banks were prohibited from buying bonds that had not been rated "investment grade" (BBB- or higher) by these firms, and many were legally restricted to buying only the highest-rated (AAA) securities.... Moreover, in 1975, the Securities and Exchange Commission (SEC) effectively conferred on the three rating firms that were in existence – Moody's, Standard and Poor's, and Fitch – oligopoly status. In this ruling and subsequent actions, the SEC ensured that only these three firms were Nationally Recognized Statistical Rating Organizations (NRSROs) – and that only an NRSRO's ratings (oftentimes, two NRSRO's ratings) would fulfil the numerous regulatory mandates... that had proliferated since 1936.

In recent years, the total number of officially recognized NRSROs has climbed to ten, but the three largest ones still enjoy a dominant position (U.S. Securities and Exchange Commission 2016). There is little chance that this could change soon. Under such conditions, regulation is a second best. Rather late in the game, as it were, the Dodd-Frank Act of 2010 set in place rules regarding their management, methodologies, ethical standards, and reporting obligations (U.S. Securities and Exchange Commission 2016).

Admittedly, one also has to take into account the fraudulent practices of many mortgage brokers and "shadow banks"[7] which deliberately misrepresented the conditions of the loans they were offering, signing up clients at a low rate without revealing contract clauses stipulating that the

---

[7] For in-depth analyses of shadow banking, report to the chapters written by Hira et al. and Busumtwi-Sam in this volume.

rates could be adjusted upward.[8] It is difficult to evaluate the impact of these dishonest methods on the housing crisis because one cannot separate the activities of the brokers from the systemic conditions under which they operated but, in this respect, the role of the GSEs was crucial. It is undeniable that they made things worse when the housing bubble burst in 2007: interest rates began to climb back up in 2006, and house prices, which had peaked in 2006, declined sharply in 2007—around 15–20% down as compared to 2006, as a consequence of both the hike in mortgage rates and an oversupply of new houses. House owners who could barely keep up with their payments still had the option of selling their properties and getting out of debt before the market collapsed, but they were no longer able to do so. Mortgage-based assets became "toxic." In August 2007, American Home Mortgage filed for bankruptcy, and the stock market began to slide. After Lehman Brothers went bankrupt in September 2008, the shockwave spread throughout the American banking system, but also reverberated in many other countries—Canada being one of the few exceptions. These facts are well known and, for my purpose here, there is no need to explore them further.

At first sight, the "malinvestment" hypothesis seems confirmed in this instance, although the fit is not perfect; one could raise questions about the reasons why malinvestment was largely confined to the housing market. In fact, despite large corporate profits, investment was deficient in other sectors, leading to what some have called a "savings glut" which could be viewed as a market-induced cause of low interest rates. But there is evidence (such as statements by the Chairman of the Federal Reserve during that period, Alan Greenspan) that the Federal Reserve was intentionally keeping rates low rather than merely reacting to a "savings glut." However, alternative theories—especially the post-Keynesian approach— also deserve examination.

Alternative Views: A Rebuttal

Some economists have chosen to put more emphasis on the fundamental uncertainty that characterizes financial markets and the banking industry than government failures, although these two lines of thinking are not

---

[8] These fraudulent practices and the passivity of the US government in responding to complaints are well documented in Engel and McCoy (2011).

necessarily incompatible. Building on the works of Hyman Minsky ([1986] 2008), some post-Keynesians have revisited Keynes' teachings about uncertainty and irrational trends in financial markets.[9] But contrary to the Austrians, post-Keynesians are more prone to locate the source of uncertainty in the private sector. They posit that disequilibrium—rather than the neoclassical emphasis on a tendency towards equilibrium—best describes the actual performance of the economic system. Booms are followed by busts. A crucial mechanism at play here is the role of the banks in the creation of money through credit, and the irrational behaviour of economic actors willing to borrow above and beyond their ability to carry their debt load—until the "Minsky moment" when the house of cards comes tumbling down. In brief, even though reality is always a little more complex than that, the amount of private debt rises up to a point where it is no longer sustainable, and a crisis ensues. That seems to fit the situation of the early 2000s rather well, except for the fact that even in the US there was not really a generalized boom in sectors other than the housing sector, and no boom took place in most of the OECD countries (King 2016, 307). If so, the only concession to the government failure hypothesis that post-Keynesians are willing to contemplate is the inability of policy makers to put a lid on the euphoric climate that propels borrowing by entrepreneurs and consumers alike.

Although his policy prescriptions differ from those advocated by post-Keynesians (see below), Mervyn King (2016) shares with them the idea that the economy is more prone to disequilibrium—because of the complexity of monetary issues—than the neoclassical model of markets for goods and services smoothly moving towards equilibrium. More specifically, the error that bankers committed in America, in Britain and much of Western Europe was to confuse risk with uncertainty. They extended credit beyond what (with the benefit of hindsight) was unsuitable because they became too confident in the ability of their mathematical models to control risk.

What about the pure and simple market failure hypothesis? Proponents of this thesis advance that the regime put in place in the wake of the Great Depression of the 1930s "produced a stable US financial system – for 50 years, no major financial crisis was experienced" (Moosa 2015, 48). One

---

[9] Steve Keen (2013), who counts himself among the few economists who anticipated the financial crisis, credits Minsky's works for the accuracy of his diagnosis.

of the key features of this regime in the US was the Glass-Steagall Act which established a separation between commercial and investment banking. The Gramm-Leach-Bliley Act passed in 1999 under President Clinton abolished the Glass-Steagall Act and prevented the Securities and Exchange Commission (SEC) from regulating investment bank holding companies; then the post-war regime further unravelled under the Bush Administration as an under-funded SEC took a back seat, and Congress failed to put in place any new rule concerning derivatives and other new financial products. On the international scene, cross-border financial transactions also became less controlled and more extensive. Some would want to argue that this was a government failure in a negative form: a choice of doing nothing whereas new rules were needed to deal with evolving financial markets. In Paul Krugman's (2012, ch. 4) words, nothing stood in the way of the bankers "going wild." However, this point can be pushed too far. As explained by Koppl (2014, 30), all this "'deregulation' left in place the [Federal Deposit Insurance Corporation] FDIC"[10] whose very existence is a major source of moral hazard, that is, encouraging risky behaviours, even if unintentionally, by reducing their costs (see Gaillard and Michalek in this volume). In this instance, a general belief that banks would be bailed out in the event of a downturn encourages imprudent practices. Moreover, one cannot always assume that regulators have access to the information they need to design efficient regulations; in the real world, ad hoc regulations do not always produce better results than the absence of regulations. And this all happened against the background of the Federal Reserve's overly lax monetary policy as discussed.

Path Dependence: Doomed to Revisit Past Failures or to Coast on Past Success?

The effects of policy decisions are magnified or deflected by institutional rules and political conventions. Ill-considered political choices—what I have so far referred to as government failures—can have more or less destabilizing results depending on the context. Deregulation occurred in a unique institutional and historical setting. A comparison between the US and Canada brings this point home (Bordo et al. 2015). Recent debates about deregulation should not hide from view a long record of legislative

---

[10] The value of the deposits guaranteed by the FDIC was doubled in 1980.

action at the federal and state levels directed at banks and financial institutions that goes back to the nineteenth century. The American banking system has a long history of bankruptcies or near failures (Hendrickson 2011). States have the constitutional power to regulate banks, and, because of recurring populist pressure on state legislatures to resist the intrusion of national banks in the local (mostly agrarian for much of the nineteenth century) economies, US banks have historically been denied the option of growing large enough to diversify and build sizeable reserves. The result is an exceptionally complicated but also rather fragile American banking system. By contrast, the Canadian banking system has been remarkably stable—perhaps the most stable in the world.[11] According to Calomiris and Haber (2014), the reason is that Canadian banks were allowed to grow and establish branches in every province where they wished to do so. While there was historically some populist opposition to the banks in the Western Provinces, they never gained sufficient political power to deflect the more or less benign and supportive regulations the central government adopted in overseeing banks that quickly established themselves as major players in the Canadian economy.[12] It was not until 1935 that the Bank of Canada was established as Canada's central bank—compared to 1913 for the creation of the Federal Reserve—and on the whole its policies have occasioned less political controversies than the Federal Reserve.[13]

A remarkably successful feature of the Canadian banking system consists of the periodic (re-)issuance of the bank's charters. Canadian banks are granted charters valid for only ten years; at the end of this period, they must provide an account of their performance, which gives them an incentive to manage risks prudently. But this also provides an opportunity for the banks to make their case for the inclusion in the renewed charter of new provisions more adapted to changing economic circumstances. The

[11] Canadian banks went through the Great Depression of the 1930s and the Great Recession of the late 2000s relatively unscathed.

[12] The Western Provinces (where populist hostility to banks has had a stronger footing) have always had a minority of seats in Parliament; moreover, monetary policy and banking is an exclusively federal jurisdiction in Canada.

[13] The best-known example of a conflict between politicians and the Bank of Canada happened in 1961; to protest pressures from Prime Minister John Diefenbaker to lower the interest rate, the governor of the Bank of Canada, James Coyne, resigned. However, in the long run, this episode has strengthened the independence of the Bank.

soundness of the Canadian banking system is confirmed by Bragues (2016, 138) who showed that the Austrian hypothesis of "malinvestment" applies better to the US than Canada, largely because of the differences in the institutional frameworks in which these two countries formulate and implement policies about credit, financial markets, and so on.[14]

The Canadian example reminds us that both government and market failures always occur against an institutional and cultural background that is itself a concatenation of past successes and failures on the part of myriads of political and economic actors. Perhaps, therefore, it is more appropriate to speak of path dependence than of a clear-cut dichotomy between government and market failures.[15] In other words, while the government failure thesis fits the facts of the 2007–2008 financial crisis rather well, it may simply be another episode in a series of predictable failures that are rooted in the complex structure of the American financial system itself.

IN THE WAKE OF THE CRISIS AND BEYOND: AN ABUNDANCE OF REFORM PROPOSALS AND POLICY EXPERIMENTS BUT LITTLE CLARITY AND EVEN LESS CERTAINTY

To a large extent, the differences of opinions about what reforms need to be undertaken to deal with the financial crisis closely matches the opposition between those who attribute the crisis to the failures of deliberate interventionist policies and those who argue that exaggeratedly self-interested players in the financial sector took advantage of opportunities created by deregulation and an overall laissez-faire climate. Austrian economists, advocates of the public choice paradigm, and many pro-market conservative economists belong to the school of thought that argues that little or no stimulus is required to grow the economy again (i.e., no interventionist fiscal or monetary policy is warranted). Beyond that, they believe the capacity of governments to regulate financial markets ought to be severely curtailed. Post-Keynesians form the core of the second school, but they have many allies among more orthodox economists and policy analysts. Proponents of the latter approach support interventionist fiscal and monetary policies and recommend re-regulating financial markets.

[14] On the healthier Canadian mortgage market, see also Young (2016).
[15] Path dependence is the main theme in Bordo et al.'s (2015) analysis of the causes of the stability of the Canadian banking system in comparison to the American system.

Surprisingly, both schools converge on one issue (but for different reasons): they are opposed to giving a free rein to bankers to make risky loans and to keep on expanding credit.

I hereafter examine the key ideas that these schools of thought advance as well as their political impact and political feasibility. Just as the arguments of the first school about the origins of the crisis (failed interventionism) have generally received less coverage than those of their intellectual adversaries, their policy proposals for reforming the regulatory system and financial markets have had little impact so far. Until very recently, they were politically unfeasible. The current Republican majority in the US Congress and some members of the Trump Administration, however, seem to be willing to implement a few of these ideas. This is not to say that the Trump Administration has a coherent set of goals with which all conservative economists agree. The post-Keynesians and more conventional Keynesians, on the other hand, were quite influential during the first term of the Obama presidency. They have been on the defensive more recently. Outside of the US, it is difficult to identify a clear pattern except to note that radical libertarian views—which I describe in more detail below—have had little traction in most jurisdictions outside of the US. Governments and central bankers in Europe and elsewhere appear to be vacillating between different priorities or economic doctrines, such as fiscal expansion or austerity (see Mitchell 2015; Aslund and Djankov 2017 for two opposite views regarding the optimal economic policies for Europe).

In commenting on these matters, my purpose is not to argue in favour of a specific political agenda. It is rather to underline the bedevilling complexity of the issues at stake and the limited set of options at the disposal of policy makers and private sector actors tasked with managing many other considerations beyond the advice they receive from academic economists. I begin with a brief discussion of remedies proposed by economists who are more inclined to see the origin of crises in government failures and, consequently, recommend even more deregulation and competition than mainstream "neoliberals."

Preventing Future Policy Failures by Reining in the "Big Players"

A thread running through the reforms proposed by the advocates of greater market freedom is that the role played by "Big Players" in the financial sector should be reduced. This is a theme developed at length by

Koppl (2002, 2014). "A Big Player is big in the sense that it influences the market" but "it is insensitive to the discipline of profit and loss; and it is arbitrary in the sense that its actions are based on discretion rather than any set of rules" (Koppl 2002, 120). Big Players, as defined by Koppl, include the many financial regulators, the Federal Reserve Board, the government-sponsored Fannie Mae and Freddie Mac, and to a lesser extent the credit rating agencies. Private firms enjoying a protected monopoly or oligopolistic situation would qualify, but at least in North America almost none are to be found in financial markets with the possible exception of the rating agencies. In other words, the Big Players should not be confused with big financial institutions such as the so-called systemically important financial institutions (SIFIs). It is not that "bigness" is not a potential problem—the "too big to fail" syndrome is obviously a major issue—but the decisions reached by SIFIs are not arbitrary but are in fact responsive to market conditions. Inversely, public authorities (e.g., the Federal Reserve Board of Governors) would cease to qualify as Big Players as Koppl defines them if they were bound by official, known, and stable rules, such as those that would be included in a monetary constitution. Big Players can also be identified in most other jurisdictions (e.g., the UK, the EU, and Japan). As regulatory agencies and the central banks became more active and exercised more discretion, there occurred a "separation of expectations formation [about the management of money] from underlying economic fundamentals" (Koppl 2002, 188). Koppl outlines goals that must be achieved to limit the discretionary power of the Big Players: (i) more fiscal discipline; (ii) move towards the denationalization of money (as discussed below); and (iii) more competition among regulators—for example, in the case of the US, ending the exclusive mandate of the SEC to regulate publicly traded firms and allowing state-level agencies to play a greater role (see Romano 1998, 2402),[16] or ending the oligopoly of the three dominant credit rating agencies.

The Big Players that public choice and Austrian economists are the most eager to downsize are the central bankers. The general idea is that "one clear lesson from the Great Recession… is that political control of money can do grave damage, even though it is taken for granted by the

---

[16] Chris Brummer (2008) explores the interesting potential for international competition among securities regulators as stock exchanges are increasingly competing for investors on a global basis.

political class and the intellectuals" (Horwitz 2011, 331). Most central bankers are guaranteed considerable decision-making autonomy once appointed. But the appointment process itself remains political.[17] The Austrians and their followers argue for the abolition of central banks altogether and the implementation of a system of "free banking." Public choice theorists, for their part, would be content with a severe curtailment of the functions of central banks by means of the "constitutionalisation of money" (Buchanan 2010).

Several decades ago, Friedrich Hayek (1976) advanced the idea of introducing competition in the use of currencies. His first step in that direction was to suggest that instead of establishing a single currency throughout what was still then called the European Common Market, each Common Market country should allow domestic transactions to be carried out in whichever currency people would prefer; thus a resident of Milan, Italy, for example, would have been able to buy a car with Deutsche marks. The rationale for this scheme being that the national central banks would be discouraged from inflating their home currencies for fear consumers and/or investors would switch to another one. But Hayek did not stop there. He went on to recommend doing away with the central banks' monopoly to issue money altogether. In other words, private banks could issue instruments of payments just as central banks do and all such instruments would compete in the markets for goods and services. This would provide a strong disincentive to abuse monetary policy for political purposes and prevent unsound investments not supported by a sufficient amount of savings. Interest rates would no longer be arbitrarily set by the monetary authorities but would converge towards their "natural" value.[18] If so, at least according to the Austrian business cycle theory, financial crises would be far less severe. Hayek (1976, 13) was the first one to acknowledge that he "was still very far from having solved all the problems which the existence of multiple concurrent currencies would raise." He considered that a second-best solution would be a gold standard administered by a central bank, even though he regarded gold as a "wobbly anchor" (Hayek 1976, 82–83).

---

[17] See the appointment by President Trump of Jerome Powell as Federal Reserve Chairman (Swanson and Appelbaum 2017).

[18] Keynesians are prone to refute the idea that there is such a thing as a natural rate of interest and assume that the rate is whatever the monetary authority decides; see Rochon (2016).

Hayek's "denationalization" is another term for "free banking"—a practice which was rather common in the nineteenth century and which is again attracting some attention because of the rise of unregulated digital currencies such as Bitcoin (Fung et al. 2017). Perhaps the most compelling argument in favour of free banking is that:

> Even if banks are rapacious, their self-motivated actions lead them quickly to redeem excess notes from other over-expanding banks to penalize them. Hence knavery is leveraged to provide a decentralized, self-enforcing accountability system that aims to correct monetary disequilibrium while also releasing relevant information to them through the changes in their reserves. (Paniagua 2016a, 23)

Whatever theoretical merits free banking may present, however, there is no point in dwelling on them because its political feasibility is very much in doubt (Paniagua 2016a, 26). Short of free banking, there still is the option of limiting the power of banks to leverage the deposits they are entrusted with. A few British policymakers have shown interest in this idea. There has been some support among Tories for better protecting the property rights of depositors although, so far, no legislative changes have resulted from their isolated initiatives.[19] Arguably more feasible is the scheme proposed by Mervyn King, former Governor of the Bank of England. He argues that making central banks more independent, lifting restriction on the flow of capital across borders, and allowing "banks both to diversify into new products and regions and to expand in size," thereby spreading risks, had contradictory consequences—some of which good, some bad, and some ugly (King 2016, 22). "The Good was a period between about 1990 and 2007 of unprecedented stability of both output and inflation – the Great Stability" (ibid., see above). "The Bad was the rise in debt levels" (ibid.). Finally, the "Ugly was the development of an extremely fragile banking system" (ibid., 23). The Bad and the Ugly combined in 2008 to defeat the Good (ibid., 24). The problem for King is the

---

[19] The Earl of Caithness and the Tory MPs Douglas Carswell and Steve Baker introduced bills, respectively, in the House of Lords (in 2008) and the House of Commons (in 2010), which proposed to give depositors more control over the use to which their bank deposits could be put; none of these bills were passed into law. Carswell later joined the UK Independence Party (UKIP) before eventually deciding to sit as an independent MP but did not run in the 2017 general election.

capacity that banks possess to create even more uncertainty than would in any event exist in complex economies. While he suggests that banks engage in a sort of alchemy along the lines of what critics of fractional reserve banking have long argued, he sees drawbacks in the idea of requiring commercial banks to back up 100% of their deposits with matching reserves. His alternative plan can be summarized as "no unconditional bailouts." He thinks that central banks, instead of acting as lenders of last resort, should become "pawnbrokers for all seasons" (King 2016, 269). In a time of crisis, banks could expect loans from the central bank only if they have collaterals in the form of reserves and assets, the value of which would be agreed upon in advance between the financial institutions and the central bank. This would set a limit to the banks' proclivity to take risks since they would know in advance the maximum amount of liquidity that would be made available to them in the event they need help from the central bank. Presumably, they would over time manage their assets and liabilities to avoid exceeding the limit beyond which the central bank would not come to their rescue. Outside of the UK, the most decisive move towards abolishing fractional reserve banking took place in Switzerland: a popular initiative to preclude commercial banks from creating lines of credit drew enough signatures in 2015 to begin the process that is constitutionally required to set up a referendum; but the Swiss Federal Council—the first step in that process—quashed the proposal in 2016.[20]

James Buchanan was sceptical about free banking and less worried about fractional reserve banking. He and public choice economists who follow in his path advocate instead the "constitutionalisation of money" (Buchanan 2010; Kohler et al. 2015). Buchanan wished to protect money from political manipulations but thought that market competition with regard to the issuance of currencies would lead to "monetary anarchy" (Buchanan 2010, 251). He argued that conventional thinking on constitutional matters has neglected "security in the value of money" (ibid., 253). Constitutionalization would not only entrench the independence of a central bank but also limit its discretionary powers by proclaiming that its only objective would be "maintenance in the value of the monetary unit" (ibid., 257). An objection to this sensible idea is that the judiciary

[20] It was dubbed the "sovereign money" initiative because only the national bank, as arm of the sovereign state, would have retained the power to create money.

may be ill-prepared to estimate the extent to which a monetary unit has "maintained" its value. Another is that its political feasibility is questionable. Constitutionalizing fiscal and monetary policy would be near impossible in many countries where constitutional amendments involve complicated procedures fraught with political risks.[21] However, a "monetary constitution" is not necessarily coterminous with a formal political constitution. As Paniagua (2016b, fn. 9 and fn. 16) explains, such a "constitution" could consist, at least in part, of unwritten conventional rules. What matters is less the strictly legal nature of monetary constitutional rules than their legitimacy and the ease (or rather lack thereof) with which they can be altered. The "constitutional" character of monetary rules lies in the expectation of stability they entail. In the case of Canada or the US, all that is required is the existence of a broad consensus that the fiscal and monetary instruments should not be used for short-term stabilization purposes (e.g., a political convention that budgets must be balanced).[22] Since the Treaty of Maastricht (1992), the rules upon which the European Monetary Union is founded have gradually taken the appearance of a monetary constitution. A commonly accepted principle is the independence of the European Central Bank (ECB). But there is a great deal of disagreement about what other principles should be entrenched in the European monetary constitution. Many economists and policy makers in Germany would prefer to put in place a regime somewhat similar to what Buchanan had in mind; that is to say, norms guaranteeing a sustainable non-inflationary growth of money supply with little regard for short-term economic objectives. But the rise of left- and right-wing populisms and more benign expressions of economic nationalism push in the opposite direction, that is, to make the ECB more responsive to economic trends and more accountable to the Council of Ministers, the European Parliament, and ultimately majority public opinion (Knupp 2011).

Experts and opinion leaders on the other side of the ideological divide will no doubt find reasons to take issue with these admittedly conservative proposals. But I would suggest that the Hayekian "knowledge problem"—

---

[21] In 2010, Congressmen Jeb Hensarling and Mike Pence (the then-future Vice-President) introduced a constitutional amendment—The Spending Limit Amendment—that would limit the growth of federal public spending to the rate of growth of the economy. Needless to say, it has little chance of ever being adopted.

[22] Over the past 25 years, Ottawa has stayed much closer to that objective than Washington.

the fact that policy makers rarely have sufficient knowledge to anticipate all the consequences of their decisions[23]—is a problem that transcends ideological barriers. Ironically, it also casts doubt on the presumed benefits of a radical and sudden return to free banking.

In fact, government failures are not always caused by overregulation and/or excessive interventionism: they may be due to poorly conceived or executed policy instruments. The consequence is that the solution is not necessarily less government intervention but better designed policies and regulations. But the knowledge problem cannot be easily circumvented; the information about, and familiarity with, the issues at stake are always incomplete and often inadequate.[24] This is why Austrian economists insist that the only solution is to have less regulations in place instead of always trying to come up with better ones.

It is interesting to compare the Austrian theory with Erik Gerding's (2014) Regulatory Instability Hypothesis. According to Gerding, financial regulations are typically enacted in the aftermath of an asset bubble but over time, as the recovery takes hold, and until the next one inevitably comes along, they are viewed as being unsuited to the new circumstances, and some rules may indeed turn out to be poorly thought out. Interest groups lobby to have them repealed or firms find ways around them ("regulation arbitrage"). But when the bubble bursts, the outcome is very damaging to the economy. Gerding, who provides a wealth of evidence to support his thesis, does not entirely side with the Austrians because he does not conclude that regulations ought to be kept to a strict minimum but concedes that no regulation can altogether prevent the occurrence of asset bubbles. The best institutional design principles should be applied to the more modest goal of drafting rules that can dampen their effects.

If indeed the knowledge problem is unavoidable, regulatory reforms that enhance rather than clip the powers of the Big Players are likely to miss their mark. Pragmatists may want to retort that reality is a little more nuanced. As noted above, the Canadian financial system seems to rest on

---

[23] An illustration is the Federal Reserve's inadequate rating prior to 2008 of mortgage-based securities counting towards the maintenance of reserves under the risk-based capital rules stipulated in the "Basel I" accord (Hogan and Manish 2016).

[24] Another way of describing this challenge is the well-known principal-agent problem which, in this instance, is a triple one involving (i) asymmetries of information between the public and elected officials, (ii) between the elected officials and the regulators, and (iii) between the banks and the regulators.

a sound regulatory foundation, although its soundness is due in part to the fact that originally rules were kept at a minimum, and even today remain flexible[25] because of the opportunities created every ten years by the renegotiation of the banks' charters—a process which limits the risks of both political dogmatism and regulatory capture (for the latter issue, see Cohn's chapter in this volume). All the same, policy makers ignore the knowledge problem at their own peril. But, as I explain hereafter, scepticism about the virtues of government interventionism and regulatory oversight has not been heeded in recent years. This ironically looks like a replay of the 1930s Hayek vs. Keynes controversy. In the early 1930s, Hayek was a respected economist teaching at the London School of Economics whose ideas were beginning to receive considerable attention. His very critical review of Keynes' *A Treatise on Money* (1930) prompted Keynes to write a rebuttal but soon after Keynes himself realized that this work was flawed. However, Keynes' *General Theory* (1936) was much more successful and Hayek's influence among economists waned for many years after that. But in the decades leading up to the 2008 crisis, Hayek's non-interventionist conception of the market as a "spontaneous order" had arguably eclipsed Keynesian interventionism, and yet as soon as the crisis occurred, Keynesianism was hastily rediscovered.

The Rise and Fall (?) of Keynesianism

Post-Keynesians object to the idea of deregulating financial markets and "letting the chips fall where they may" for theoretical reasons. They are convinced that investors and bankers tend to act in ways that, although seemingly rational in the short term, are destabilizing and counterproductive in the end. Such myopic, herd-like behaviours (harking back to Keynes' famous comments on "animal spirits") and the cancerous growth of the financial sector they produce must in their view be kept in check. In the wake of the 2007–2008 crisis, the political mood in all affected countries was far more receptive to these ideas than to those who blamed the Big Players in the public sphere.

---

[25] By "flexible" I do not mean to imply that Canadian regulations are not constraining nor that Canadian banks are free to take unsustainable risks but rather that errors due to the knowledge problem can be adjusted and that new challenges met in an agreed manner.

The response to the crisis was traditionally Keynesian in the fiscal area and more inspired by post-Keynesianism with respect to regulatory reforms. There was no mood for market absolutism in the wake of the 2007–2008 financial crisis. Massive bailouts and the injection of liquidity in the financial sector began under President George W. Bush. President Barack Obama succeeded in defeating his Republican opponent in 2008 by promising to pay more attention to "Main Street" than to "Wall Street." The first Obama Administration pursued a policy of fiscal stimulus, for example, implementing the various components of the Troubled Assets Relief Program (TARP) initiated in the last months of the Bush Administration and spearheading the *American Recovery and Reinvestment Act* (ARRA) of 2009. Canada and the EU countries also pursued fiscal stimulus policies of various kinds. However, there have been significant differences among advanced economies in the degree to which fiscal and/or monetary instruments were aggressively applied. These differences are largely explainable by the size of the "policy space" available to policy makers and/or central bankers. As Romer and Romer (2018) show with a wealth of data, countries with very large public debts (e.g., Japan) have not been able to stimulate their economies as efficiently as countries burdened with less debt (e.g., the US or Norway). Similarly, countries with already extremely low interest rates are obviously less able to lower them even further. But as a timid recovery began to take place, the policy makers' compass began to oscillate chaotically as they received conflicting advice and found themselves pushed and pulled in various directions. A turn towards austerity was noticeable in the US after the Republicans regained control of the House of Representatives—although the Obama Administration continued to push for investments in education and health care—and in the Southern European countries, under pressure from the IMF, the ECB, and the leaders of the larger Eurozone economies (see Mitchell 2015 for a harsh analysis of austerity). For somewhat different reasons, the British government moved in the same direction. In other words, public debt moved back to the top of the policy agenda. And yet, even more recently, electoral promises of massive public infrastructure investment were made, notably in the US, Canada, and France, but their implementation remains to be seen. In brief, fiscal Keynesianism regained some of the lustre it lost in the 1970s and 1980s but is far from being unchallenged. Inflation may no longer be a negligible threat while levels of public and private debt continue to be a concern. But this is only one

of the facets of a general climate of uncertainty and serious policy contra-
dictions in the global economy.

On the monetary front, the Federal Reserve embarked on an aggressive
policy of "quantitative easing" to accompany the fiscal stimulus and kept
interest rates quite low until 2017. In contrast to the pre-2007 situation,
this did not pose a risk because the economic recovery was still unfolding.
The Federal Reserve has raised rates since December 2015 but at a very
slow pace. Similar trends can be observed elsewhere (e.g., China). The
European Central Bank (ECB) was criticized by some European governments for not creating enough liquidity to support a sluggish recovery
immediately after the crisis and is holding steady at the time of writing.

Trends affecting financial regulation are no less confusing, at least with
respect to the US and Europe. In July 2010, the *Dodd-Frank Wall Street
Reform and Consumer Protection Act* was passed. It is a massive piece of
legislation (848 pages long) which imposes 390 requirements out of
which only 279 have been finalized at the time of writing. Dodd-Frank did
slightly increase the reserve requirement for American banks but did not
alter the role of the Federal Reserve as lender of last resort. This role is a
double-edged sword. On the one hand, it constitutes a safeguard against
systemic risk (i.e., a global collapse of the economic system). On the other
hand, it perpetuates moral hazard, which is certainly the most persistent
challenge for policymakers as well as citizens.

It is noteworthy that the Dodd-Frank Act paved the way to the so-
called Volcker rule. This regulation prohibits proprietary trading by banks,
that is, risky trading with the bank's own money, and limits their ownership of hedge funds. Dodd-Frank also creates a new institutional mechanism for overseeing the operation of Wall Street, most notably the Financial
Stability Oversight Council which has been granted significant authority
to constrain excessive risk in the financial system. For instance, the Council
has the authority to designate a nonbank financial firm for tough new
supervision to help minimize the risk of such a firm threatening the stability of the financial system (US Department of the Treasury 2017).

Many players in the financial industry have expressed their dissatisfac-
tion about Dodd-Frank. Not only is it a source of inefficiencies, particularly in its effects on small banks which face onerous reporting obligations
even though they are unlikely to cause the collapse of the American financial system, but it creates many opportunities for arbitrary decisions by the

regulators (Koppl 2014).[26] One of President Trump's first executive orders was indirectly aimed at Dodd-Frank; it instructed the Treasury Department to "identify whether existing regulations align with the new administration's goals, including fostering 'economic growth and vibrant financial markets'" (Protess 2017). The new chairman of the Commodity Futures Trading Commission, J. Christopher Giancarlo, is indeed expected to ease some of the rules. Congress has also weighed in. Congressman Jeb Hensarling, Chairman of the House Financial Services Committee, has introduced a bill titled the *Financial CHOICE Act* (as in Creating Hope and Opportunity for Investors, Consumers, and Entrepreneurs). The Financial CHOICE Act is intended to achieve a grand bargain whereby American Banks would be required to moderate their leverage (i.e., increasing their capital and liquidity requirements) in exchange for lessening or eliminating many of the regulations built into the Dodd-Frank Act, such as (i) the Volcker rule, (ii) the limits placed on the banks' ownership of hedge funds, and (iii) the "stress tests" imposed by the Federal Reserve. In their thorough review of the Financial CHOICE Act, Richardson et al. (2017, 5) conclude that while it would make the American financial system more efficient—something they welcome—it would also make it less safe. The main reason for such concern is that the Act does not distinguish between the riskier and less risky practices that would be deregulated. At the very least, the grand bargain mentioned above should start with a much more substantial increase in the reserve requirements.[27] To add to the confusion, while initiatives like the Financial CHOICE Act point in the direction of deregulation, the White House has signalled that it would be willing to bring back the principle enacted in the 1933 Glass-Steagall Act, which was repealed in 1999.[28]

Financial reform in Europe, at the time of writing, is still a work in progress because of the difficulties involved in reaching a consensus among

[26] Admittedly, a few checks and balances are built into the Dodd-Frank Act; for instance, the decisions of the Consumer Financial Protection Bureau can be appealed to the Financial Stability Oversight Council.

[27] Moreover, neither Dodd-Frank nor CHOICE address the fragile status of the GSEs (Fannie Mae and Freddie Mac), which have been in conservatorships since 2008 but whose involvement in the financial system remains important.

[28] The Glass-Steagall Act insulated banking activities from investment activities. The architects of Dodd-Frank considered reinstating Glass-Steagall in 2009–2010 but rejected this option because, in their view, it would not have prevented the 2007 crisis.

all the nations involved. These disparities reflect different degrees of commitment to the post-Keynesian doctrine and its insistence on the need to protect investors from their own irrationality, as well as different opinions about the centralization of policy making in the EU. Many pieces of legislation were introduced in the aftermath of the crisis; the careful review of each would take us beyond the scope of this chapter. However, some measures deserve more examination. In 2014, the EU adopted the *Bank Recovery and Resolution Directive* (the Directive), which is designed to help policy makers deal with bank failures at the national level and across boundaries.[29] Among other provisions, the Directive includes regulations comparable to the Volcker rule in order to prevent banks from engaging in proprietary trading and other more targeted "ring-fencing" provisions. Foot dragging by the UK is part of the reason for this delay, but the positions defended by the UK fit within a broader debate between those who want tighter regulations and those who are reluctant to move in the direction of a greater centralization of authority at the European level. As Aneta Spendzharova (2016, 228) observes, partial solutions to the "too big to fail" problem led to various sets of proposed reforms (e.g., capital adequacy rules, bank supervision, bank resolution regimes, etc.). Those "have constrained the opportunities to design a coherent EU framework regulating bank structures."

It is noteworthy that Japan deregulated its financial market in the 2000s. After the 2008 turmoil, which shook Japan less than other Western economies, some regulations were tightened, especially with respect to the use of derivatives, but Prime Minister Abe still aims at developing domestic capital markets to attract investors and start-ups. In this context, there is little to expect from Japanese regulators.

Lastly, at the international level it should be noted that the so-called Basel III agreement imposes on banks a higher leverage threshold than was the case with the much-criticized Basel II agreement, requiring them at all times to maintain a ratio of at least 4.5% between common equity and risk-weighted assets. These standards are in the process of being put into effect in many jurisdictions. But critics argue that the way in which

---

[29] The more comprehensive package entitled *Structural Measures Improving the Resilience of the EU Credit Institutions*, which was first proposed by the European Commission in January 2014, has still to be approved by the European Parliament at the time of writing.

the banks are allowed to weigh the risks still leaves too much room for risky decisions.

The above remarks are not intended to present a comprehensive overview of all the efforts undertaken in all the major economies in order to avert a major financial crisis. Instead, these somewhat eclectic comments suggest that the clear-cut priorities of the advocates of market competition and of a reduced role for Big Players are almost entirely rejected by policy makers. In fact, pragmatic and ad hoc policy responses using a variety of methods seem to be more reliable than rigid and dogmatic regulatory frameworks that may prove to be flawed in some unexpected manner.

CONCLUSION

The challenges facing all who would propose reforms have not been made simpler by recent social and political trends. The current surge of populist parties or movements in many (if not most) advanced countries threatens an economic recovery that is much less robust than the boom of US and European stock exchange indices could suggest. Inequalities go on widening, job markets are still weak in European countries, and private and public debt levels remain at very high levels there. In addition to these fundamental macro-economic weaknesses, regulatory rules do not seem to be correctly designed to prevent a new financial crisis.

In the face of such uncertainty, the spectre of government failure looms large. Prudence would recommend not taking chances with the public debt, refraining from threatening the independence of central banks, or otherwise confusing economic actors about the direction of fiscal and monetary policies. Doing less, however, does not equate with suddenly abdicating all responsibilities. Curbing the power of the Big Players by introducing more competition, as advocated by those who have more faith in markets than in governments, might be a sound policy; however, returning to free banking or the gold standard could very well have unintended consequences. Experimenting with more modest yet still innovative schemes trending in a similar direction, such as the one proposed by Mervyn King, is more advisable. It is also encouraging that European leaders have resisted the simplistic idea that the ECB should oversee *all* banks in the Eurozone and so far have agreed that responsibilities should be assigned on the basis of the size of the banks, allowing experimentation at the national level in the case of the smaller banks. Whether all this diversity can be managed in a way that maintains some coherence and predictability, however, is an open question. When rules proliferate or are constantly adjusted, a government failure—one that is caused by conflicting signals sent from different sources in a global economy where investment flows are increasingly transnational—becomes more menacing.

An uncertain political climate makes a sustained move towards stable monetary rules more challenging. This lack of stability is certainly the most troubling aspect of the current system. The Great Recession is now behind us but what lessons have been learned is unclear. Whether top policy makers are populist (e.g., President Donald Trump), are hedged by populist pressures (e.g., Prime Minister Theresa May), or are "centrists" attempting to satisfy disparate expectations (e.g., Prime Minister Justin Trudeau or President Emmanuel Macron), the preferred direction for the future of the global financial system is uncertain (see Fisher and Taub 2017). In fact, anti-establishment sentiments work both ways: they are consistent with massive spending initiatives, protectionism, and "draining the swamp" of Wall Street, on the one hand. Anti-bureaucratic sentiments can also be harnessed to the cause of deregulation, lower taxes, and investor-friendly policies. Confusing signals from the Trump Administration are especially symptomatic: they seem to indicate a willingness to experiment with both fiscal imbalance—at the risk of dramatically increasing the public debt of the US—and a quasi-Austrian determination to let the chips fall where they may in the financial sector (e.g., committing to not bailing out failed companies). No one knows for certain when the next bubble is going to burst, but it remains to be seen whether we are more prepared now than we were for the bursting of the previous one.

Rather than advancing specific policy prescriptions, I would like to make some methodological recommendations. First, the thread that runs through this chapter is that global finance is a devilishly complex subject, and its complexity unfolds at two levels: (i) when one tries to make sense of the mechanisms of the global economy and of the role of the financial sector within it and (ii) when one considers the daunting problem for policy makers who, regardless of the merits of the technical solutions they wish to put forward, have to manoeuvre through the political institutions within which they operate, be it the "checks and balances" embedded in the US government, the institutions of the EU, or international organizations. We may not fully understand the problems at hand but, even if we do, "solutions" are rarely viewed as such by all parties involved.

Therefore, my advice is twofold: to invest intellectually in approaches that deal with complexity and strategic interactions, namely, complexity theory and game theory, but also to adopt a more *self-critical* stance and to search for ways to dialogue with colleagues in a variety of other disciplines, from psychology to anthropology, who work from very different but sometimes illuminating perspectives.

I allude to game theory for two reasons: it is a rich source of materials on institutional design (for an example among many others, see Roth 2002). But even if one does not wish to deploy the mathematical models that this literature has produced, there are epistemological insights that should be useful to those who wish to understand how government failures in general and regulatory failures in particular occur. Many of the recent advances in game theory revolves around the problems caused by the lack of consistency or alignment between the beliefs of players who enter a competitive situation thinking that they are "playing" another game than the one their opponents believe they are engaged in: regulators look at macro-economic variables, financial institutions and firms are guided by the interests of their shareholders, elected officials seek re-election, interest groups raise their own concerns, and so on. Those who see the result of these interactions taking the form of government failure seek market-based solutions but are frustrated in reaching that goal by sociopolitical constraints. Those who seek to remedy market failures sometimes receive political support for their policy goals but are frustrated by the unintended economic consequences of their interventionist policies. In the end, business and political cycles reinforce each other, in ways that other chapters in this volume explore. There is no obvious solution to this dilemma, but paying closer attention to strategic thinking is a necessary first step towards robust second-best institutional rules and policies.

The usual style of discourse, but one that I would suggest has led us into this impasse, is to forcefully argue in favour of a specific type of reform in pursuit of marginal improvement. Analysts are trained to provide logical and evidence-based arguments supporting an *optimal* solution. In this chapter, I have emphasized the merits of some of the theoretical arguments and factual evidence put forward by libertarian economists. But the lack of political traction of such proposals prompts me to suggest a more pragmatic approach. And that is to think carefully about how *second-best* solutions can be achieved. It is in this respect that a detour through the literatures on complexity, strategic thinking, behavioural economics, and so on can be immensely useful. Paying more attention to the motivations of all the actors involved, the psychological mechanisms at play in most conflicts, and so on, could be a way to formulate potentially more workable measures. The key is to discover how to "nudge" people who hold different positions towards some sort of agreement to at least enter into a more productive dialogue. Thus, if market-based rather than interventionist policies are theoretically preferable, and indeed make sense to most economists, it must also be acknowledged that many political and social actors are more concerned with fairness than with efficiency. It is not enough to point the finger at the mistakes made at Fannie Mae or Freddie Mac, for example. It is also crucial to understand why, for example, attempting to make it possible for a low-income household to obtain a mortgage was such an important priority for so many Democratic as well as Republican elected officials and civil society groups.

Inversely, proponents of stricter financial regulations, more transparency, and more controls over financial institutions, which could be perceived as being inimical to entrepreneurship, must offer ways of improving economic efficiency in other areas, for instance by removing trade barriers, lowering corporate taxes, and so on. The dogmatic pursuit of a one-dimensional programme of reform is usually not a winning strategy. The failure of so-called neoliberal policies in the 2000s is undoubtedly a striking illustration of the limits of those "monolithic", one-dimensional economic policies (see Kotz 2015). Political economists must think more about how their recommendations can generate agreement around second-best options than about showing that the solutions to the problems they have identified are technically unassailable, let alone ideologically pure. In a second-best world, government failures cannot be ruled out, markets are less than perfectly competitive, and financial crises cannot be fully averted, but they are less likely to be catastrophic.

Acknowledgements Ted Cohn, Norbert Gaillard, and Anil Hira

REFERENCES

Aslund, Anders and Simeon Djankov. 2017. *Europe's Growth Challenge*. Oxford and New York: Oxford University Press.
Bator, Francis M. 1958. The Anatomy of Market Failure. *Quarterly Journal of Economics*. 72(3): 351–379.
Bernanke, Ben S. and Frederic S. Mishkin. 1997. Inflation Targeting: A New Framework for Monetary Policy? *Journal of Economic Perspectives*. 11(2): 97–116.

Bordo, Michael D., Angela Redish, and Hugh Rockoff. 2015. Why Didn't Canada Have a Banking Crisis in 2008 (or in 1930, or 1907, or...)? *Economic History Review.* 68(1): 218–243.

Bragues, George. 2016. The Political Regime Factor in Austrian Business Cycle Theory: Historically Accounting for the US and Canadian Experiences of the 2007–2009 Financial Crisis. In Steven Horwitz (Ed.). *Studies in Austrian Macroeconomics.* Vol. 20 of the series Advances in Austrian Economics. Bingley, UK: Emerald Group Publishing.

Brummer, Chris. 2008. Stock Exchanges and the New Markets for Securities Laws. *University of Chicago Law Review.* 75(4): 1435–1491.

Buchanan, James. 2010. The Constitutionalisation of Money. *Cato Journal.* 30(2): 251–258.

Calomiris, Charles W. and Stephen H. Haber. 2014. *Fragile by Design: The Political Origins of Banking Crises and Scarce Credit.* Princeton: Princeton University Press.

Coase, Ronald. 1960. The Problem of Social Cost. *Journal of Law and Economics.* 3: 1–44.

Colander, David, Michael Goldberg, Armin Haas, Katarina Juselius, Alan Kirman, Thomas Lux, and Brigitte Sloth. 2009. The Financial Crisis and the Systemic Failure of the Economics Profession. *Critical Review.* 21(2–3): 249–267.

Engel, Kathleen C. and Patricia A. McCoy. 2011. *The Subprime Virus: Reckless Credit, Regulatory Failure, and Next Step.* New York: Oxford University Press.

Fisher, Max and Amanda Taub. 2017. Uncertainty, More Than Populism, Is New Normal in Western Politics. *New York Times.* June 10.

Friedman, Jeffrey. 2009. A Crisis of Politics, Not Economics: Complexity, Ignorance and Policy Failure. *Critical Review.* 21(2–3): 127–183.

Fung, Ben, Scott Hendry and Warren E. Weber. 2017. Canadian Bank Notes and Dominion Notes: Lessons for Digital Currencies. *Staff Working Paper 2017-5,* Bank of Canada.

Gaillard, Norbert J. and William J. Harrington. 2016. Efficient, Commonsense Actions to Foster Accurate Credit Ratings. *Capital Markets Law Journal.* 11(1): 38–59.

Gerding, Erik F. 2014. *Law, Bubbles, and Financial Regulation.* London: Routledge.

Hayek, Friedrich A. 1976. *Denationalisation of Money.* London: Institute of Economic Affairs.

Hendrickson, J.M. 2011. *Regulation and Instability in US Commercial Banking: A History of Crises.* New York City: Palgrave Macmillan.

Hogan, Thomas L. and G.P. Manish. 2016. Banking Regulations and Knowledge Problems. In Steven Horwitz (Ed.). *Studies in Austrian Macroeconomics.* Vol. 20 of the series Advances in Austrian Economics. Bingley, UK: Emerald Group Publishing.

Horwitz, Steven. 2011. Do We Need a Distinct Monetary Constitution? *Journal of Economic Behavior and Organisation*. 80(2): 331–338.

Jablecki, Juliusz. 2009. The Impact of Basel I Capital Requirements on Bank Behavior and the Efficacy of Monetary Policy. *International Journal of Economic Sciences and Applied Research*. 2(1): 16–35.

Keen, Steve. 2013. Predicting the 'Global Financial Crisis': Post-Keynesian Macroeconomics. *Economic Record*. 89(285): 228–254.

King, Mervyn. 2016. *The End of Alchemy: Money, Banking and the Future of the Global Economy*. London: Little, Brown.

Knupp, Christopher. 2011. The ECB and its Monetary Policy: Between Nostalgia and Anti-Growth Policy. Paper for the 15th FMM Conference, From crisis to growth? The challenge of imbalances, debt, and limited resources, available at https://www.boeckler.de/pdf/v_2011_10_27_knupp.pdf

Kohler, Ekkehard, Victor J. Vanberg, and Lawrence H. White. 2015. *Renewing the Search for a Monetary Constitution: Reforming Government's Role in the Monetary System*. Washington, D.C.: Cato Institute Press.

Koppl, Roger. 2002. *Big Players and the Economic Theory of Expectations*. London: Palgrave.

Koppl, Roger. 2014. *From Crisis to Confidence: Macroeconomics after the Crash*. London: Institute of Economic Affairs.

Kotz, David M. 2015. *The Rise and Fall of Neoliberal Capitalism*. Cambridge, MA and London: Harvard University Press.

Krugman, Paul. 2012. *End this Depression Now!* New York: W. W. Norton.

Mian, Atif and Amir Sufi. 2014. *House of Debt: How They (and You) Caused the Great Recession, and How We Can Prevent It from Happening Again*. Chicago: University of Chicago Press.

Minsky, Hyman P. [1986] 2008. *Stabilizing and Unstable Economy*. New York: McGraw-Hill.

Mitchell, William. 2015. *Eurozone Dystopia – Groupthink and Denial on a Grand Scale*. Cheltenham and Northampton: Edward Elgar.

Moosa, Imad A. 2015. *Good Regulation, Bad Regulation: The Anatomy of Financial Regulation*. London: Palgrave Macmillan.

Oppers, Stefan Erik 2002. The Austrian Theory of Business Cycles: Old Lessons from Modern Economic Policy? *IMF Working Papers WP/02/2*.

Paniagua, Pablo. 2016a. The Robust Political Economy of Central Banking and Free Banking. *Review of Austrian Economics*. 29(1): 15–32.

Paniagua, Pablo. 2016b. The Stability Properties of Monetary Constitutions. *Journal des Economistes et des Etudes Humaines*. 22(2): 113–138.

Protess, Ben. 2017. Trump Picks a Regulator Who Could Help Reshape Dodd-Frank Act. *The New York Times*. March 14.

Reinhart, Carmen, and Kenneth Rogoff. 2009. *This Time is Different: Eight Centuries of Financial Folly*. Princeton: Princeton University Press.

Richardson, Matthew P., Kermit L. Schoenholtz, Bruce Tuckman, and Lawrence J. White. 2017. *Regulating Wall Street: CHOICE Act vs. Dodd-Frank*. New York: NYU Stern and NYU Law School Faculty.

Rochon, Louis-Philippe. 2016. In Pursuit of the Holy Grail: Monetary Policy, the Natural Rate of Interest, and Quantitative Easing. *Studies in Political Economy*. 97(1): 87–94.

Romano, Roberta. 1998. Empowering Investors: A Market Approach to Securities Regulation. *Yale Law Journal*. 107(5): 2359–2430.

Romer, Christina D. and David H. Romer. 2018. Phillips Lecture – Why Some Times Are Different: Macroeconomic Policy and the Aftermath of Financial Crises. *Economica*. 85(337): 1–40.

Roth, Alvin E. 2002. The Economist as Engineer: Game Theory, Experimentation, and Computation as Tools for Design Economics. *Econometrica*. 70(4): 1341–1378.

Spendzharova, Aneta B. 2016. Regulatory Cascading: Limitations of Policy Design in European Banking Structural Reforms. *Policy and Society*. 35(3): 227–237.

Swanson, Ana and Binyamin Appelbaum. 2017. Trump Announces Jerome Powell as New Fed Chairman. *New York Times*. November 2.

U.S. Department of the Treasury. 2017. Financial Stability Oversight Council: About FSOC, available at https://www.treasury.gov/initiatives/fsoc/about/Pages/default.aspx

U.S. Securities and Exchange Commission. 2016. 2016 Summary Report of the Commission's Staff Examination of Each Nationally Recognized Statistical Rating Organization. Washington, D.C.

Wallison, Peter J. 2009. Cause and Effect: Government Policies and the Financial Crisis. *Critical Review*. 21(2–3): 365–376.

Young, Andrew T. 2016. Canadian versus US Mortgage Markets: A Comparative Study from an Austrian Perspective. In Steven Horwitz (Ed.). *Studies in Austrian Macroeconomics*. Vol. 20 of the series Advances in Austrian Economics. Bingley, UK: Emerald Group Publishing.

CHAPTER 3

The Effects of Regulatory Capture on Banking Regulations: A Level-of-Analysis Approach

Theodore H. Cohn

INTRODUCTION

Financial regulation refers to the laws, rules, and enforcement procedures associated with the functioning of financial institutions and markets. Regulatory failure occurs when regulators and politicians fail to serve the public interest because of their actions or inaction: They may impose unnecessary or ill-advised regulations; they may fail to impose necessary regulations; or they may dismantle necessary regulations. Several theories of regulation are prominent in the literature, including the public interest, regulatory capture, special interest groups, and credible commitment theories (Moosa 2015, 7–15; Christensen 2011, 96–110; Mattli and Woods 2009, 1–43). This chapter focuses on the effects of regulatory capture on banking regulations. *Regulatory capture* occurs when regulators and politicians consistently and systematically give preference to the regulated interests over the public interest. A number of studies describe

T. H. Cohn (✉)
Department of Political Science, Simon Fraser University, Burnaby, BC, Canada
e-mail: cohn@sfu.ca

© The Author(s) 2019

A. Hira et al. (eds.), *The Failure of Financial Regulation*,
International Political Economy Series,
https://doi.org/10.1007/978-3-030-05680-3_3

regulatory capture as one of the factors contributing to the 2008 global financial crisis.

This chapter has two main objectives in line with those of the volume. First, I examine the effects of regulatory capture on banking regulations at both the domestic (US) and global levels. I assess the validity of a hypothesis closely associated with regulatory capture theory—that capture resulted in the banking deregulation which was a major factor contributing to the 2008 financial crisis. I also assess the degree to which capture remains an issue since the 2008 crisis.

The worst financial crises usually involve banks, because they are often highly leveraged; that is, they have large amounts of debt relative to assets or income. Leverage enables banks to increase their returns on investment, but it can also result in increased risk-taking and moral hazard. Banks are also often associated with financial crises because there is an inherent mismatch between their borrowing and lending behaviour. By lending out funds, commercial banks earn returns on the created bank loans while performing the important function of credit creation. However, the funding for such loans consist of deposits that people can withdraw on short notice. If depositors (or investors in regard to investment banks) lose confidence and withdraw their funds (or reduce or cease making deposits) bank failures can result. While sovereign defaults and exchange rate crises have been much more common in developing economies, banking crises are "an equal-opportunity menace, affecting rich and poor countries alike" (Reinhart and Rogoff 2009, xxvii). Regulatory capture in the case of banks can therefore have serious and widespread consequences.

The second primary objective of this chapter is to address an apparent gap in the literature. Most international political economy (IPE) research focuses on regulatory capture through two levels of analysis: the national and global levels. This chapter seeks to also examine capture at the individual level. In *Man, the State and War,* Kenneth Waltz seeks answers to the causes of war by looking "within man, within the structure of the separate states, within the state system" (Waltz 1959, 12). Drawing on Waltz, this chapter argues that only by looking at all three levels can we adequately assess regulatory capture theory. As the chapter progresses, it will become clear that the three levels are overlapping and interactive. However, I begin by discussing regulatory capture theory generally, and criticisms of the theory, particularly as it relates to banking.

Regulatory Capture Theory

Regulatory capture theory proposes that regulators may consistently and systematically give priority to a regulated industry's interests over the public interest; that is, the regulators are "captured" by the regulated. In a seminal study, George Stigler wrote that an industry often acquires regulation which "is designed and operated for" the industry's benefit. For example, "every industry or occupation that has enough political power" will seek state regulations that benefit well-established firms and limit the entry of new rival firms (Stigler 1971, 3 and 5). Scholars often concluded from early studies such as Stigler's that the solution to regulatory capture was to discontinue or avoid regulations that benefited industries at the expense of the public interest. No regulation was preferable to a captured regulatory agency that carried with it the authority of the government. However, "corrosive capture" that results in the dismantling of regulation is more common in regard to banking issues (Carpenter and Moss 2014, 16). A number of studies contend that deregulation resulting from capture enabled banks to engage in risky innovations that contributed to the 2008 financial crisis. As discussed, this is the hypothesis to be examined in this chapter.

Regulatory capture theorists are concerned about both market and government failures. *Market failure* occurs when the market fails to produce an optimal allocation of resources; for example, the market may produce private benefits that have huge social costs. *Government failure* occurs when government intervention does not correct market failure efficiently, when it is unwarranted because the market is performing adequately, or when it produces unintended negative consequences (on government failure, see the analysis developed by Dobuzinskis in this volume). Regulatory capture theorists view capture as an indication of government failure, because government regulators give preference to private interests of the regulated over the general public interest. However, they also warn that inadequate government regulation enables banks to engage in risky activities contributing to market failure.

Capture theorists seek to explain why and how capture occurs. The general public's influence on banking regulators is *diffuse*, because most citizens have little incentive to influence the regulators and because the marginal benefit of the regulation may be very small. The influence of banks on the regulators by contrast is *concentrated*, because the regulations directly affect them and the marginal benefit to their profits can be significant. Banks and other financial institutions are in fact "one of the most concentrated and well-organized interest groups in modern societies" (Drezner 2014, 87). Rational choice theorists argue that concentrated interests of industries have more influence over policy makers than diffuse interests of the public because politicians adopt policies that improve their chances for re-election (Cohn 2016, 91; Moosa 2015, 10–13). Regulated banks can also capture the regulators by providing them with benefits such as offers of more lucrative jobs as bank employees or lobbyists. This is referred to as *material capture*, because it assumes that regulators and politicians as rational, self-interested actors gain something materially (e.g., financial benefits) from favouring regulated banking interests over the general public interest. Material capture sometimes borders on corruption, that is, dishonest or fraudulent behaviour. However, regulators who are subject to material capture are not necessarily corrupt. Some theorists argue that cognitive or cultural capture is also important (Baker 2010, 653–654; Engstrom 2013, 31–32; Kwak 2014). *Cultural capture* occurs when regulators and politicians develop more shared belief systems with the regulated banks through the colonizing of ideas; this can result in decisions favouring the regulated over the public interest. Regulators may be unaware of the degree to which their worldviews are influenced by the regulated (Kwak 2014, 78–80; Engstrom 2013, 32).

CRITICISMS OF REGULATORY CAPTURE THEORY

Some scholars contend that the regulatory capture concept is too widely used in IPE. For example, Kevin Young argues that "while some literature expresses some mild reservations about regulatory capture, the concept is relatively ubiquitous and relatively unquestioned in the existing IPE literature" (Young 2012, 666). Daniel Carpenter and David Moss assert that a major problem with regulatory capture research "is not merely its tendency to overstate the evidence for capture, but its lack of nuance in describing how and to what degree capture works in particular settings" (Carpenter and Moss 2014, 9). They argue that capture only occurs if the regulated industry "actively and knowingly" pushes "regulation away from the public interest" (Carpenter and Moss 2014, 13–14). It is also important to distinguish between "hard" and "soft" capture. *Hard capture* goes so much against the public interest that it might be best to replace the regulatory agency or stop trying to regulate an industry. *Soft capture* decreases the degree to which regulation benefits the public interest, but on balance the regulatory agency still enhances social welfare (Carpenter and Moss 2014, 11–12; Engstrom 2013, 33). The most widespread criticism is that IPE scholars do not do rigorous empirical studies before concluding that capture has occurred.

Claims of regulatory capture should of course be subject to rigorous empirical examination whenever possible. Alan Blinder, a Princeton University economist, writes that he has "long been distressed by the high correlation between economists' political views and their allegedly objective research findings" (Blinder 2014, 56–57). IPE scholars examining material capture are also affected by their political views, and their empirical studies sometimes result in contradictory conclusions. Furthermore, cultural capture is also important, even though it is more difficult to demonstrate empirically than material capture. The importance of cultural capture raises questions about Carpenter and Moss's contention that capture can only occur if regulated industries "actively and knowingly push regulation away from the public interest" (Carpenter and Moss 2014, 13–14). With cultural capture, regulators and politicians internalize the preferences of the private sector not necessarily because of "a conscious and deliberate strategy of capture," but because of "formal and informal practices of public-private interaction and agreement among an increasingly coherent and transnational policy community" (Tsingou 2008, 59). Carpenter and Moss are correct that the evidence of capture is stronger if we can show that the regulated industries actively and knowingly push regulation away from the public interest. However, it is not always possible to demonstrate (or measure) this in regard to cultural capture.

Another criticism of capture theory is that it overemphasizes the effect of private financial interests in determining regulatory outcomes. Eric Helleiner points to an alternative explanation for regulatory outcomes that is state-centric, focusing "on power and politics among and within influential states" (Helleiner 2014, 19). In accordance with Helleiner's view, this chapter shows that private banking interests are unlikely to succeed in regulatory capture without the support of government actors. A final criticism is that the definition of capture as privileging a regulated industry's interests over the public interest does not identify what "public interest" means. It can be argued that the subjective determination of "the public interest" contributes to the correlation noted by Blinder. Some critics even reject the idea that there is an identifiable public interest, asserting that individuals and special interest groups espouse a diversity of interests (Engstrom 2013, 31; Mattli and Woods 2009, 13).

Although there is no universally accepted definition of the public interest, it is a useful concept when discussing regulatory capture. The public interest as commonly understood in most developed countries has several characteristics. First, it is associated with due process standards. Groups and individuals are more likely to accept a decision as being in the public interest if they have the opportunity for input and consultation. Inclusive forums with broad-ranging consultation are less susceptible to regulatory capture and more likely to serve the public interest than exclusive forums that privilege the regulated industries. Second, the public interest is better served by informed and educated citizens who are interested in expressing their views and are able to elect their representatives. Third, the public interest is rooted in welfare economics, which depicts government regulation as a response to market failure. Market failure may result from anticompetitive behaviour, information asymmetries, or failure to provide public goods. State regulation serves the public interest when it provides remedies for these market deficiencies (Mattli and Woods 2009, 12–26; Carpenter and Moss 2014, 13–16; Morgan and Yeung 2007, 18). In this chapter, I define the "public interest" as the opportunity for input, and the welfare of the community as a whole as compared to the input and welfare of the private banking industry.

This chapter examines the strengths and shortcomings of capture theory by assessing the validity of the hypothesis that regulatory capture resulted in banking deregulation that contributed to the 2008 financial crisis. To assess this hypothesis, it is necessary to focus on the individual, national, and global levels. Special attention is given to the individual level because it has received little attention in the IPE literature. My discussion of each level focuses mainly on the period before the 2008 financial crisis, but also examines the post-crisis period. I also point to the interaction among the three levels.

THE INDIVIDUAL LEVEL

The individual level deals with issues related to individual regulators who occupy key positions. The worldviews of important regulators can have a significant effect on the regulatory process (Barth et al. 2012, 6). For example, banking regulators may be orthodox or interventionist liberals. Orthodox liberals support "negative freedom," or freedom of the market to function with minimal interference from the state. Interventionist liberals, by contrast, support some government involvement to promote more equity and justice in a free market economy (Cohn 2016, 77–78). Whereas interventionist liberals focus on market as well as government failure, orthodox liberals tend to be fixated on government failure.

A regulator's worldview, of course, never fits fully within one type of liberalism, but regulators can lean more towards one type. To demonstrate how a regulator's worldview can affect the regulatory process, I focus here on Alan Greenspan, who was Chair of the Board of Governors of the United States (US) *Federal Reserve* (the *Fed*).

The Greenspan Case

As noted in Chap. 1, the Fed, founded in 1913, is the main financial regulator of US banking and financial institutions. Greenspan was the Fed Chair for five terms under four US Presidents (Ronald Reagan, George H.W. Bush, Bill Clinton, and George W. Bush), from August 1987 to January 2006. William McChesney Martin was the only Fed Chair who served slightly longer than Greenspan, from 1951 to 1970. However, banking, credit, and the Fed became much more important during Greenspan's tenure (Mallaby 2016, 5). Greenspan is a complex individual whose views have evolved over time, and there are competing interpretations of his worldview. Sebastian Mallaby, in his biography *The Man Who Knew*, asserts that Greenspan "never was a simple efficient market believer, and he sometimes voiced grave doubts about the risks in financial innovation" (Mallaby 2016, 7). Timothy Geithner, who worked closely with Greenspan in the 1990s, by contrast writes that Greenspan had "an almost theological belief that markets were rational and efficient, as well as a deep skepticism that government supervision and regulation could make them safer" (Geithner 2014, 85). Despite these competing interpretations, Greenspan was inclined to see the world more through an orthodox than an interventionist liberal lens, and he was a close associate of Ayn Rand. Even when he was Fed Chair, Greenspan regularly expressed an "aversion to regulation" (Engel and McCoy 2011, 189). His faith in financial innovation outweighed his interest in regulation, and he believed that the market could best regulate itself. In his key position, Greenspan's worldview was a significant factor in the banking deregulation before the 2008 financial crisis.

The appointment of individuals to key regulatory positions provides an opening for capture, because lobbyists "can promote certain candidates for appointment to a given position or block others who might not share their views" (Lavelle 2013, 131). In terms of my hypothesis, regulated banking institutions are likely to favour orthodox liberals as regulators who would be inclined to promote deregulation. This was certainly the case when Greenspan was appointed Fed Chair in 1987. The events leading up to the Greenspan appointment attest to this fact. After almost 5000 banks failed during the Great Depression, the US Congress passed the *Glass-Steagall Act* (the *Bank Act of 1933*), which separated commercial and investment banking. The *Federal Deposit Insurance Corporation* (*FDIC*) was established in 1933 to protect commercial banks from panic-induced bank runs, but the banks had to accept tight federal regulations in return. Although the *Securities and Exchange Commission* (*SEC*) would regulate investment banks, the regulation was looser and did not focus on ensuring the banks' health and stability. Commercial banks tried to circumvent the Glass-Steagall constraints, but for several decades the US Congress limited their activities. In the 1970s, however, banks became more aggressive in pushing back against Glass-Steagall, and Congress began to lose some of its resolve. Joseph Stiglitz writes in his book *Freefall* that Greenspan's appointment was closely related to the moves towards deregulation:

> When President Ronald Reagan appointed Greenspan chairman of the Federal Reserve in 1987, he was looking for someone committed to deregulation. Paul Volcker, who had been the Fed chairman previously, had earned high marks as a central banker for bringing the U.S. inflation rate down.... Normally, such an accomplishment would have earned automatic reappointment. But Volcker understood the importance of regulations, and Reagan wanted someone who would work to strip them away. (Stiglitz 2010, xvii)

Stiglitz does not tell the full story as to why Greenspan was appointed in 1987. President Jimmy Carter had nominated Volcker to be Chair of the Fed in 1979, and in 1983 President Reagan had to decide whether to renominate him for a second term. Greenspan, who was already being considered for the position, was a Republican like Reagan, while Volcker was a Democrat. Reagan nevertheless renominated Volcker in 1983, largely because of his success in controlling inflation (Mallaby 2016, 286–293). Thus, other forces besides Reagan's political affiliation and personal views played a role in his 1987 decision to replace Volcker with Greenspan. The events leading up to Reagan's 1987 decision show that banking institutions had a major role in Greenspan's appointment.

In 1984 JP Morgan launched a forceful drive for the deregulation of Glass-Steagall, which prevented commercial banks from underwriting and dealing with securities. Wall Street was increasingly involved with packaging mortgages and other loans as tradable securities, and JP Morgan as a commercial bank viewed dealing with securities as essential to maintaining its competitiveness. Volcker wanted to prevent commercial banks from moving rapidly into securities, while Greenspan by contrast was a JP Morgan Director who was generally supportive of the firm's position. To increase the pressure on Volcker, Bankers Trust and Citicorp joined with JP Morgan in formally requesting that the Fed permit them to set up securities affiliates. Volcker resisted this pressure and delayed responding to their request for more than two years. However, President Reagan, Secretary of the Treasury James Baker, and leading Republican senators supported the banks' petition to move into securities, and Volcker was increasingly isolated. In 1987, the Fed Board of Governors held several votes in which the majority supported the banks' petition for deregulation and in each case, Volcker voted with the minority. Thus, sentiments shifted against Volcker, he was persuaded not to seek a third term as Fed Chair, and Greenspan was offered the position (Mallaby 2016, 311–318; Eichengreen 2015; Nash 1987).

The assertive campaign by JP Morgan and some other banks ties in with my hypothesis, because they helped ensure that President Reagan would appoint a new Fed Chair who would not oppose deregulating Glass-Steagall. Greenspan in fact later wrote that "since I was an outlier in my libertarian opposition to most regulation, I planned to be largely passive in such matters and allow other Federal Reserve governors to take the lead" (Greenspan 2007, 373). Greenspan's appointment was a case of cultural capture, which occurs when individuals (e.g., Greenspan) are appointed or promoted to key regulatory positions because their beliefs and approach are well aligned with the culture and preferences of the regulated banks. Individuals whose belief systems differ from the regulated (e.g., Volcker) are not appointed or reappointed. However, this case also points to the limitations of regulatory capture theory, because the banks would not have been successful in securing Greenspan's appointment without the state-centric support of Republicans. Public-private cooperation between Republican political leaders and several major banks was necessary to ensure that Greenspan would replace Volcker as Fed Chair. His appointment had a major effect on banking deregulation as the following discussion demonstrates. (On the sweetening role of regulators, see Gaillard and Michalek in this volume.)

After 1987, banks became more assertive, the US Congress became more open to financial deregulation, and the Fed under Greenspan expanded loopholes that enabled commercial banks to encroach on the functions of investment banks. Investment banks in return sought to encroach on commercial banking activities. The moves towards deregulation culminated in the *Gramm-Leach-Bliley Act* (the *Financial Services Modernization Act of 1999*), which repealed most of Glass-Steagall by removing the remaining barriers between commercial and investment banking; that is, holding companies could now own subsidiaries engaged in both types of banking. Since the banks' operations could no longer be clearly separated, the government guarantee of commercial banks was effectively extended to investment banking. Deposits could be invested in risky assets with assurance that the FDIC would make up the losses. The effective extension of FDIC insurance to investment banking activities contributed to moral hazard and helped set the stage for the 2008 financial crisis (Johnson and Kwak 2011, 82–86; on moral hazard, see Gaillard and Michalek in this volume).

Although Greenspan's belief that banks could best regulate themselves was a major factor in his appointment as Fed Chair, cultural capture has its limits in explaining his behaviour. For example, when the Fed decided to raise interest rates in 1994, the effects were highly destabilizing. Greenspan's subsequent failure to raise interest rates in later years resulted partly from his 1994 experience. Greenspan also sometimes warned against risky financial investments and innovations, and he coined the term *irrational exuberance* in a 1996 speech to the American Enterprise Institute when he asked: "How do we know when irrational exuberance has unduly escalated asset values, which then become subject to unexpected and prolonged contractions" (Greenspan 1996)? Greenspan's use of the term calls to mind the earlier warnings of Hyman Minsky in his *financial instability hypothesis*, and of Charles Kindleberger's argument against debt-financed "euphoria," which could eventually result in a major economic downturn (Minsky 1982, 120–125; Kindleberger and Aliber 2005, 97–105; Keen 1995, 607). Stock markets around the world initially fell in response to Greenspan's warning against "irrational exuberance," and he never used the term again in public (Shiller 2005a, b, 1–2). However, Greenspan also stated in his 1996 speech that "we as central bankers need not be concerned if a collapsing financial asset bubble does not threaten to impair the real economy" (Greenspan 1996). Stock markets recovered rapidly when it became clear that Greenspan would not take measures to dampen speculation and risk-taking. Our perception of whether or not government intervention is needed to avert a collapsing financial asset bubble depends partly on our worldview, and Greenspan continued to support the easing of financial regulations in the period leading up to the 2008 financial crisis.

Deregulation under Greenspan also resulted to a degree from factors beyond his control. For example, Mallaby asserts that Greenspan "welcomed the advent of options, swaps, and new-fangled securities... partly because he felt he had no choice... technological change and globalisation made it impossible to resist the explosion of trading in derivatives" (Mallaby 2016, 7–8). Although technological change did impose some regulatory constraints on Greenspan, he was given fair warning that more regulation was needed. In 1994, Orange County, California, and companies such as Procter & Gamble and Gibson Greeting Cards suffered major losses from derivatives trade; and Orange County eventually had to file for the largest US municipal bankruptcy in history. As developed in Chap. 1, in 1998, Brooksley Born, the head of the US *Commodity Futures Trading Commission* (*CFTC*), responded to these events by warning against the growing market for *over-the-counter* (*OTC*) *derivatives*. Whereas the CFTC regulated public *exchange-traded* or *standardized derivatives*, OTC derivatives were private contracts that were subject to less stringent legislation. Thus, Born argued that the CFTC should also regulate OTC derivatives. Greenspan, Treasury Secretary Robert Rubin, Deputy Treasury Secretary Larry Summers, and Wall Street bankers strongly opposed Born's efforts, and they persuaded the Republican Congress to impose a moratorium prohibiting the regulation of OTC derivatives (Johnson and Kwak 2011, 7–10, 134–147; Mallaby 2016, 465). Greenspan, Rubin, and Summers believed that firms "had good incentives to manage derivatives carefully, and that government interference in private transactions could stifle innovation in a dynamic industry" (Geithner 2014, 87). However, the failure to regulate certain OTC derivatives—credit default swaps—was a major cause of the 2008 financial crisis. Greenspan's failure to heed Born's warnings about OTC derivatives resulted largely from his worldview.

After Greenspan's period as Fed Chair ended in January 2006, he continued to support the self-regulating market, writing that he hoped "one of the casualties" of the financial crisis would "not be reliance on...

financial self-regulation, as the fundamental balance mechanism for global finance" (Greenspan 2008). In October 2008, however, Greenspan gave a startling admission to some "self-doubts" in a House of Representatives committee hearing on the financial crisis. The committee Chair, Democratic Representative Henry Waxman, and Greenspan had the following exchange (U.S. House of Representatives 2008):

> *Waxman*:   You had the authority to prevent irresponsible lending practices that led to the subprime mortgage crisis. You were advised to do so by many others. Now, our whole economy is paying the price. Do you feel that your ideology pushed you to make decisions that you wish you had not made?
>
> *Greenspan*:   Yes, I found a flaw. I don't know how significant or permanent it is, but I have been very distressed by that fact.
>
> *Waxman*:   In other words, you found that your view of the world, your ideology, was not right, it was not working.
>
> *Greenspan*:   Precisely. That's precisely the reason I was shocked, because I had been going for 40 years or more with very considerable evidence that it was working very well.

In 2010, Greenspan offered some explanations for the Fed's behaviour before the 2008 financial crisis:

> The failure to anticipate the length and depth of the emerging bubble should not have come as a surprise. Although we like to pretend otherwise, policy makers, and indeed forecasters in general, are doing exceptionally well if we can get market projections essentially right 70 percent of the time. But that means we get them wrong 30 percent of the time. In 18½ years at the Federal Reserve, I certainly had my share of the latter. (Greenspan 2010, 209, fn. 16)

Greenspan also wrote that "the previous U.S. recession, in 1990–91, was the second most shallow… this experience led the Federal Reserve and many a sophisticated investor to believe that future contractions would also prove no worse than a typical postwar recession" (Greenspan 2010, 211).

Greenspan of course has a point, because most policy makers and academics did not anticipate the 2008 crisis. However, regulators' projections are affected not only by limits to their knowledge and experience but also by their worldviews. Thus, Greenspan's strong belief in market rationality and efficiency caused him to overlook signs of the impending 2008 crisis. He "became a cheerleader for more consumer credit and more subprime loans in particular" (Engel and McCoy 2011, 192), and he argued that too much emphasis on regulation and stability would stifle growth and innovation (Greenspan 2010, 244). In 1996, however, Robert Shiller warned the Fed of the dangers of an emerging bubble in the US stock market, and in 2004 he warned the Fed of an emerging bubble in the housing market. The FBI also issued public warnings about widespread fraud in assets related to subprime mortgages, and internal documents at the Fed show that by 2004 it knew of the growing problems related to subprime mortgages. Despite these warnings, the Fed continued to give priority to financial innovation over regulation (Carroll 2010, 259; Barth et al. 2012, 93).

The Post-Crisis Period

Has capture at the individual level contributed to banking deregulation since the 2008 financial crisis? As discussed, capture theory indicates that concentrated banking interests have more influence over regulators than diffuse public interests. After major financial crises, regulatory issues become more politicized, and the public becomes more focused on exerting influence (Helleiner and Pagliari 2010, 11). The passage of the 2010 US *Dodd-Frank Wall Street Reform and Consumer Protection Act* was in part a reaction to public anger over the financial crisis. The Act's provisions extend over 2300 pages, and some of the main points can be briefly summarized here: (i) A *Financial Stability Oversight Council* and *Orderly Liquidation Authority* monitors the financial stability of banks considered too big to fail (TBTF) and has the authority to break up large banks that pose a systemic risk (see Gaillard and Michalek on TBTF in this volume). (ii) A *Consumer Financial Protection Bureau* (*CFPB*) seeks to prevent predatory lending for mortgages and other purposes by banks and other firms. (iii) The *Volcker Rule* is designed to prevent banks from engaging in the types of speculative activities that contributed to the 2008 financial crisis. It prevents banks from conducting some investment activities with their own accounts ("proprietary trading"), and limits their ownership and activities in regard to private equity and hedge funds. The implementation of Dodd-Frank through necessary regulations has been only partially completed and, with Donald Trump's election as President, its future is highly uncertain.

Trump's ideas are not clearly articulated, and he has delivered mixed messages. For example, during the election campaign, he indicated that he would resurrect Glass-Steagall. However, Trump and a number of Congressional Republicans have adamantly opposed Dodd-Frank. Just as some major US banks had railed against Glass-Steagall and actively worked towards its repeal when Greenspan was appointed Fed Chair, today many banks similarly oppose Dodd-Frank. There are some interesting parallels between decisions taken by the Trump and Reagan administrations. As in the case of Greenspan, Trump and Congressional Republicans have appointed to key positions individuals who share the major banks' commitment to weakening financial regulation. As was the case under Reagan, this public-private cooperation under Trump results largely from the sharing of worldviews. Under Reagan, JP Morgan led the banks' opposition to Glass-Steagall and had a major role in Greenspan's appointment as Fed Chair. Under Trump, Jamie Dimon of JP Morgan Chase has been a vocal critic of Dodd-Frank, and he has considerable influence with the President. After a White House meeting with business executives in February 2017, Trump stated that "we expect to be cutting a lot out of Dodd-Frank," and that "there's nobody better to tell me about Dodd-Frank than Jamie [Dimon]" (White 2017). Shortly afterwards, Trump appointed former Goldman Sachs banker Steven Mnuchin as Treasury Secretary, and issued an executive order directing him to undertake a comprehensive review of Dodd-Frank.

Several examples show that banks and other financial institutions are trying to ensure that those who are in key positions in the Trump administration will contribute to a deregulatory environment. First, in February 2017, Daniel Tarullo, the top Fed official charged with bank regulation, said that he would resign more than four years before his term ended. Tarullo said that he had planned to step down early; but he was strict about implementing Dodd-Frank, and his views diverged from those of Trump, Republican legislators, and the major banks (Jopson 2017). A second example is Trump's decision to replace Janet Yellen with Jerome Powell as the next Fed Chair. Whereas Yellen is a Democrat, Powell has long-term ties to the Republican Party and the financial industry. Trump's replacement of Yellen is unusual, because since World War II every other Fed Chair who completed their first four-year term was nominated for a second. Presidents Ronald Reagan, Bill Clinton, and Barack Obama all reappointed sitting Chairs who were members of the opposite party. Powell will also be the first Fed Chair in 40 years who does not have an economics degree, whereas Yellen has a PhD in economics from Yale University. Furthermore, Yellen's performance has been quite impressive, with economic growth, falling unemployment, and low inflation during her tenure. In appointing Powell, "Trump wanted to avoid the explosive political reaction that appointing Yellen to a second term was sure to provoke" from Wall Street bankers (Greider 2017). Granted, Powell is a centrist who has consistently supported Yellen's approach to monetary policy in his position as Fed Governor. However, he has indicated that he will loosen regulation somewhat on banking and finance, and his long-term ties with Wall Street bankers raise questions as to how far he will go in terms of deregulation. In 1999, Powell became a partner at the Carlyle Group, an asset management firm, and his 2016 financial disclosure form revealed his net worth to be about $55 million. Whereas Yellen's publicly available calendar shows that she has only met with Wall Street bankers a few times in 2017, a copy of Powell's calendar reveals that he has had formal meetings or calls at least 50 times in 2017 with the heads of Wall Street investment banks (Swanson and Appelbaum 2017; Long 2017).

Even more striking than the Yellen-Powell case is a third example: the conflict over selecting the next Director of the Consumer Financial Protection Bureau. Created under Dodd-Frank, the CFPB is designed to protect consumers from abusive lending practices of banks and other companies. Under its assertive Director, Richard Cordray, the CFPB has extracted almost $12 billion for 29 million consumers in compensation for predatory lending. The CFPB's most high-profile case was a $100 million fine levied against Wells Fargo Bank for pressuring its sales people to open thousands of unauthorized consumer accounts. Major banks have strongly opposed the CFPB, with the support of most Congressional Republicans. When Cordray announced his resignation in late November 2017, he indicated that his Deputy Director, Leandra English, would become the next Director under the Dodd-Frank rules. However, the Trump administration argued that the Dodd-Frank rules do not displace the President's authority under the Federal Vacancies Reform Act, and Trump named his budget Director, Mick Mulvaney, as the acting head of the CFPB. Mulvaney had referred to the CFPB in 2014 as a "sick, sad joke," and he once voted to abolish the regulator. The courts sided with Trump, leaving Mulvaney as the acting Director. Shortly after taking office, Mulvaney instituted a 30-day freeze on taking new initiatives and reversed CFPB efforts to have the mortgage lender Nationwide put up cash based on a judicial decision against it (Kolhatkar 2017; Silver-Greenberg and Cowley 2017).

In sum, our case study of Greenspan offers strong confirmation for the hypothesis that regulatory capture at the individual level resulted in banking deregulation that contributed to the 2008 financial crisis. This form of capture meets Carpenter and Moss's standards, because there is evidence that the regulated industries are "actively and knowingly" pushing "regulation away from the public interest" (Carpenter and Moss 2014, 13–14). However, limitations persist when capture theory is applied to the individual level. First, regulatory outcomes depend not only on private financial interests but also on state-centric factors such as the views of top political leaders. Public-private cooperation between political leaders and the banks is essential for regulatory capture in the appointment process. A second limitation is that some aspects of Greenspan's role cannot be explained in terms of cultural capture: As Fed Chair, he sometimes warned against risky financial innovations; technological change imposed limits on his regulatory abilities; and he was not alone in failing to foresee the 2008 financial crisis. Despite these limitations, capture theory helps to explain many aspects of Greenspan's behaviour as Fed Chair. And, despite the 2008 financial crisis, capture seems to have a major role in explaining President Trump's propensity to appoint regulators that are committed to banking deregulation. I now turn to a discussion of capture at the national level.

The National Level

To assess the hypothesis that capture at the national level resulted in banking deregulation that contributed to the 2008 financial crisis, I examine material and combined material/cultural capture at the national level.

Material Capture

Lobbying and financial contributions may result in material capture, because of the financial and electoral benefits accruing to politicians (Johnson and Kwak 2011, 90–92). For example, one study shows that lobbying and *Political Action Committee* (*PAC*) expenditures by regulated firms were associated with statistically significant changes in legislative voting before the 2008 financial crisis. More intense lobbying and higher PAC expenditures increased the likelihood that legislators would favour financial deregulation (Igan and Mishra 2014). Another study finds that those lobbying the most intensively represented financial institutions engaged in riskier mortgage lending practices before the 2008 crisis, had worse outcomes afterwards, and benefited most from US bailout programmes; this is a prime example of moral hazard (Igan et al. 2011). The financial sector has been the largest contributor to US political campaigns during the last 25 years; and major banks that favoured financial deregulation were the largest source of campaign contributions from the 1970s to the early 2000s. Although the Democrats endorsed the 1933 Glass-Steagall Act, there was some partisan convergence with the Republicans favouring deregulation beginning in the 1980s. Increased banking sector campaign support for the Democrats was one factor behind this convergence (Keller and Kelly 2015, 438). Examples of this convergence were President Bill Clinton's support for the deregulatory 1994 *Riegle-Neal Interstate Banking and Branching Efficiency Act*, and his appointment of former Goldman Sachs co-Chair Robert Rubin as Treasury Secretary. The deregulatory campaign escalated when banking contributions increased in the 1990s, and Congressional members who received more financial sector donations were more likely to vote to repeal Glass-Steagall. As a result, more than 90 per cent of Republicans and 70 per cent of Democrats supported the Congressional bill to repeal what remained of Glass-Steagall (Keller and Kelly 2015). Material capture was therefore a significant factor leading to the banking deregulation that contributed to the 2008 financial crisis.

After the 2008 crisis, the increased financial sector campaign support for Democrats continued. Barack Obama's 2008 campaign for President received about $42.2 million from Wall Street bankers and other financial insiders, and the question arises whether this campaign support affected Obama's behaviour in line with regulatory capture theory. Although civil suits were filed against major banks during the Obama administration, top bankers were generally not subject to criminal charges for their role in the financial crisis. The government was also accused of bailing out Wall Street more than Main Street, and its "rescue operations ensured that many private interests rebounded from the crisis quickly and retained enormous influence in post-crisis regulatory debates" (Helleiner 2014, 13). Furthermore, Obama appointed a number of Wall Street executives to important government and regulatory positions. However, Obama was an interventionist liberal in many respects, and he had an uneven relationship with Wall Street executives. A growing source of friction was the fact that Obama signed and continued to support the Dodd-Frank Act. Thus, capture theory at the national level has its limits in explaining the Obama administration's behaviour.

A second example of material capture at the national level relates to the *credit rating agencies* (*CRAs*). Three CRAs are dominant: *Standard and Poor's* (*S&P*) and *Moody's Investors Service* (*Moody's*) are the largest, followed by *Fitch Ratings* (*Fitch*). The "Big 3" CRAs are viewed as an authoritative source of judgements, and their influence grew substantially in 1975 when the SEC designated them as *Nationally Recognized Statistical Ratings Organizations* (*NRSROs*). CRAs with the NRSRO label had a major role in determining the minimum capital levels financial firms needed to trade in certain securities. Investors also viewed the NRSRO rating as a sign of government approval, and this gave the Big 3 a virtual "monopoly" in credit ratings. Although the SEC has added more CRAs to its NRSRO list over the years, the Big 3 control around 95 per cent of the credit ratings market. Their influence has grown because financial market liberalization has increased investors' exposure to risk, and data about investment in innovative financial instruments can be overwhelming (Mullard 2012, 86–87; Sinclair 2005, 1–8; CFR Staff 2015, 1–2).

The CRAs assess a debt issuer's ability and willingness to make timely payments of principal and interest on its securities. It is often assumed that the rating process is technical; but the CRAs rely on qualitative as well as quantitative findings, and their final ratings are largely qualitative. They usually provide ratings as a letter grade, with AAA the highest and safest designation. For several decades the Big 3 followed a *subscriber-pays model* that required large institutions investing in securities to pay for their ratings. In the 1970s, however, they shifted to an *issuer-pays model*, in which financial institutions issuing securities pay fees to the CRAs for their ratings. This change occurred because security issuers needed certain ratings to sell their securities to regulated financial institutions, and they were more willing than investors to pay for CRA services (CFR Staff 2015; Gaillard and Harrington 2016). The Big 3 failed to foresee the Enron and WorldCom bankruptcies in 2001 and 2002; and when the US subprime mortgage crisis morphed into the 2008 financial crisis, many observers viewed the CRAs as one of the culprits. They had given AAA credit ratings to risky structured finance transactions—for example, *mortgage-backed securities* (*MBSs*) and *collateralized debt obligations* (*CDOs*)—and investors from around the world purchased them. The CRAs were charged with failing to identify the riskiness of the new financial products, and for downgrading MBSs and CDOs much too late.

Evidence indicates that material capture had a major role in the Big 3's higher rating of securities. Since the Big 3 operate on an issuer-pays model, they relied on the regulated banks for much of their business. If S&P gave bank securities lower ratings than Moody's, the banks would go to Moody's instead. Thus, the CRAs had an incentive to overrate securities (Blinder 2013, 79–81). The effects of Moody's change from a subscriber-pays to an issuer-pays model in 1970 and of S&P making this change in 1974 provide empirical support for this argument. Moody's ratings were higher than S&P's from 1970 to 1974, but the two CRAs' ratings no longer differed after S&P changed to an issuer-pays model. The equalization of ratings resulted from "an increase in S&P's ratings around 1974, rather than from any change in Moody's ratings" (Jiang et al. 2012, 608). Thus, the issuer-pays model resulted in higher CRA ratings, which could help to explain the Big 3's failure to downgrade risky MBSs and CDOs in a timely manner.

Testimonial evidence also provides support for material capture. Eric Kolchinsky worked at Moody's for eight years and was a Moody's Managing Director for the business line that rated subprime-backed CDOs for most of 2007. In striking testimony before the Financial Crisis Inquiry Commission, Kolchinsky asserted that the issuer-pays model resulted in regulatory capture:

> The failure of the rating agencies can be seen as an example of "regulatory capture" – a term used by economists to describe a scenario where a regulator acts in the benefit of the regulated instead of the public interest. In this case, the "quasi" regulators were the rating agencies, the "regulated" included banks and broker/dealers, and the public interest lay in the guarantee which taxpayers provide for the financial system. (Kolchinsky 2010, 1)

Other factors in addition to capture had a role in CRA rating errors such as incompetence, lack of research, and limited staff time:

> Despite the increasing number of deals and the increasing complexity, our group did not receive adequate resources. By 2007, we were barely keeping up with the deal flow and the developments in the market. Many analysts, under pressure from bankers and their high deal loads began to do the bare minimum of work required. We did not have the time to do any meaningful research into all the emerging credit issues. (Kolchinsky 2010, 4)

Staff time was limited because of pressure the Big 3 felt to compete with each other. Thus, the CRAs worked to answer all credit rating requests because "of senior management's directive to maintain and increase market share" (Kolchinsky 2010, 2–3).

Is material capture still an issue for the CRAs since the 2008 financial crisis? In response to the crisis, Dodd-Frank includes requirements to address certain problems with the credit rating system. The SEC has responded with new rules for CRAs, but it has been slow to act and has implemented only some of the Dodd-Frank requirements. Major issues such as the CRAs' use of unsolicited ratings as part of their competitive strategies have not been addressed. Furthermore, investors are unwilling to take a more active role in assessing credit risk. The Big 3 therefore still operate largely on an issuer-pays model, which affects their objectivity and independence in their role in financial regulation. Although the CRAs' methodologies have become more quantitative and transparent, the issuer-pays system makes them susceptible to material capture. Recently, claims were being made that the CRAs were resuming the practice of providing positive ratings to increase business (Gaillard 2017; Gaillard and Harrington 2016; Kruck 2016; Adelson and Jacob 2015; Helleiner 2014, 107–108).

The examples of material capture at the national level provide support for the hypothesis that capture led to banking deregulation that contributed to the financial crisis. Material capture assumes that regulators and politicians are rational actors pursuing their self-interest, and empirical studies show that financial and electoral rewards affected their regulatory decisions. However, financial rewards were not the only factors affecting the CRAs. They also were concerned about their reputations for issuing reliable assessments, they had insufficient staff to assess the securities they rated, and the CRAs were not alone in failing to foresee the 2008 financial crisis. Similarly, the limitations in capture theory are also seen in Obama's having passed and continuing to support the Dodd-Frank Act over the objections of some major bankers even though he had received substantial Wall Street funding for his 2008 election campaign. Despite these limitations of capture theory, the evidence is quite strong for material capture at the national level. Thus, the Obama administration in many respects "preferred" Wall Street over Main Street; and the CRAs' overrating of securities continues to stem largely from financial rewards they receive for inflated ratings (see Gaillard and Michalek in this volume). Material capture at the national level, as well as cultural capture at the individual level, help to explain the appointment of individuals committed to banking deregulation.

Combined Material/Cultural Capture

An example of combined material/cultural capture stems from the "revolving door" between regulators and the banking industry. As financial issues became more complex and central to the economy, the US government had to hire people with modern financial expertise who were usually from the banking industry. This became a revolving door, because regulators could benefit financially from moving from their positions either back to the banking industry or to banking for the first time. For example, every past President of the New York Federal Reserve except the first President (Benjamin Strong, who died in office) worked in a financial institution afterwards. The lure of higher salaries was a source of material capture, but the revolving door was also a source of cultural capture, ensuring that regulators shared the banking sector's worldview in many respects (Barth et al. 2012, 89; Johnson and Kwak 2011, 92–96). Even without the revolving door, regulators often defer to the judgement of bankers because of their assumed expertise, and the regulators increasingly view financial issues from the same perspective as the regulated. This is especially true during periods of prosperity when we come to believe that "this time is different" (Reinhart and Rogoff 2009).

The revolving door also involves the movement of US government regulators into the lobbying industry. Lobbyists who were previously with the government can use their political contacts to generate lobbying revenue. One study finds that "lobbyists connected to U.S. senators suffer a 24 percent drop in generated employment when their previous employer leaves the Senate," and that "ex-staffers are less likely to work in the lobbying industry after their connected senators exit Congress" (Blanes i Vidal et al. 2012, 3732). Legislators' links with revolving door lobbyists are based on mutual trust and similar worldviews, and they "tend to listen to lobbyists who tell them what they want to hear" (Lavelle 2011, 37; 2013, 20–25). Lobbyists who were previously employed by legislators are also more effective in persuading them to support banking deregulation. Thus, "by hiring connected lobbyists rather than unconnected ones gets firms in the financial industry more value for their money" (Igan and Mishra 2014, 1080).

The US government continues to depend on people from the banking industry in hiring regulators, and the revolving door therefore is "alive and well" since the 2008 financial crisis. For example, the Obama administration's hiring included Secretary of the Treasury Jacob Lew (Citigroup), US Trade Representative Michael Froman (Citigroup), White House Chief of Staff William Daley (JP Morgan Chase), and CFTC Chair Gary Gensler (Goldman Sachs) (Eisinger 2014; Kiely 2012; Davidson and Lee 2014). Trump has appointed Joseph Otting (formerly an executive at several US banks) as Comptroller of the Currency, and he has also appointed individuals to key regulatory positions who have important linkages with banks. For example, he appointed Walter J. Clayton as Chair of the SEC. Clayton's entire career has been in corporate boardrooms, and his regulatory experience has been in advising banks on dealing with governments. Despite Trump's criticism of Goldman Sachs during the election campaign, his appointments with Goldman Sachs linkages have included Mnuchin for Treasury Secretary, Clayton to lead the SEC, Gary Cohn as Director of the National Economic Council, Stephen Bannon as Chief White House Strategist, and Dina Powell as Deputy National Security Adviser. Lloyd Blankfein, the CEO of Goldman Sachs, has indicated that it attaches considerable importance to public service for its employees. Nevertheless, the appointment of key financial regulators from Goldman Sachs and other banking institutions contributes to the revolving door, and to possibilities for regulatory capture.

These examples of combined material/cultural capture at the national level do not meet Carpenter and Moss's requirement that the regulated industry must "actively and knowingly push regulation away from the public interest" (Carpenter and Moss 2014, 13–14). At the individual level, this chapter presented evidence that JP Morgan and several other banks deliberately pressured for the appointment of Greenspan rather than Volcker as the Fed Chair in 1987 because Greenspan was more inclined to favour banking deregulation, and that such efforts were successful. The revolving door at the national level, by contrast, stems partly from the fact that individuals in the banking industry have more expertise to serve as regulators. Nevertheless, the revolving door enables key regulators from Goldman Sachs and other banks to expedite banking deregulation. Cultural capture is also a factor, because regulators who were formerly in the banking industry are likely to have similar worldviews with their former colleagues; and many return by the revolving door to banking positions after their stint as regulators. The revolving door at the national level is often less visible than the higher profile appointments of key individual regulators; in fact, lower profile hires, orders, and appointments can accelerate the move towards banking deregulation. For example, the Treasury Department is making it easier for banks and other financial firms to avoid being identified as "too big to fail," which subjects them to greater oversight, and the SEC is limiting the power of regional Directors to issue subpoenas (Goldstein and Cowley 2017).

THE GLOBAL LEVEL

After providing some background on global banking regulation, this section assesses the hypothesis that capture at the global level resulted in banking deregulation that contributed to the 2008 financial crisis. I then examine whether capture by banks and bank associations has been more contained at the global level since the 2008 crisis. This section also discusses the linkages between regulatory capture at all three levels.

The Pre-Crisis Period

Exchange controls and other direct restrictions on financial flows gradually decreased after World War II, but banking continued to be regulated at the national level. Cooperation among national governments and central banks was therefore necessary to deal with financial globalization. The need for such cooperation increased when the OPEC raised oil prices after the 1973 Middle East war, because international banks recycled a large share of OPEC's petrodollars as loans to oil-importing developing countries. In 1974 the *Bank for International Settlements* (*BIS*) formed the *Basel Committee on Banking Supervision* (*BCBS*). The BCBS facilitates global financial cooperation, and provides non-binding recommendations to member countries for banking regulation and supervision (Goodhart 2011, 10–12). When the BCBS was formed, its members included the G10 countries—Belgium, Canada, France, Germany, Italy, Japan, the Netherlands, Sweden, the UK, and the US—plus Luxembourg and Switzerland. After the 2008 financial crisis, new members were added to the BCBS, including Argentina, Australia, Brazil, China, Hong Kong, India, Indonesia, Mexico, Russia, Saudi Arabia, Singapore, South Africa, South Korea, and Turkey.

The first BCBS's effort to regulate banks focused on two concerns: the risk posed to global financial stability from internationally active banks with low capital levels, and the competitive advantages that some banks had because of lower capital requirements. This effort resulted in the 1988 *Basel I Accord*, which raised the capital ratios for internationally active banks. After Basel I was established, three issues sparked the negotiation of the 2004 *Basel II Accord*: the boom of the securitization of mortgages and other loans by major banks; the development by leading banks of their own credit risk models and other risk management techniques; and financial contagion risk, as illustrated by the 1997 Asian financial crisis (Tarullo 2008, 45–46 and 88). Basel II refined the capital adequacy calculations used for smaller banks, and permitted the larger, more sophisticated banks to base their minimum capital requirements on their own *internal ratings-based (IRB)* approach. After the 2008 financial crisis, the BCBS negotiated the *Basel III Accord* to limit the type of risk-taking by global financial institutions that contributed to the crisis. I first discuss Basel II, and then turn to a discussion of Basel III after the financial crisis.

During the Basel II negotiations, the BCBS included central bankers and bank regulators from 13 developed countries. The revolving door, and personal linkages between regulators and the regulated banks facilitated capture in Basel II. For example, the *Institute for International Finance (IIF)*, a transnational association of banks and other financial institutions, exerted influence over the BCBS's regulatory plans through close personal linkages. The IIF's headquarters are in Washington, DC, but it now also has regional offices in the UK, Beijing, Dubai, and Singapore. Examples of the IIF's personal linkages with BCBS regulators include the following: The Bank of England's Peter Cooke was the BCBS Chair from 1977 to 1988, and also a co-founder of the IIF. Cooke helped steer the BCBS negotiations to the 1988 Basel I agreement. In the mid-1990s, the BCBS Chair Tommaso Padoa-Schioppa of the Bank of Italy had close personal ties with the IIF's Managing Director, Charles Dallara. Most importantly, the IIF's Dallara also developed a close friendship with the New York Federal Reserve's William McDonough, who was the BCBS Chair during most of the Basel II negotiations. With clear intent to exert influence, the IIF established a Steering Committee on Regulatory Capital to advise the BCBS on drafting the Basel II agreement. McDonough as BCBS Chair facilitated the IIF's efforts by giving it "unprecedented access to the Committee from the earliest stages of the reform process" (Lall 2012, 619; Goodhart 2011, 146–194). Furthermore, the IIF by several accounts in fact wrote the first draft of Basel II, and had considerable influence over the final agreement (Tsingou 2008, 62; Baker 2010, 650). The

BCBS was also highly susceptible to cultural capture, with participants at Basel II meetings often stating that markets were efficient and largely self-regulating and that policies promoting capital account liberalization and financial innovation were highly beneficial (Baker 2010, 653–654).

The IIF's influence was also evident in the final Basel II agreement. For the first time the BCBS permitted larger banks to estimate some aspects of credit risk with their own IRB approach. Initially, some BCBS regulators and US Federal Reserve and Bank of England economists doubted that an IRB system would be reliable and transparent. The IIF, however, lobbied aggressively, and "by mid-2000, every member of the committee had come around to the IIF's view and the working group on credit risk began informal work with the IIF to formally incorporate internal ratings into Basel II" (Lall 2012, 622). Smaller banks lacked the resources to adopt an approved IRB approach, and they had to maintain higher minimum capital requirements than the majors under the standardized ratings-based system. Since the major banks could maintain lower capital levels, this gave them a competitive advantage over smaller banks. The large international banks also had a preemptive advantage over smaller banks in putting forth their proposals because of their numerous linkages with the regulators. These linkages resulted partly from the fact that the BCBS was lacking in expertise to develop its own IRB-type approach, and it therefore depended on ideas and other input from the leading banks when considering the issue (Lall 2012; Tarullo 2008, 136).

There is also evidence that capture at the global, national, and individual levels was intertwined in the formulation of Basel II. American and British representatives on the BCBS had considerable influence because of their proximity as home-country regulators to the Wall Street and London banking centres. The leading American and British banks in turn had influence on their representatives, and this enabled them to help shape the BCBS policy debates (Baker 2010, 650–651).

The US position on Basel II shows that to understand regulatory capture at the global level it is necessary to examine domestic as well as international politics. In the private arena, smaller US banks were at a competitive disadvantage because they did not qualify for the IRB approach available to the leading US banks. In the public arena, US federal banking supervision is divided among four different agencies that disagreed on several Basel II issues. However, the Fed used the international process to overcome the reluctance of other US bank supervisors to accept the use of internally based models. As a result, by late 1999, "the U.S.

members of the Basel Committee, particularly the Federal Reserve, were advocating more strongly than ever a far-reaching shift to an IRB approach" (Tarullo 2008, 100, 103, 135).

Individual US regulators in key positions also affected Basel II. In a 1999 talk to the American Bankers Association, Greenspan supported the IRB approach, stating that the "banks' internal risk-management systems can... be used to enhance assessments of a bank's capital adequacy." He advised the bankers that the Basel II concepts "are beginning to congeal and deserve your close attention, especially if you wish to influence the eventual outcome of the deliberations" (Greenspan 1999).

In some respects, global regulatory capture can be greater than national capture because transnational banks and bank associations have considerable resources for exerting influence, and the political and regulatory control mechanisms are much weaker at the global than the national level (Goldbach 2015, 1090). National legislatures also have little control over the BCBS, because BCBS members come from independent regulatory agencies rather than governments. Thus, the Basel II meetings were conducted in private, with no record of who attended, what they discussed, or what interest groups had influence. Although national legislators had some authority to refuse final approval of the Basel II accord, the highly technical nature of the issues precluded them from having a significant role in the different stages of the negotiating process (Lall 2012, 619–621).

Despite the strong evidence of regulatory capture in the formulation of Basel II, capture theory has its limits in explaining banking regulatory decisions at the global level, as it does at the individual and national levels. These limits are evident in several case studies Young has conducted of the Basel II negotiations. In one case study, Young examines IIF efforts, with the support of the *International Swaps and Derivatives Association* (*ISDA*), to get the BCBS to endorse a full internal model approach to capital adequacy requirements for the leading banks. The ISDA was created in 1985 to enable institutions in the private negotiated derivatives market to network and improve the market. Although the IIF and ISDA captured the BCBS's attention, investigations by the BCBS, US Fed, and Bank of England convinced the BCBS to adopt an IRB approach that was not *fully* based on internal ratings. Thus, Basel II's capital requirements were higher than those favoured by the major banks (Young 2012, 672–674). In a second case study, the IIF and ISDA urged the BCBS to adopt a regulatory model that would fully utilize major banks' internal risk ratings. Although the BCBS drew upon the banks' ideas, it determined that the banks' risk models were overly optimistic, and it opted for a more stringent model. In a third case study, the BCBS proposed a regulatory charge for operational risk. Whereas credit risk relates to risk in extending credit, operational risk involves possible bank failure because of internal or external issues or events. The IIF and ISDA lobbied against an explicit charge for operational risk, but the US Fed supported the BCBS position that such a charge would induce banks to devote more attention to operational risk. In this case, the IIF and ISDA could not present a unified front, because a small number of IIF working group members were open to the BCBS proposal. Thus, the Basel II model on operational risk was more stringent than the model most banks preferred (Young 2012, 674–679).

Another limitation of capture theory is that regulated banks and bank associations are not the only private groups that have a vested interest in influencing some financial policy and regulatory decisions. Finance is so central to the economy that many business groups that make investments and depend on access to credit have a strong interest in some regulatory decisions. Empirical studies of banking and OTC derivatives regulation show that other business and non-business groups can have a significant effect on policy outcomes. The positions of these interest groups can therefore affect the ability of banks to achieve their regulatory objectives. If the banking industry can form coalitions with other like-minded business interests, their influence over the regulators may increase. However, if the banking industry's objectives conflict with those of other business and non-business groups, their ability to achieve their objectives will decrease. The plurality of groups interested in regulatory decisions and the views and influence of the various groups can therefore affect the degree to which regulatory capture occurs (Pagliari and Young 2014).

Although the large banks did not get everything they wanted from Basel II, they achieved their main objectives. As discussed, they were able to rely *primarily* on their own IRB-based approach to determine their minimum capital requirements. The model most used was inadequate for assessing risk, and was a major factor contributing to the financial crisis. The BCBS also made the highly questionable decision to enable banks to have lower capital requirements for securitized assets. The rationale was that a securitized bundle of mortgages would be highly diversified and contain many mortgages that were rated highly by the CRAs. As discussed, the CRAs themselves were subject to material capture, and their inflated ratings were also a central factor contributing to the US subprime mortgage crisis. Another problem confronting the BCBS is that it depends on national governments to implement its decisions, and regulatory capture can delay the national implementation of global decisions. For example, the US did not issue its final regulations for Basel II's implementation until April 2008, and with the financial crisis that followed, Basel II was never fully implemented (Barth et al. 2012, 52–53 and 187). In sum, there is considerable evidence that regulatory capture at the global level, in concert with capture at the national and individual levels, contributed to the 2008 financial crisis.

The Post-Crisis Period

After Lehman Brothers collapsed in September 2008, the Group of 20 (G20) responded to public pressure for financial reform by calling on the BCBS to replace Basel II with a stronger agreement. With an enlarged membership that includes all G20 countries, the BCBS released preliminary proposals for Basel III in December 2009. Following negotiations, the BCBS issued the Basel III accord in September 2010, and revised it in June 2011. The major banks were dissatisfied with the Basel III preliminary proposals, and the 2010 Basel III accord actually proposed more regulations than Basel II. This is not surprising, because sentiments shifted towards more regulation after the 2008 financial crisis. To examine whether regulatory capture continued to have a role after the financial crisis, this section examines two questions: (i) Did the banking industry succeed in diluting the Basel III preliminary proposals in the final accord? (ii) Will Basel III help repair the financial architecture?

Several studies indicate that the leading banks were successful in diluting the preliminary Basel III proposals in the final accord. As was the case with Basel II, the banks and bank associations had considerable influence in the BCBS negotiations and in framing the final Basel III agreement. In accord with regulatory capture theory, the concentrated interests of the leading banks carried more weight than the diffuse interests of other stakeholders and the general public. As economic growth resumed after the 2008 crisis, the public demand for reform subsided, and this enabled the IIF to regain its influence. Thus, the IIF Steering Committee on Regulatory Capital had a central role in dealing with the BCBS and in leading the banking industry response to the Basel III reform proposals (Institute of International Finance 2017). A number of personal linkages gave banking interests an advantage in Basel III, as they had in Basel II. For example,

Marc Saidenberg, who was Head of Regulatory Policy at Merrill Lynch and an IIF committee member until 2008, was a prominent BCBS member. Saidenberg was actively involved in the development of the Basel III capital and liquidity standards. These personal linkages gave the IIF and other financial interest groups first mover advantage in the Basel III negotiations. As was the case for Basel II, the global negotiations were more susceptible to regulatory capture because the preliminary Basel III proposals were vetted in subcommittees without adequate transparency to domestic stakeholders (Lall 2012, 625–632).

The influence of financial interests was also evident in the final Basel III accord. Basel III did introduce some new standards for banks. For example, capital requirements were increased; minimum leverage ratios were introduced; there were new rules on liquidity to protect banks in difficult periods; and counter-cyclical buffers were supported to encourage banks to increase their capital during growth periods. Basel III also added a provision to impose additional capital charges on systemically important financial institutions (SIFIs) to decrease threats to the financial system. Despite these provisions, there is evidence that financial interests were successful in diluting the BCBS's new standards and requirements. Examples include the following: (i) Basel III continues to permit major banks to use their own IRB models for risk assessment of assets. By using a more permissive model, banks could lower their capital requirements. (ii) Minimum capital ratios for banks are raised, but not sufficiently to avoid future crises. (iii) Basel III minimum leverage ratios could be insufficient to prevent severe bank indebtedness. (iv) The added capital surcharge for SIFIs is inadequate, and only states could implement it (Helleiner 2014, 101–103). According to some "direct participants in the Basel process," industry lobbying had a role "in producing a much more minimal Basel III than originally envisaged" (Baker 2013, 427).

As with the individual and national levels, regulatory capture theory does have its limits in explaining the factors that moulded the final Basel III agreement. The IIF and other banking groups had less influence in Basel III for several reasons. First, by the time of the Basel III negotiations, the BCBS's own staff had developed significant expertise in banking regulation, so they were less dependent on the regulated banks. Second, the BCBS regulators sometimes reacted negatively to the aggressive lobbying by the banking sector in Basel III. Third, as was the case with Basel II, other business and non-business interests influenced the Basel III negotiations, and their objectives sometimes differed from those of the major banks. A diversity of groups pressured for financial regulation after the 2008 financial crisis, and the leading banks therefore had to adopt more subtle advocacy strategies in the Basel III negotiations. As the salience of regulatory issues receded somewhat, banking groups re-established a dialogue with the BCBS, but in the new regulatory environment, they shifted focus in two respects: They began to promote self-regulatory banking reform initiatives in order to help set the agenda and relieve themselves from public pressure for reform; and they shifted from trying to block regulatory reforms to arguing for a longer period to implement reforms. Despite the new limitations on the banking sector's influence, there is evidence that the financial sector's effort at delaying implementation has been successful. For example, the various parts of Basel III will be phased in gradually, extending to 2019, and a number of countries have delayed issuing final regulations in accordance with the agreement. Achieving these delays will enable the banking industry to upgrade its advocacy efforts as the regulatory issues become less salient, and perhaps reverse some of the changes incorporated in Basel III (Drezner 2014, 92–94; Young 2013).

In sum, there is compelling evidence that the IIF and ISDA met Carpenter and Moss's requirement for capture, since they "actively and knowingly" pushed "regulation away from the public interest" in Basel II and Basel III (Carpenter and Moss 2014, 13–14). In fact, the efforts of the IIF and ISDA were successful insofar as the BCBS endorsed an approach in Basel II and Basel III that permitted the major banks to rely primarily on their own internal ratings for risk assessment of assets. Regulatory capture occurred because capture "does not mean that private interests always get their way" (Underhill 2015, 467; Goldbach 2015, 1123, fn. 1). Although the bankers did not get everything they wanted, the content of global standards in the agreement largely reflected banking interests. In Basel III, banking groups had to shift from blocking reforms to pressure for a longer time to implement reforms. However, they have been quite successful in delaying the implementation of some significant Basel III provisions. With cultural capture, it is more difficult to demonstrate that financial interests have "actively and knowingly" pushed "regulation away from the public interest." Nevertheless, cultural capture played a significant role in the formulation and implementation of the Basel II and III agreements, with banking lobbyists having greater access to BCBS regulators because of a "shared intellectual bubble" (Young 2012, 681).

CONCLUSION

Drawing on the example of Waltz in *Man, The State and War*, this chapter seeks to fill a gap in IPE research by focusing on regulatory capture by banks and banking groups at the *individual*, as well as the national and global levels. Only by looking at all three levels can we adequately assess regulatory capture theory, the evidence for and against capture, and the conditions under which capture occurs. Based on these findings, I can provide improved prescriptions for addressing regulatory capture in banking regulation. After briefly reviewing some of the findings in this chapter, I propose such prescriptions.

This chapter finds compelling evidence of cultural capture by banks at the individual level. For example, some large US banks pressured like-minded Republican political leaders to appoint Greenspan as Fed Chair in 1987, and *not* to reappoint Volcker. The banks preferred Greenspan because his worldview was more favourable to banking deregulation than Volcker's, and the deregulation that followed was a major factor leading to the 2008 financial crisis. Although this was primarily a case of cultural capture, material and cultural capture are closely intertwined and it is sometimes difficult to distinguish them. For example, adhering "to the President's ideology can enhance an administrator's post-government employment prospects, making him or her more attractive to think tanks, corporations, and other similar employers" (Shapiro 2012, 230).

The chapter presents evidence of material capture, and combined material/cultural capture at the national level. Material capture assumes that regulators and politicians are pursuing their self-interest, and empirical studies show that financial and electoral rewards had a major effect on the banking deregulatory decisions of regulators, politicians, and CRAs at the national level. The "revolving door" was a prime example of combined material/cultural capture at the national level. At the global level, this chapter presents evidence that capture contributed to weakening the regulatory reforms in the final Basel II agreement.

The analysis also points to the fact that capture at the individual, national, and global levels are intertwined. At the individual level, Greenspan supported relying on the major banks' internal risk management systems in Basel II, and he advised US bankers to devote attention to influencing the outcome of the global deliberations. The leading American and British banks did seek to influence their representatives, enabling them to help shape the BCBS policy debates. The American and

British representatives on the BCBS had considerable influence in formulating the Basel II accord because they were regulators close to the Wall Street and London banking centres.

Despite the wide scope and severity of the 2008 financial crisis, there is considerable evidence that regulatory capture is contributing to banking deregulation again in the post-crisis era: This is a clearly persistent issue that policy makers should address. Public pressure for more regulation immediately after the crisis resulted in the Dodd-Frank Act in the US and in the Basel III negotiations at the global level. However, as the effects of the 2008 crisis gradually receded, the public interest in regulation became more diffuse, and the regulated banks' concentrated interests—as served through the capture channels described above—began to dominate. At the individual level, President Trump by his own admission has taken advice from bank executives such as JP Morgan's Jamie Dimon in his appointment of key regulators. And while much of the post-crisis regulatory architecture, including Dodd-Frank, remains intact, Trump's appointments are weakening major parts of it. At the national level, regulatory capture persists via bank lobbying and financial contributions, the CRAs, and the revolving door. At the global level, banking groups such the IIF gradually regained influence in the Basel III negotiations via a combination of declining public interest and a change in tactics by the bankers. Thus, there is considerable evidence to support Helleiner's finding that the 2008 financial crisis has been "more of a status quo event than a transformative one" (Helleiner 2014, 2).

Nevertheless, we also find the explanatory limits of capture theory. For example, regulatory outcomes depend not only on private financial interests but also on state-centric factors such as the views of political leaders. Furthermore, the capture concept is highly normative as well as descriptive, because it involves the accusation that regulators fail to serve the public interest (Shapiro 2012, 223). Thus, analysts with differing political views may disagree on the significance of the regulatory changes even when they agree on their substance. Despite the shortcomings of the theory, this chapter has pointed to considerable evidence that capture by banks was a major factor leading to deregulation that contributed to the 2008 financial crisis.

Too much regulation can have adverse effects on banking innovation and credit availability, so it is important to assess the degree of capture before prescribing solutions. For example, it is necessary to determine whether the capture is hard or soft. Hard capture goes so much against the public interest that regulatory changes are necessary to deal with it. Soft capture, where interpretation and implementation of regulation are influenced, may go somewhat against the public interest, but still have longer-term effects that on balance are welfare-enhancing. The prescriptions that follow are designed to deal with the type of hard capture that contributed to the 2008 financial crisis and yet persists.

As discussed, the dependence of regulators on the expertise of the regulated banks increases the opportunity for—and extent of—capture. For example, when regulatory agencies hire bankers to deal with complicated financial innovations, a revolving door develops which can give regulated banks undue influence over regulatory decisions. Even without the revolving door, regulators must often rely on the expertise and views of bankers, and the regulators' worldviews may become similar to those of the bankers in the process. As emphasized, a former senior analyst at Moody's reported that in the lead up to the financial crisis, the CRA staff did not have the time and resources to adequately assess the complex credit issues confronting them and would often use and rely on the models provided by the bankers. One solution to this problem is to have better funded regulatory agencies that can develop more in-house expertise on banking issues, and thus become less dependent on banking interests. For example, by the time of the Basel III negotiations, the BCBS's own staff had developed more expertise in banking regulation, so they were less dependent on the regulated banks.

In terms of resources, the source of financing for a regulator can also be a crucial issue. When the Big 3 CRAs shifted from a subscriber-pays to an issuer-pays model for their ratings, material capture assumed a much bigger role in their rating of securities. Because the securities-issuing banks paid fees to the CRAs for their ratings, the Big 3 relied on the regulated banks for much of their business. If S&P gave bank securities lower ratings than Moody's, the banks would go to Moody's instead. Thus, before the 2008 financial crisis, the CRAs failed to downgrade risky MBSs and CDOs until it was too late. Since the financial crisis, the CRAs' methodologies have become more quantitative and transparent, but it was reported that the CRAs were resuming the practice of providing positive ratings to increase business. To reduce material capture, alternative business models should be developed, which might involve a return to the investor-pays model or the implementation of a clearing house system to rate structured finance deals (see Mathis et al. 2009).

Increased transparency of regulatory decisions may also decrease capture. Lack of transparency was especially problematic in the Basel II and Basel III meetings, which were conducted in private, with no record of who attended, what they discussed, or what interest groups had influence. Sufficient transparency can also be a problem in developed countries with complex regulatory systems; for example, US federal banking supervision is divided among four different agencies. Two simple requirements would help. First, the US Congress should require agencies to provide information on the number of times they meet with banks as compared to groups representing consumers and other interests. Next, agencies should be required to publish periodic reports on the degree to which they achieve their legislatively mandated objectives. In addition, well-documented media coverage can help to discourage elected officials from becoming beholden to special interests by keeping the public well informed (Shapiro 2012, 257). The media had an important role in reporting on regulatory capture that contributed to the 2008 financial crisis. (On the role of media coverage, see Hira et al. in this volume.) Increasing transparency may remain a bigger challenge at the global level because the BCBS members come from independent regulatory agencies and are not answerable to national legislatures. In this case, international agreement among major countries in a forum such as the G20 would be necessary.

Capture develops because concentrated banking interests usually have exorbitant influence over regulators and politicians. As a result, concrete measures should be taken to ensure that a diversity of business and non-business interests are represented in regulatory processes. Efforts should also be made to employ a diversity of sources of expertise, including academics, to independently assess the views espoused by the regulated banks.

To slow or eliminate the revolving door, minimum "waiting" periods should be imposed as to when regulators could be hired as lobbyists for or employees of firms they are or have been regulating. If regulators receive much better remuneration and employment conditions, this could also decrease their incentive to be hired by the regulated banks.

Other types of reforms deserve examination. Although it would probably not gain much support in the US today, imposing limits on lobbying and campaign contributions would reduce the excessive influence of banking interests (see Hasen 2016).

Ideally, during periods of prosperity, measures should automatically take effect to constrain excessive leverage and risk-taking by banks, and to ensure that the security of consumers and other citizens is adequately insulated from these risk-taking activities. By the same token, further research focusing on "shadow banks" and financial intermediaries (such as hedge funds), unlisted derivatives, and on unregulated activities by regulated institutions (such as credit default swaps) must be done. Dodd-Frank is designed to regulate banks, but it devotes insufficient attention to shadow banks, whose very existence is in part a response to regulation. In view of the growing role of shadow banking in finance, it is necessary to devote more attention to regulatory capture by the shadow banking system (Turner 2016).

The current deregulatory climate in the US with the Trump administration and the Republican-led Congress does not bode well for instituting many of these reforms at present. As asset prices in the US and elsewhere are again rising parabolically, without necessary reforms banking regulatory capture could once again contribute to another major financial crisis (Lachman 2017).

Acknowledgements Anil Hira, Kathryn Lavelle, Norbert Gaillard, Leslie Armijo, Laurent Dobuzinskis, and Rick Michalek

References

Adelson, Mark and David Jacob. 2015. Strengthening Credit Rating Integrity. *Journal of Financial Regulation and Compliance.* 23(4): 338–353.

Baker, Andrew. 2010. Restraining Regulatory Capture? Anglo-America, Crisis Politics and Trajectories of Change in Global Financial Governance. *International Affairs.* 86(3): 647–663.

Baker, Andrew. 2013. The Gradual Transformation? The Incremental Dynamics of Macroprudential Regulation. *Regulation & Governance.* 7(4): 417–434.

Barth, James R., Gerald Caprio Jr., and Ross Levine. 2012. *Guardians of Finance.* Cambridge, MA: MIT Press.

Blanes i Vidal, Jordi, Mirko Draca, and Christian Fons-Rosen. 2012. Revolving Door Lobbyists. *American Economic Review.* 102(7): 3731–3748.

Blinder, Alan S. 2013. *After the Music Stopped.* New York: Penguin.

Blinder, Alan S. 2014. What's the Matter with Economics? *New York Review of Books.* 61(20). December 18: 55–57.

Carpenter, Daniel and David A. Moss. 2014. Introduction. In Daniel Carpenter and David A. Moss (Eds.). *Preventing Regulatory Capture,* 1–22. New York: Cambridge University Press.

Carroll, Christopher. 2010. Comments and Discussion. *Brookings Papers on Economic Activity.* Spring: 259.

Christensen, Jorgen Gronnegard. 2011. Competing Theories of Regulatory Governance: Reconsidering Public Interest Theory of Regulation. In David Levi-Faur (Ed.). *Handbook on the Politics of Regulation*, 96–110. Northampton, MA: Edward Elgar.

Cohn, Theodore H. 2016. *Global Political Economy: Theory and Practice*, 7th ed. New York: Routledge.

Council on Foreign Relations (CFR) Staff. 2015. The Credit Rating Controversy. CFR Backgrounder. February 19, available at http://www.cfr.org/financial-crises/credit-rating-controversy/p22328

Davidson, Kate and M. J. Lee. 2014. Citi on the Potomac. *Politico*. February 26.

Drezner, Daniel W. 2014. *The System Worked*. New York: Oxford University Press.

Eichengreen, Barry. 2015. Financial Crisis: Revisiting the Banking Rules that Died with a Thousand Cuts. *Fortune*. January 16.

Eisinger, Jesse. 2014. Why Only One Top Banker Went to Jail for the Financial Crisis. *New York Times*. April 30.

Engel, Kathleen C. and Patrica A. McCoy. 2011. *The Subprime Virus*. New York: Oxford University Press.

Engstrom, David Freeman. 2013. Corralling Capture. *Harvard Journal of Law and Public Policy*. 36(1): 31–39.

Gaillard, Norbert J. 2017. Credible Sovereign Ratings: Beyond Statistics and Regulations. *European Business Law Review*. 28(1): 5–18.

Gaillard, Norbert J. and William J. Harrington. 2016. Efficient, Commonsense Actions to Foster Accurate Credit Ratings. *Capital Markets Law Journal*. 11(1): 38–59.

Geithner, Timothy F. 2014. *Stress Test: Reflections on Financial Crises*. New York: Crown Publishers.

Goldbach, Roman. 2015. Asymmetric Influence in Global Banking Regulation. *Review of International Political Economy*. 22(6): 1087–1127.

Goldstein, Matthew and Stacy Cowley. 2017. Casting Wall Street as Victim, Trump Leads Deregulatory Charge. *New York Times*. November 27.

Goodhart, Charles. 2011. *The Basel Committee on Banking Supervision*. New York: Cambridge University Press.

Greenspan, Alan. 1996. Remarks as Federal Reserve Board Chairman at the Annual Dinner and Francis Boyer Lecture of the American Enterprise Institute for Public Policy Research, Washington, D.C., December 5, available at https://www.federalreserve.gov/board/docs/speeches/1996/19961205.htm

Greenspan, Alan. 1999. The Evolution of Bank Supervision. Remarks by Federal Reserve Board Chairman before the American Bankers Association, Phoenix, Arizona, October 11, available at https://www.federalreserve.gov/board-docs/speeches/1999/19991011.htm

Greenspan, Alan. 2007. *The Age of Turbulence*. New York: Penguin Press.

Greenspan, Alan. 2008. We Will Never Have a Perfect Model of Risk. *Financial Times*. March 16.

Greenspan, Alan. 2010. The Crisis. *Brookings Papers on Economic Activity*. Spring: 201–246.

Greider, William. 2017. How Trump Stiffed the Bankers with Federal Reserve Appointment. *The Nation*. November 9.

Hasen, Richard. 2016. *Plutocrats United: Campaign Money, the Supreme Court, and the Distortion of American Elections*. Yale: Yale University Press.

Helleiner, Eric. 2014. *The Status Quo Crisis*. New York: Oxford University Press.

Helleiner, Eric and Stefano Pagliari. 2010. Crisis and Reform of International Financial Regulation. In Eric Helleiner, Stefano Pagliari, and Hubert Zimmermann (Eds.). *Global Finance Crisis*, 1–17. New York: Routledge.

Igan, Deniz and Prachi Mishra. 2014. Wall Street, Capitol Hill, and K Street: Political Influence and Financial Regulation. *Journal of Law and Economics*. 57(4): 1063–1084.

Igan, Deniz, Prachi Mishra, and Thierry Tressel. 2011. A Fistful of Dollars: Lobbying and the Financial Crisis. *NBER Macroeconomics Annual*. 26(1): 195–230.

Institute of International Finance. 2017. IIF Steering Committee on Regulatory Capital (SCRC), available at https://www.iif.com/content/iif-steering-committee-regulatory-capital-scrc

Jiang, John (Xuefeng), Mary Harris Stanford, and Yuan Xie. 2012. Does It Matter Who Pays for Bond Ratings? Historical Evidence. *Journal of Financial Economics*. 105(3): 607–621.

Johnson, Simon and James Kwak. 2011. *13 Bankers*. New York: Vintage Books.

Jopson, Barney. 2017. Tarullo Says Trump's Wall St. Principles 'Good Starting Point'. *Financial Times*. February 13.

Keen, Steve. 1995. Finance and Economic Breakdown: Modeling Minsky's 'Financial Instability Hypothesis'. *Journal of Post Keynesian Economics*. 17(4): 607–635.

Keller, Eric and Nathan J. Kelly. 2015. Partisan Politics, Financial Deregulation, and the New Gilded Age. *Political Research Quarterly*. 68(3): 428–442.

Kiely, Eugene. 2012. Obama White House 'Full of Wall Street Executives'? Factcheck: A Project of The Annenberg Public Policy Center. February 29, available at http://www.factcheck.org/2012/02/obama-white-house-full-of-wall-street-executives

Kindleberger, Charles P. and Robert Z. Aliber. 2005. *Manias, Panics and Crashes: A History of Financial Crises, 5th ed*. Hoboken, NJ: John Wiley & Sons.

Kolchinsky, Eric. 2010. Statement and Testimony before the Financial Crisis Inquiry Commission on Credibility of Credit Ratings, The Investment Decisions Made on Those Ratings, and the Financial Crisis. June 2, available at https://fcic-static.law.stanford.edu/cdn_media/fcic-testimony/2010-0602-Kolchinsky.pdf

Kolhatkar, Sheelah. 2017. What is the Fate of the Consumer Financial Protection Bureau? *The New Yorker*. September 7.

Kruck, Andreas. 2016. Resilient Blunderers: Credit Rating Fiascos and Rating Agencies' Institutionalized Status as Private Authorities. *Journal of European Public Policy*. 23(5): 753–770.

Kwak, James. 2014. Cultural Capture and the Financial Crisis. In Daniel Carpenter and David A. Moss (Eds.). *Preventing Regulatory Capture*, 71–98. New York: Cambridge University Press.

Lachman, Desmond. 2017. The Global Economy is Partying Like It's 2008. *New York Times*. December 13.

Lall, Ranjit. 2012. From Failure to Failure: The Politics of International Banking Regulation. *Review of International Political Economy*. 19(4): 609–638.

Lavelle, Kathryn C. 2011. *Legislating International Organization: The US Congress, the IMF, and the World Bank*. New York: Oxford University Press.

Lavelle, Kathryn C. 2013. *Money and Banks in the American Political System*. New York: Cambridge University Press.

Long, Heather. 2017. Trump's Fed Nominee Jerome Powell Met 50 Times with Wall Street Execs this Year: Is that a Problem? *Washington Post* wonkblog. November 28.

Mallaby, Sebastian. 2016. *The Man Who Knew: The Life and Times of Alan Greenspan*. New York: Penguin Press.

Mathis, Jérôme, James McAndrews, and Jean-Charles Rochet. 2009. Rating The Raters: Are Reputation Concerns Powerful Enough to Discipline Rating Agencies? *Journal of Monetary Economics*. 56(5): 657–674.

Mattli, Walter and Ngaire Woods. 2009. In Whose Benefit? Explaining Regulatory Change in Global Politics. In Walter Mattli and Ngaire Woods (Eds.). *The Politics of Global regulation*, 1–43. Princeton: Princeton University Press.

Minsky, Hyman P. 1982. *Can "It" Happen Again? Essays on Instability and Finance*. New York: M.E. Sharpe.

Moosa, Imad A. 2015. *Good Regulation, Bad Regulation*. New York: Palgrave Macmillan.

Morgan, Bronwen and Karen Yeung. 2007. *An Introduction to Law and Regulation*. New York: Cambridge University Press.

Mullard, Maurice. 2012. The Credit Rating Agencies and Their Contribution to the Financial Crisis. *The Political Quarterly*. 83(1): 77–95.

Nash, Nathaniel C. 1987. Bank Curbs Eased in Volcker Defeat. *New York Times*. May 1.

Pagliari, Stefano and Kevin L. Young. 2014. Leveraged Interests: Financial Industry Power and the Role of Private Sector Coalitions. *Review of International Political Economy*. 21(3): 575–610.

Reinhart, Carmen, and Kenneth Rogoff. 2009. *This Time is Different: Eight Centuries of Financial Folly*. Princeton: Princeton University Press.

Shapiro, Sidney A. 2012. The Complexity of Regulatory Capture: Diagnosis, Causality, and Remediation. *Roger Williams University Law Review*. 102(1): 221–257.

Shiller, Robert J. 2005a. Definition of Irrational Exuberance, available at http://www.irrationalexuberance.com/definition.htm

Shiller, Robert J. 2005b. *Irrational Exuberance*, 2nd ed. Princeton: Princeton University Press.

Silver-Greenberg, Jessica and Stacy Cowley. 2017. Consumer Bureau's New Leader Steers a Sudden Reversal. *New York Times*. December 5.

Sinclair, Timothy J. 2005. *The New Masters of Capital*. Ithaca, NY: Cornell University Press.

Stigler, George J. 1971. The Theory of Economic Regulation. *Bell Journal of Economics and Management Science*. 2(1): 3–21.

Stiglitz, Joseph E. 2010. *Freefall: America, Free Markets, and the Sinking of the World Economy*. New York and London: W.W. Norton.

Swanson, Ana and Binyamin Appelbaum. 2017. Trump Announces Jerome Powell as New Fed Chairman. *New York Times*. November 2.

Tarullo, Daniel K. 2008. *Banking on Basel*. Washington, DC: Peterson Institute for International Economics.

Tsingou, Eleni. 2008. Transnational Private Governance and the Basel Process. In Jean-Christophe Graz and Andreas Nolke (Eds.). *Transnational Private Governance and its Limits*, 58–68. New York: Routledge.

Turner, Adair. 2016. *Between Debt and the Devil – Money, Credit, and Fixing Global Finance*. Princeton: Princeton University Press.

Underhill, Geoffrey R.D. 2015. The Emerging Post-Crisis Financial Architecture: The Path-Dependency of Ideational Adverse Selection. *British Journal of Politics and International Relations*. 17(3): 461–493.

U.S. House of Representatives. 2008. "The Financial Crisis and the Role of Federal Regulators." Hearing before the Committee on Oversight and Government Reform. 110th Congress, 2nd Session, October 23, available at https://www.gpo.gov/fdsys/pkg/CHRG-110hhrg55764/html/CHRG-110hhrg55764.htm

Waltz, Kenneth N. 1959. *Man, the State and War*. New York: Columbia University Press.

White, Gillian B. 2017. Trump Begins to Chip Away at Banking Regulations. *The Atlantic*. February 3.

Young, Kevin. 2012. Transnational Regulatory Capture? An Empirical Examination of the Transnational Lobbying of the Basel Committee on Banking Supervision. *Review of International Political Economy*. 19(4): 663–688.

Young, Kevin. 2013. Financial Industry Groups' Adaptation to the Post-Crisis Regulatory Environment: Changing Approaches to the Policy Cycle. *Regulation & Governance*. 7(4): 417–434.

CHAPTER 4

How and Why Moral Hazard Has Distorted Financial Regulation

Norbert Gaillard and Richard J. Michalek

INTRODUCTION

The emerging dominance of finance, and *finance capitalism*, in the late twentieth century can briefly be described as the rational response to the acceleration in the use of and need for debt. From the late 1960s and throughout the 1970s, any number of novel, unforeseen and/or disruptive trends and events altered the traditional function of finance and the roles of the primary economic actors. The end of the Bretton Woods fixed rate exchange regime allowed new opportunities for central banks to manipulate their currencies and support their country's international competitiveness. The oil shock of 1973 and the relatively passive response from the Federal Reserve amplified the levels of inflation in commodities and in consumer goods. At the outset of the 1980s, foreign competition, particularly from Japan and the nascent Asian tigers, raised the awareness of the US financial sector to the opportunities from incipient internationalization and further pressured US industry, even as the aggressive

N. Gaillard (✉)
NG Consulting, Paris, France
e-mail: gaillard@alumni.princeton.edu

R. J. Michalek
RJM Consulting, New York City, NY, USA

© The Author(s) 2019
A. Hira et al. (eds.), *The Failure of Financial Regulation*,
International Political Economy Series,
https://doi.org/10.1007/978-3-030-05680-3_4

targeting of money supply by the Volcker-chaired Federal Reserve throttled inflation, but at a cost of the most severe recession (at the time) since the Great Depression.

Both public and private US indebtedness began to grow at an increasing multiple of their correlates, income and productivity (see Fig. 4.1). Whether or not the increased use of deficit financing in the public sphere was originally intended to be temporary, the political benefits of sustaining and extending government services (the expectation for which is truly "sticky downwards"), such use has in hindsight become permanent. And the parallel development of increased and increasing private debt (both at the consumer and corporate levels) may result from similar needs: the consumer has (perpetually) postponed downward adjustments to standards of living, while corporations have augmented their "real asset" operating earnings with *financially engineered* earnings and savings.

For consumers, the "income deficit" has been filled by credit card debt, increasingly accommodative auto loans, student loans, and a panoply of mortgage products. The burgeoning industry of "financial services" has

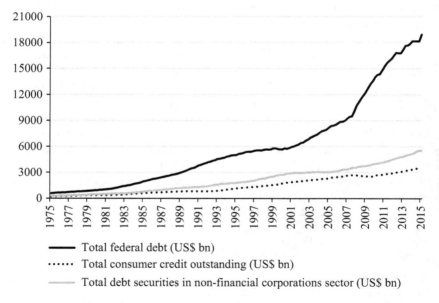

Fig. 4.1 Public and private debts, 1975–2015. Note: Quarterly data. (Source: Federal Reserve)

been only too happy to create the next deficit-bridging product. At the corporate levels, newly minted masters of business administration filled the corporate finance departments, as leveraged buyouts, mergers and acquisitions, and other recession-generated restructurings accelerated. Transactions using "OPM" (other people's money) became ever larger, and the culture bolder, and intermediation powered the growth of banks and bank balance sheets. *Financial disintermediation* then followed,[1] and new forms of debt from securitisation further expanded total debt.[2]

However, the growth of financial activity came at a cost. Recent scholarship has shown that while the early studies demonstrating the benefits of financial development on growth in general were valid, there is increasing evidence that, beyond a certain level, the development of the finance industry has clearly negative effects on the real economy (Philippon and Reshef 2013).

This chapter goes beyond these findings and advocates that "financialisation" (i.e., the process by which financial service participants, institutions, and markets increase in size and influence) and the resulting trend of *finance capitalism* has been essentially driven by moral hazard and, more precisely, by the emergent "too big to fail" (TBTF) banks.[3] The influence of these entities has grown so much that it has distorted the relations with regulators (at the expense of the latter), amplified the indebtedness of economic actors (at the expense of the latter too), and increased systemic risk.[4] This in turn has exacerbated further moral hazard and trapped the US economy into a vicious cycle where mega-banks take more

[1] Disintermediation means bank customers directly engage in financial activities without the guidance and support of—and without paying fees to—intermediary financial institutions, such as banks and savings and loan associations.

[2] Securitisation is the process of collecting and transforming individually illiquid assets into a pool of collateral supporting the issuance of senior and subordinated debt and equity interests. Common examples of securitisation include mortgage-backed securities (MBS), and asset-backed securities (ABS) secured by, for example, credit card account receivables.

[3] Moral hazard occurs when one entity takes greater than proportionate risks because another entity bears *or is made to bear* the cost of those risks. In this chapter, moral hazard primarily refers to a specific situation, namely, that of US systemic banks, which take excessive risks because they are confident they will not be allowed to fail in case of severe financial distress. See Rowell and Connelly (2012) for a study of the term "moral hazard".

[4] Systemic risk is the possibility that an event at a bank or company level could trigger the collapse of the economy.

and more risks but know they will not be allowed to fail in the event of crisis.[5]

The next section investigates how some US banks became TBTF and "instrumentalized" (if not "weaponized") financial innovation to push their own interests. In the following section, we argue that the major regulators became "lenient partners" (what we call "sweeteners") to TBTF banks. These gatekeepers implemented permissive policies to avert market disruptions and avoid interfering in TBTF banks' strategies, but consequently encouraged increased risk-taking. The last section advances some recommendations to fight moral hazard, directly and indirectly. We support the idea that we need to step back from "finance for all" and find a route to *optimal* finance at the domestic and global levels.

THE TRIUMPH OF "TOO BIG TO FAIL" BANKS

Banks and financial institutions have a long and storied history of needing special assistance in times of crisis (see Chap. 1 of this volume). Flores (2010) and Dowd and Hutchinson (2010) describe the Bank of England's rescue of Barings Bros in 1890 as perhaps the first explicit acknowledgement of an institution as being too big and/or too important to be allowed to fail. Subsequent and particularly noteworthy examples in the US of "special assistance" preceding the financial crisis of 2008 include JP Morgan's resolution of the 1907 panic following the failure of Knickerbocker Trust, the US Congress' creation of the Resolution Trust Corporation to resolve the savings and loan crisis in the 1980s, and the failure (and subsequent resolution) of Continental Illinois National Bank and Trust Company in 1984 (discussed below).

Superficially, the key characteristics to ensuring membership in the class of institutions deserving such special assistance (at least prior to the establishment of regulations defining "systemically important financial institutions", or SIFIs) have been size and interconnectedness. In fact, the term "too big to fail" is in effect the offspring of the original 1950 concept of a failing bank being "essential" to its community and thereby being eligible

---

[5] We focus exclusively on the US economic and financial system because consumer credit, structured finance products, excessive leverage, and the TBTF phenomenon emerged and developed dramatically in the US before spreading, to a lesser extent, to other developed countries.

to receive a direct infusion of funds (rather than face closure or the forced acquisition by a more well-capitalized bank).[6]

Consideration of the possible "disruption to the community" morphed into concern for systemic risk as banks grew larger through multiple acquisitions and mergers (Federal Deposit Insurance Corporation—FDIC 1997, Chapter 7). With the accelerating accumulation of debt (financial assets to the banks) from the 1980s, the increased competition from niche providers (offering credit card services, discount brokerage, and mutual fund investments), and the realization that the government would exercise its power to prevent systemic risk created by a large bank failure, the importance of size as a component of competitive advantage came into focus.[7]

1984 and the Triumph of Moral Hazard

The 1974 failure and subsequent rescue of the Franklin National Bank (with deposits reaching $1.4 billion) convinced US regulators that the stability of the US banking system might be ending. Riskier business activities (e.g., direct lease financing, underwriting of revenue bonds, and foreign operations) combined with the disintegration of the Bretton Woods system in 1971 and the 1973 recession were weakening a growing number of banks.

Shortly after this episode, several economists argued that as banking crises were increasingly sharp, US regulators would have to revise their lender-of-last-resort policy in the near future and directly bail out large banks (see Horvitz 1975; Humphrey 1975; Mayer 1975). Their analyses proved accurate when the Continental Illinois National Bank and Trust Company (CINB) failed in 1984.

Pursuing a rapid growth strategy from the late 1970s, CINB became the largest commercial and industrial lender in the US by 1981. Because regulations prohibited banks and bank holding companies from interstate branching and owning banks across state lines, the common strategy was

---

[6] Federal Deposit Insurance Corporation (FDIC 1997, 248). The FDIC's Annual Report for 1950 indicated that it was "the intent of the Corporation to use this authority sparingly".

[7] The consequence of hypergrowth strategies was the increasing concentration in the financial sector. This remains a major challenge of the re-globalization era. James Busumtwi-Sam provides a striking illustration in Chap. 5, showing that remittance flows are in the hands of a very small group of international money transfer operators.

to acquire assets (loans) from banks outside the state. CINB invested heavily in oil and gas exploration and other speculative energy-related loans and purchased $1 billion of such loans from Penn Square Bank, an Oklahoma bank that failed in July 1982 (FDIC 1997, 241). CINB also had exposure to Latin American debt, which was adversely affected by Mexico's sovereign default in August 1982.[8]

Efforts to stabilize its balance sheet continued throughout 1982 and 1983, but by the end of the first quarter of 1984, CINB reported an increase in nonperforming loans to $2.3 billion, igniting rumours of pending insolvency and a run by depositors. Prior to the investor panic, CINB had over $28 billion in deposits, including over $20 billion that exceeded the $100,000 limit at that time for FDIC insurance. In anticipation and in reaction to the deterioration of the balance sheet, depositors withdrew nearly $11 billion in 1984. Despite over $3.6 billion in direct borrowing from the Federal Reserve Bank of Chicago, and a $4.5 billion line of credit arranged from 16 of the nation's largest banks, the run continued. The FDIC estimated that well over 2000 banks were minority investors in CINB with 179 having invested amounts equal to more than 50% of their own equity capital (FDIC 1997, 250). The FDIC then announced it would extend deposit insurance to depositors and other bank creditors even where the exposure exceeded $100,000 (Swary 1986, 471–472). Subsequent to successfully halting the immediate crisis, and after unsuccessfully attempting to find an acquiring bank, the FDIC committed to purchasing bad loans from CINB's balance sheet, conditioned however on the removal and replacement of senior managers and submission to government ownership.[9]

The CINB crisis, and the response by the FDIC, represented an important turning point in bank regulation and, more importantly, strategic planning by bank management. Because of the expressed concern for "spillover" effects and contagion impacting the greater financial system and the general economy, banks now had an effective ceiling to the risk presented by their activities. In fact, during the congressional hearings

[8] See https://www.federalreservehistory.org/essays/failure_of_continental_illinois

[9] The purchase of the 'bad loans' and the assumption of control represented a new response to a failing bank. Prior to the CINB crisis, the FDIC had three options: liquidate the bank and pay insured depositors (only), arrange for an acquiring bank to assume the liabilities (and thus protect uninsured depositors), or directly inject funds.

following CINB's rescue, the Comptroller of the Currency explicitly stated that regulators were unlikely to allow the nation's largest banks to fail, to which Congressman Stewart McKinney sarcastically responded, "let us not bandy words. We have created a new kind of bank. It is called too big to fail, TBTF, and it is a wonderful bank".[10]

The creation of TBTF institutions had three major consequences. First, it magnified the power of top managers in US banks. Second, it encouraged hypergrowth strategies in order to immunize against financial crisis. Third, it accelerated financialisation, encouraging and deepening the US economy's addiction to debt while increasing its dependency on the health of those institutions.

A New Paradigm with New "Masters"

In 1981, the proportion of the financial service corporations' earnings of the S&P 500 Index companies was approximately 5%. A decade later, that proportion had doubled. By 1997, the proportion had doubled again to 20%, and by 2007, earnings from financial corporations comprised 27% of the total earnings of the 500 companies comprising this benchmark index (Dowd and Hutchinson 2010, 151).

Hyperbolic earnings generated a self-serving explanation: that senior managers and executive talent were primarily responsible. Compliant boards anxious to maintain the trend responded affirmatively to such explanations. CEO compensation and the competition for talent rose dramatically in the 1980s, and "performance-based" bonuses were widely installed. Executive salaries over the period of 1980–2004 increased at an average rate of 8.5% per year in real terms, while profits grew at 2.9% (Bogle 2005, 17–18). In 1980, the average US CEO salary was 42 times that of an average worker; by 2008 that CEO could expect *520* times the annual compensation of their average worker (Bogle 2009). These figures *do not* include executive "perks" and amenities such as country club dues, luxury apartments, personal use of corporate jet, retirement stipends, and so on. As early as the late 1980s, it appeared that the bigger the bank, the higher the salary of its CEO. The premium was (ironically) referred to as pay for "hazardous duty" (Liscio 1987)!

---

[10] See https://www.federalreservehistory.org/essays/failure_of_continental_illinois and Carrington (1984).

Managerial control of compensation is perhaps the most explicit abuse of the power of the shareholder owners' agents. But other "privileges" appeared. Share buybacks, writing off losses by labelling them "extraordinary" (and thereby avoiding the income statement), reducing long-term research and development investment, outsourcing services to nations with lower labour costs, manipulating taxable earnings through offshore transactions, and issuing executive stock options with favourable targets all became common strategies used by the "C-suite".

With so much of the leadership focusing on short-term results necessary to maximize performance-based metrics (with little to no regard to the longer-term consequences of the strategies pursued), the culture in finance followed the leaders down the slippery slope. "Maximizing shareholder value" has been the fig leaf covering any number of devolutions towards the morally hazardous short-term environment that banking and finance have come to occupy.[11]

At least some of that devolution from the top derives from *who* is at the top, and from the 1980s the balance of power in the "C-suites" had shifted. Increasingly, the CEOs for the biggest Wall Street banks were coming up through trading, and not through investment banking.[12] And the trader mentality at the top inspired "mirroring behaviour" down the chain of command, particularly when doing so was in the best interests of those eager to move up that chain of command. Combine trading mentality with its focus on share price and short-term results, together with the trend away from partnership structures and towards publicly traded ownership (where the capital at risk is "other people's money"), and the trader culture thrives. Within a trader culture steeped in the "markets are efficient" philosophy, great rewards can only come from ever greater risk. In

---

[11] See statement of Richard Michalek, US Senate, Permanent Subcommittee on Investigations, *Hearing on Wall Street and the Financial Crisis: The Role of Credit Rating Agencies*, 23 April 2010, p. 44: Senator Levin: "OK. And then, what does [IBG-YBG] mean?" Richard Michalek: "IBG-YBG was explained to me to mean", "I'll be gone, you'll be gone. So why are you making life difficult right now over this particular comment?" [...] "When it was originally told to me, I did not realize how that thinking really was driving much of what was going on, actually". Senator Levin: "Short-term thinking". Mr. Michalek: "Short term, get this deal done, get this quarter closed, get this bonus booked, because I do not know whether or not my group is going to be here at the end of next quarter, so I have to think of this next bonus".

[12] For a scathing description of a battle for power exemplifying the then-current shift in cultures, see Auletta (1985).

that context, risk is embraced and the moral calculus shifts from "we can't go until we have confirmed this is permitted" to "we won't stop unless it is confirmed to be prohibited".

The newfound personal wealth among the managerial class combined with the growing sophistication from tax-advantaged structuring to lay the seeds of what later would become the global scandals of tax avoidance in the tax havens for senior city employees, and, ultimately, the Panama Papers and the Paradise Papers (refer to Hira et al.'s chapter in this volume). In the US, the tax regulation known as "check the box" permitted entities structured as "hybrid entities" to be taxed differently in different jurisdictions (Oosterhuis 2005). In an environment steeped in moral hazard, where lawyers are given the task to "confirm it's not prohibited", it is but a short step from the corporate use of offshore tax havens for captive structured finance (SF) subsidiaries involved in fee generation to the deployment of personal offshore shell corporations for the improvement of one's global after-tax net income. In fact, the notoriety of the opportunism expressed by the use of offshore tax havens to enrich the high-net-worth individual has contributed to the broad brush populist condemnation of the "elites" who seemingly pay no taxes and serve no jail time. That disapprobation has tainted corporate use of international transactions aiming for a similar tax benefit (cf. Apple Corporation and its reported "billions" held in offshore subsidiary accounts) and has contributed to the deep suspicion if not outright rejection of all things mislabelled "globalization".

The TBTF banks' corporate hubris expanded with each new complex cross-border multi-jurisdictional deal and especially structured finance transactions. The dialogue with regulators, and with the rating agencies, soon altered as nearly every solicitation would begin with an explanation of what the banks were interested in doing. The relatively undercompensated and overworked government employee would be placed in a position of being asked—often by the bank's high-powered Wall Street counsel—whether or not this novel first-impression transaction was *anywhere prohibited*. Keeping in mind that the government employee, in many instances, coveted the bank employee (or its counsel's) job, it is not hard to understand how the banks could come to see the regulators and the rating agencies as necessary pawns to be politely courted, and then played (see Cohn's chapter and below).

Financial Innovation

The 1980s may have marked the onset of aggressive financial engineering and the first generation of new products, but it was the period after the 1980s through to the financial crisis of 2008 that most exploited the development and *marketing* of such products. The rent-seeking short-term culture spread through financial innovation and through the increasing international competition between and among the global money centre banks.

Creative finance as a tool came from the combination of increasing debt levels, and new, unprecedented, low levels of both inflation and interest rates. Managers answered commercial challenges with financial solutions diverting real asset resources to finance (Cecchetti and Kharroubi 2015). Leveraging the expertise attained in solving corporate challenges of the late 1970s and early 1980s (refinancings, currency hedges, interest rate swaps, buyouts, takeovers), financial institutions turned towards the creation of consumer products. Most significantly, they embraced the origination of new products supported by *securitisation*.

The acceptance and use of debt and household credit was driven by, and helped to drive, the expansion of financial services and can be considered the seedbed of securitisation. Based on a "value added" measure, the US Bureau of Economic Analysis has reported that the financial services sector contributed 8.3% to the US GDP in 2006, as compared to 4.9% in 1980 (Greenwood and Scharfstein 2013, 3). The credit boom between 1991 and 2007 cannot be overstated: domestic private sector debt more than tripled from $10.3 trillion to $39.9 trillion with financial and household sectors leading the way (Wilmarth 2010, 726).[13] The International Monetary Fund (IMF 2009) estimated that US private sector issuance of *asset-backed securities* (ABS), *commercial and residential mortgage-backed securities* (CMBS and RMBS), and *collateralized debt obligations* (CDOs) from 2000 to 2007 totalled approximately $9 trillion. In fact, the growth in financial services can be considered a recognition of *fee income* as a new and critical source of earnings for the participating institutions.[14]

---

[13] It is worth noting that abundant liquidity on US capital markets was (and is still) partly driven by capital flows from China. See http://www.cnbc.com/2014/09/17/why-chinese-money-is-flooding-american-markets.html

[14] Fee income of the largest US banks rose from 40% of total earnings in 1995 to 75% of total earnings in 2007 (Wilmarth 2009, 995). See also Greenwood and Scharfstein (2013, 5 et seq.).

The consequences of excessive mortgage indebtedness are still ricocheting through the US economy, but the overuse and *overprovision* of consumer credit does not end with residential mortgages. Both auto loans and student loans have mushroomed, with the latter especially raising much concern (Mezza and Sommer 2015).

The Race to Become (and Remain) TBTF

The globalization and growth of finance capitalism feeds off the common recognition at financial institutions around the globe that there is a positive correlation between assets under management and earnings growth. Through the use of complex derivatives and structured finance innovation, risk managers increasingly became balkanized "Cassandras" within their own institutions. Senior management succumbed to the false sense of security even as the increasingly unwieldy, unregulated, and destabilizing products chased diminishing marginal returns in larger and larger transactions.

The technology of securitisation, where ever-larger pools of presumably diverse financial assets are acquired, the purchase of which is funded by notes structured according to the anticipated cashflows from those assets, permitted the entrance of new funding sources for capital. The particularly innovative element of this technology was the creation of a balance sheet out of "thin air". While traditional lending had forever required the pre-existing balance sheet of a well-capitalized lending institution, securitisation required only the agreement of investors regarding where they stood in line in respect of the cashflows *to be generated* by the assembled pool of financial assets.[15] With no meaningful overhead (no customer service, no state or federal banking regime to comply with, and no employees other than the contractually engaged agents needed to service the cashflows and dispose of nonperforming assets), securitisation offered "nonbank" finance companies significant competitive advantages.

One critical feature of the typical securitisation is often underemphasized, but neatly captures the insidious moral hazard: structuring and originating fees and expenses are primarily paid upfront and ahead of the

---

[15] The importance of a "third party risk assessor" grew in proportion with the development of securitisation. See below.

risk-compensating returns due to even the most senior classes of indebtedness. The moral hazard embedded in this ordering of cashflows meant that originating and structuring parties exerted all possible efforts to get a deal to the closing date (i.e., the date of the funding by the issuance of debt and other capital instruments). While the ultimate returns earned by the issued indebtedness were primarily a function of the debt's duration, the returns to the originators, structurers, and deal agents (e.g., trustees) were primarily *dichotomous*: a failed closing could mean zero returns for the time, money, and effort expended. The incentive to successfully close increasingly dominated the negotiations for all parties because a failure to close represented an *immediate total* loss, while any consequent deterioration in risk management, gatekeeping quality, or reputation meant a *future marginal* loss to the transacting institution, regulatory regime, and fiduciary culture.

The larger banks recognized that the cost-effective path to further asset accumulation offered by securitisation involved the sponsorship of structured finance issuance as part of their activities. With extraordinarily promising returns, the race to universal banking (i.e., mega-bank size) was the ultimate, decisive step. The concept of "one-stop-shopping" for financial services grew throughout the 1980s and 1990s as smaller "nonbanks"—exploiting the development of new niche products and advances in computer technology as well as the continuing momentum of deregulation—began competing for the attention of consumers. Discount brokerages enjoying the deregulation of commissions, new credit card banks, and new nonbank mortgage lenders and finance companies all sought to compete on price, and consumers shifted investments away from traditional bank deposits. Accordingly, the larger banks, brokerages, and life insurers began a period of consolidation and vertical integration and pursued acquisitions in order to meet the demand (Wilmarth 2002).

In this context, and from the perspective of the legal realists who recognize the susceptibility of a legislator's opinion to the interests of the donor class, the repeal of Glass-Steagall (by virtue of the passage of the Gramm-Leach-Bliley Act—GLBA—in 1999) was inevitable. The history and consequences of the repeal are well described elsewhere (see Stiglitz 2010), but for our purposes it stands as a prime example of the increasing influence financial leaders had over and within the political process (Morgenson and Rosner 2011). Following the removal of the legal restrictions prohibiting the common ownership of insurance, commercial, and investment banking, the "race" to financial services dominance in the US began in earnest.

Perhaps the most illuminating fact of the "unintended consequences" from the explicit and expected bailout of the mega-banks is found in the post-crisis changes to their capital costs and to the treatment they received from the rating agencies. After the government bailed out the mega-banks in 2009, research has shown that borrowing costs for banks with assets over $100 billion were one third to three quarters of a percentage point *lower* than that of their smaller competitors. Prior to the bailout, that advantage was reportedly less than 0.1 percentage point (see Cho 2009; Morgenson 2009; Wilmarth 2010, fn.140). By the same token, credit rating agencies (CRAs) explicitly recognized support from the government by "notching up" the ratings assigned to the TBTF banks, with upward adjustments ranging from two (Goldman Sachs Group) to four notches (Citigroup) (Wilmarth 2010, fn. 141).[16]

The overconfidence of the largest TBTF banks, as expressed by their willingness to retain ever-larger exposures to the aggressively structured securitisations, is seen in their ballooning balance sheets. Citigroup, Merrill Lynch, and UBS—a Swiss bank especially active on the US market—together held more than $175 billion of AAA-rated CDO tranches on their books in 2007. Not surprisingly, when the "music stopped",[17] all three of these institutions required extensive support from the government to avoid failing (Tett 2009, 127–129, 133–139, and 204–206).

However, starting as far back as the 1990s, the power and influence of TBTF banks took on diffuse and insidious forms, especially through their relations with de jure and de facto financial gatekeepers. Systemic banks have used and abused the "we won't stop unless it is confirmed to be prohibited" principle by arguing that any brake on their activities and financial innovation weakened their position and thus increased the likelihood of a bailout.

In this context, financial gatekeepers should have served as "inquirers". Their duties should have consisted of *detecting and eliminating the*

---

[16] For a more exhaustive analysis of the role played by the main CRAs, namely, Fitch Ratings (Fitch), Moody's Investors Service (Moody's), and Standard & Poor's (S&P), see below.

[17] In July 2007, Chuck Prince (then CEO of Citigroup) said: "When the music stops, in terms of liquidity, things will be complicated. But as long as the music is playing, you've got to get up and dance. We're still dancing". See Nakamoto and Wighton (2007).

incentives that could induce TBTF banks to increase their risk-taking simply because they knew they would be rescued in case of financial distress. Such preventive action would have involved investigating whether, for example, financial sophistication and increasing leverage were symptoms of moral hazard and thus had to be restrained. Instead, de jure and de facto regulators have (involuntarily or cynically) overlooked these aspects and instead concentrated their efforts on the non-confrontational goal of stabilizing the capital markets. The pursuit of this utmost objective has distorted their policies and transformed uncompromising gatekeepers into "lenient partners", what we call here "sweeteners".[18]

The Three "Sweeteners": Regulators, Rating Agencies, and the Federal Reserve

Three types of "sweeteners" are scrutinized: US regulators, CRAs, and the Federal Reserve Board (FRB).[19] Though purporting to act independently from one another, they have exacerbated moral hazard and the problems inherent to the TBTF era: excessive leverage, undercapitalization of financial institutions, underestimation of credit risk, and financial sophistication. In fact, the policies undertaken by US regulatory bodies, CRAs, and the FRB seemed to be driven primarily by a fear of being blamed for disrupting capital markets.[20]

The US Regulators

A very quick look at the landscape of US banking and financial regulation in the re-globalization era helps understand why regulators failed to prevent the 2007–2009 financial turmoil. First, the US regulatory structure has been traditionally balkanized. Three different federal regulators supervise banks: the FRB, the FDIC, and the Office of the Comptroller of the

---

[18] Here, our analysis is partly in line with Laurent Dobuzinskis' chapter on regulatory failure.

[19] Here, we briefly mention the FRB as regulator. Below, we will refer to it as monetary policy maker.

[20] The "go along to get along" culture combines well with the "if it ain't broke, don't fix it" rubric in the developing "revolving door" environment, where mid-level regulators and "deal-level" employees at the CRAs were eager to maintain favour with potential future employers offering significantly greater financial rewards.

Currency (OCC). They oversee state-chartered banks that are members of the Federal Reserve System; chartered banks that are not members of the Federal Reserve System but are federally insured; and national banks, respectively. In addition to these agencies, the Securities and Exchange Commission (SEC) regulates the securities industry, while the Commodity Futures Trading Commission (CFTC) oversees futures and part of the derivatives markets. This segregated structure has resulted in inter-agency disputes and duplication of certain common activities across regulators (Department of the Treasury, 2008, 3–5).[21]

Second, US regulatory bodies lacked human resources during the past decades. For example, the total number of examiners in federal and state banking agencies declined by 14% between 1979 and 1984 (FDIC 1997, 56–57). This evolution was especially deplorable as the Garn-St Germain Depository Institutions Act of 1982 deregulated banks and the total number of troubled banks soared from 217 in 1980 to 1140 in 1985 (FDIC 1997, 57). The growth of regulatory bodies' staff in the subsequent years was dwarfed by the 14-fold increase in outstanding US asset-backed, mortgage-related, and corporate bonds—from $1178 billion in 1985 to $16,601 billion in 2007—as well as by the fivefold increase in the US commercial banks' assets, from $2395 billion in 1985 to $10,983 billion in 2007 (SIFMA and Federal Reserve data).

In addition to these organizational weaknesses, US regulators were more prone to implement lenient policies to financial institutions. At first sight, the "sweetening" function of US regulators identified here might trace its roots to the traditional Stigler view on regulatory capture (see Cohn's chapter in this volume).[22] In fact, US agencies refrain from issuing any rule that might curb financial innovation and economic growth.[23] This tendency paved the way to excessive risk-taking and untrammelled financial sophistication, which contributed to nurture moral hazard.

---

[21] For a comprehensive overview of the byzantine US regulation and supervision of financial institutions, see Mason (2015).

[22] Regulatory capture is an illustration of government failure that occurs when a regulatory body promotes the financial or political interests of the firms or groups it is charged with regulating. Nobel Prize winner George Stigler developed such arguments in various research works; for example, see Stigler (1964, 1971).

[23] In the early 1990s, there was already a consensus that financial services spurred economic development. See King and Levine (1993).

In this respect, the policy followed by the SEC to regulate structured finance deals is very telling. In 1992, the SEC adopted Rule 3a-7 under the Investment Company Act of 1940 to exclude issuers that pool income-producing assets and issue securities backed by those assets from the definition of "investment company". The rule permitted structured finance issuers to offer their securities publicly in the US without registering under and complying with the Investment Company Act and its regulations. The SEC explained that Rule 3a-7 removed an unnecessary and unintended barrier to the use of structured financings in all sectors of the economy and accommodated future innovations in the securitisation market.[24]

In 2001, in response to a letter from the Capital Committee of the Securities Industry Association, the SEC eased the marketability of ABS issued by Special Purpose Vehicles (SPVs). The SEC relaxed the rule requiring a broker-dealer to deduct from its net worth 100% of the carrying value of securities it holds in its proprietary account for which there is no ready market or which cannot be publicly offered or sold without registration.[25] The SEC no-action letter stated that there would be no haircut imposed on broker-dealers holding ABS with an initial issuance size of at least $100 million and rated in one of the two highest rating categories by at least one NRSRO (nationally recognized statistical rating organization).[26] A 15% haircut would apply to ABS with an initial issuance size of at least $100 million and rated in one of the four highest categories by at least one NRSRO.[27] The no-action letter was especially generous to broker-dealers as, at the time it was released, around 87% of structured finance ratings were ranked in the investment-grade category (i.e., in the top four broad letter categories) (Moody's 2003a).

The final, baneful, step took place in 2005 when the SEC adopted Regulation AB. This new rule consolidated and codified existing interpretive positions regarding the registration, disclosure, and reporting

[24]SEC. 1992. *Exclusion from the Definition of Investment Company for Structured Financings.* Investment Company Act Release No. 19105. November 19 [57 FR 56248 (Nov. 27, 1992)].

[25]Often used in determining regulatory capital and when posting collateral, such a deduction is referred to as a "haircut".

[26]In 1975, the SEC introduced the concept of NRSRO for the purpose of categorizing debt as investment grade (or not) when calculating broker-dealer capital.

[27]SEC. 2001. *Marketability of Asset-Backed Securities Issued by Special Purpose Vehicles.* No-Action Letter. July 13.

requirements for ABS under the Securities Act of 1933 and the Securities Exchange Act of 1934. A close review of the history and enactment of Regulation AB supports the view that the SEC was unable to identify the specific challenges posed by ABS. Its approach—much more fitted for traditional corporate debt than for complex structured finance deals (Mendales 2009, 1382–1384)—turned out to be wrong and naïve, as this excerpt from the ruling shows: "Most asset types that have been securitized have homogenous characteristics, including similar terms, structures and credit characteristics, with proven histories of performance, which in turn facilitate modeling of future payments and thus analysis of yield and credit risks".[28]

The SEC's lenient policy regarding Regulation AB was not discontinued with the onset of the subprime crisis of 2007–2009. Subtitle C ("Improvements to the Regulation of Credit Rating Agencies") of Title IX ("Investor Protections and Improvements to the Regulation of Securities") of the Dodd-Frank Act of 2010 revised the role of CRAs and strengthened their supervision.[29] Section 939 strips references to ratings from several statutes. Section 939G nullifies SEC Rule 436(g), which exempted NRSRO ratings from being considered part of a registration statement prepared or certified by an expert. This last provision took immediate effect on 22 July 2010, but its operation on Regulation AB was pre-emptively suspended by the SEC in a no-action letter that was requested by and issued to Ford Motor Credit Company LLC on the same date.[30] This letter establishes that no enforcement action will be recommended if an ABS issuer omits a rating disclosure newly required under Regulation AB by operation of Section 939G and cites as the rationale the unwillingness of NRSROs to provide consent to being named as experts

---

[28] Federal Register. Part II, Securities and Exchange Commission, 17 CFR Parts 210, 228, et al.—Asset-Backed Securities; Final Rule, Vol. 70 (5), January 7, 2005, Rules and Regulations, p. 1510.

[29] For an overview of the Dodd-Frank Act and its capacity to prevent future financial crises, see Murdock (2011).

[30] We have very reliable sources indicating that the SEC itself asked the Ford Motor Credit Company LLC to submit a request for a no-action letter on the day that Rule 436(g) was to have been suspended (i.e., the day after President Obama signed the Dodd-Frank Act). The rationale was that the Dodd-Frank provision was poorly thought out and would have caused enormous damage, so the SEC had to be proactive.

(Gaillard and Harrington 2016, 46–47). This no-action letter was still in force in November 2018.

The "sweetening" actions undertaken by US regulators have been rife since the late 1980s.

- In 1989, the Federal Reserve granted authority for JP Morgan as a commercial bank to underwrite and deal in corporate debt. The following year, the bank was allowed to underwrite equities (JP Morgan 1991, 1992). These two decisions were in contradiction with the Glass-Steagall Act of 1933.
- A year before the Gramm-Leach-Bliley Act of 1999 was passed, Citicorp merged with Travelers Group creating what was, at the time, the world's largest financial services organization. Because this merger was a violation of the Glass-Steagall Act and the Bank Holding Company Act of 1956, the Federal Reserve granted Citigroup an exemption in September 1998 (Bruce 1998; O'Neal 2000; Morgenson and Rosner 2011).
- In 2000, the Financial Accounting Standards Board (FASB) issued its relevant financial accounting standard for accounting for transfers and servicing of financial assets, Statement of Financial Accounting Standards (SFAS) No. 140. This standard replaced FASB Statement 125, revised the standards of accounting for securitisations and other transfers of financial assets, and defined a simpler, easier path to ensuring off-balance sheet treatment through the creation of "qualifying special purpose entities". As the complexity of transactions increased and the ability to exploit the original SFAS 140 requirements improved, the FASB began to examine the use of special purpose vehicles under SFAS 140 and ultimately proposed certain amendments in August 2005. However, the majority of respondents to the proposed changes objected, and accordingly, the publication of a revised and amended standard was postponed (Bernard 2009).[31]
- In 2004, the SEC launched the Consolidated Supervised Entities (CSE) programme. Participation in this programme enabled broker-dealers to use their own internal risk-assessment model instead of the current net capital rule. Concretely, CSE broker-dealers, that is, major banks like Bear Stearns, Goldman Sachs, Lehman Brothers,

---

[31] For additional post-crisis analysis of SFAS 140, see Barth and Landsman (2010).

Merrill Lynch, and Morgan Stanley, managed to reduce the value of their securities positions using "optimistic" value-at-risk models, which boosted their leverage. SEC Chairman William H. Donaldson promoted this programme explaining that it would help "move from a command-and-control regulatory model to a more efficient and goal-oriented approach" (Donaldson 2004). Four years later, Donaldson's successor, Christopher Cox, announced the end of the CSE programme, admitting that it was "fundamentally flawed from the beginning, because investment banks could opt in or out of supervision voluntarily" (Cox 2008).

- Less than six months after the bankruptcy of Lehman Brothers, Chairman of the Board of Governors of the Federal Reserve System Ben Bernanke testified to the US Senate. He delivered a soothing speech and remained silent on moral hazard problems (US Senate 2009, 22). He explained that he did not contemplate any regulatory sanction against major financial institutions under the prompt corrective action (PCA) framework[32] whereas they bore part of the responsibility for the subprime crisis and were receiving funds from the Troubled Asset Relief Program (TARP). By the same token, in November 2017, Federal Reserve chair nominee Jerome Powell told the Senate Banking Committee that improvements in US bank regulation and supervision since the Great Recession had eliminated the problem of TBTF banks (Dunsmuir and Saphir 2017).

- After the subprime crisis, various investigations and testimonies revealed that US regulatory agencies had performed badly. For instance, the Office of Thrift Supervision (OTS)—created in 1989 to regulate federally chartered and state-chartered savings banks and savings and loans associations—did not stop the unsafe practices that led to the demise of Washington Mutual. Despite having identified over 500 deficiencies at Washington Mutual, the OTS "failed to take action to force the bank to improve its lending operations and even impeded oversight by the bank's backup regulator, the FDIC" (US Senate 2011, 4). Title III ("Transfer of Powers to the Comptroller

---

[32] Since 1991, federal banking regulators have been expected to take PCA to identify and address capital deficiencies at banks to minimize losses to the deposit insurance fund (DIF). PCA includes different types of penalties. A critically undercapitalized FDIC-regulated institution would be required to be taken into receivership by the FDIC.

of the Currency, the Corporation, and the Board of Governors") of the 2010 Dodd-Frank Act slightly modified the balance of powers and duties among US regulators: Section 312 mandated merger of the OTS with the OCC, the FRB, and the Consumer Financial Protection Bureau (CFPB). The OTS was dismantled in 2011.

One response to the demands made of the regulatory authorities in the US has been the increased use of and reliance upon non-governmental "self-regulation" and to the use and participation in "clearing exchanges".[33] For instance, in 2007, the SEC formally approved certain previously granted regulatory and enforcement authority held by the New York Stock Exchange and the National Association of Securities Dealers to the private corporation Financial Industry Regulatory Authority (FINRA 2007). However, the most striking illustration of the reliance on non-governmental self-regulating trade organizations in the context of structured finance is the emergence of the International Swaps and Derivatives Association (ISDA) (see Gay and Medero 1996 for more details). Created in 1985, ISDA evolved alongside the use and development of swap transactions as a key tool in managing corporate finance. By publishing for its members "standard documentation", and by developing a legally robust architecture of master agreement/annexes/confirmations, ISDA succeeded in facilitating a process where counterparties need only adhere to a single published "master agreement", and then execute a comparatively brief "confirmation" that defines and delimits the specific terms and conditions applicable to the instant transaction. Once a single master agreement between parties is entered, negotiation and modification need only address the terms contained in the necessary confirmation, thereby accelerating the transacting process dramatically. As nearly every structured finance transaction includes a derivative element (e.g., interest rate swap, currency swap and, within the hyperactivity leading into the financial crisis, credit default swaps), ISDA and its pronouncements and definitions migrated to

---

[33] As a refresher, when securities are traded through a recognized and sufficiently capitalized "exchange", the counterparties are in fact each trading with the exchange, which then bears some of the risk of non-performance by the contracting parties. Exchange members typically pay fees and post margin (collateral) to the exchange to finance administration and to ensure sufficient capital is available to assume the relatively rare failures of the trading members.

a position of central importance, despite a notable lack of enforcement power.[34]

The explosion of issuance of US (and subsequently, European) structured finance was occurring within, and may have been augmented by, the "mission-shift" of CRAs. Even while structured finance issuance was shifting towards the "commodification" stage (wherein profits are pursued through volume and increased numbers of repeat "flow deals" with "master trust" structures serially issuing subsequent duplicative transactions enabling increased issuances), several of the rating agencies were transforming into public companies newly beholden to shareholders and metrics such as "revenue per analyst". As discussed further, the organizations' and senior management's focus expanded beyond the persistent challenge of risk measurement and ratings integrity to include (and ultimately became dominated by) maintaining "market share" and "improving relationships with clients" (dominated by the TBTF banks).

The Credit Rating Agencies

The "sweetening" role played by CRAs started in the 1990s and primarily consisted of inflating ratings. There are several intertwined causes for this phenomenon: the extensive use of credit ratings among investors and regulators, the business model of CRAs, and the boom of structured finance deals.[35]

The first regulatory rule referring to credit ratings was enacted by the OCC in 1931. In the following years, an increasing number of rating-based

---

[34] Post-crisis, ISDA developed "Determination Committees" ("DCs") to hear and determine transaction disputes from contracting counterparties. According to ISDA, the "DCs" consist of 15 member institutions, 10 of which are voting *swap dealer* members and 5 are voting *non-dealer* members. The majority of disputes involve whether or not a payment-triggering "credit event" has occurred under a credit default swap transaction. All participants using ISDA documentation contractually agree to adhere to the rulings of the DCs. But as with every other ISDA agreement, recourse for any member who disputes an outcome under the ISDA document is limited to judicial resolution in a court willing to take jurisdiction. ISDA itself has no power of enforcement. See ISDA (2012).

[35] Credit ratings were first released by John Moody in 1909. The success of these credit risk indicators in the US enabled new entrants (Poor's, Standard Statistics, and Fitch) to compete with Moody's firm in the 1920s. Since Poor's and Standard Statistics merged to form Standard & Poor's (S&P) in 1941, the credit rating industry has been dominated by these three agencies. See Sinclair (2005) for an overview.

regulations were issued (see Gaillard 2016). Credit ratings are generally used for five main regulatory purposes: identifying or classifying assets, usually in the context of eligible investments or permissible asset concentrations; providing a credible evaluation of the credit risk associated with the assets purchased; calculating capital requirements; determining disclosure requirements; and determining prospectus eligibility (BIS 2009, 3–4). The introduction of the NRSRO label in 1975 favoured Fitch, Moody's, and S&P, thus strengthening the oligopolistic structure of the credit rating business. More insidiously, it contributed to inflate the ratings of US corporate issuers in the second half of the 1970s (Behr et al. 2018). Since the 1980s, "overreliance" on credit ratings among debt issuers, central bankers, and investors has exacerbated pro-cyclicality but it has also convinced financial market participants and researchers to investigate and anticipate the reaction of common stock returns and bond yields to rating changes (for example, see Hand et al. 1992).

As de facto regulators whose return to shareholders was a direct function of the number and size of transactions rated, CRAs were more prone to follow lenient rating policies and postpone downgrades.[36] The through-the-cycle methodologies advanced by Fitch, Moody's, and S&P provided "conceptual dressing" for what was primarily reluctance to bear bad news or fear of triggering massive sell-offs.[37] Moody's policy during the Greek debt crisis in April–May 2010 is a striking illustration. Moody's refrained from downgrading Greece to speculative grade because Greek sovereign bonds would then have become ineligible for Eurosystem credit operations. By the same token, the agency announced that it would not revise Greece's rating until the Eurozone/IMF bailout programme was disclosed (Gaillard 2011, 184–185).

The shift from the investor-pays to the issuer-pays model contributed to pervert the nature of CRAs. Until the late 1960s, their revenues came from investors who purchased rating reports. Following a controversy with the city of New York, S&P charged bond issuers to "cover the cost of

---

[36] In 2013, in order to reduce the conflicts of interest inherent to the credit rating business, the European Commission "explored the appropriateness of, and ways to, support a European public credit rating agency". However, this project has not materialized so far. See *Regulation (EU) No. 462/2013 of the European Parliament and of the Council of 21 May 2013 amending Regulation (EC) No. 1060/2009*, para. 43.

[37] The through-the-cycle methodology "places low weight on short-term credit shocks and thereby reduces rating volatility" (Moody's 2003b).

supporting the staff required to perform rating functions" (Harries 1968). By 1974, all three CRAs had an issuer-pays business model. Akin to what happened with the creation of the NRSRO designation, this shift led to inflated corporate ratings (Jiang et al. 2012). These nascent conflicts of interest became blatant with the development of ancillary business and structured finance products two decades later. Ancillary business generates relationship-based fees: they include credit or rating evaluations and assessment services (SEC 2013, 18–41). Almost nonexistent in 1989, they accounted for 36% of Moody's total revenue in 2000 (Moody's Corporation 2001, 13). These services were largely connected to the increasing number of structured finance ratings.[38]

The inflation of structured finance ratings best illustrates the "sweetener" role played by CRAs. The structured finance segment accounted for an increasingly dominant share of CRAs' revenue: 39% of Moody's total revenue in 2007 compared to nearly 0% in the 1980s. The concentration of the MBS underwriting business (Coffee 2011, 238) induced CRAs to be lax when rating residential RMBS and CMBS. All things equal, ratings assigned to MBS issued by the biggest firms were comparatively the most inflated. Tellingly, the rating-inflation was increasingly common knowledge as investors priced into their deals the risk that large issuers received more inflated ratings than small issuers (He et al. 2012). The extent of the inflation of SF ratings was evidenced by the magnitude of downgrades and the high default rates that hit investment-grade securities in 2008–2009. Around 34% and 43% of structured finance securities rated in the investment-grade category by S&P were downgraded in 2008 and 2009, respectively. On the other hand, 6.3% and 8.3% of structured finance securities rated in investment-grade category by S&P defaulted in 2008 and 2009, respectively, vs. 0.1% ten years earlier (S&P data).

The investigations and hearings conducted by the SEC and the US Senate in 2008–2011 confirmed that the major CRAs had failed as financial market gatekeepers (SEC 2008, 2009; US Senate 2010, 2011). Moody's and S&P used inadequate rating models to assess credit risk of RMBS. Although they knew their ratings were no longer accurate, the two firms delayed downgrades and allowed those securities to carry inflated ratings that misled investors. When the first wave of massive downgrades

---

[38] Moody's rated less than 5000 structured finance securities in 1994 vs. more than 86,000 in 2007 (Moody's 2008, 2).

was announced in July 2007, financial markets were shocked. The mechanistic reliance on credit ratings triggered sales of assets that had lost their AAA or their investment-grade status, which led to the collapse of the subprime secondary market and thus to the financial crisis of September 2008. In addition to this, the Permanent Subcommittee on Investigations of the US Senate found that Moody's and S&P were driven to inflate their ratings in order to preserve their market shares, accommodate investment bankers bringing in business, and maintain the eligibility of the assets held by institutional investors.

The "sweetening" role played by CRAs is still operating today. It is reflected in the flaws in CRAs' procedures, rating methodologies, and in the ratings themselves. Perhaps the most telling examples of the CRAs' tacit "sweetening" actions are found in their rating confirmation and affirmation letters. These letters are typically issued in response to a request from either the structuring bank (who may still hold vulnerable pieces of the rated entity's capital structure that it was unable to onsell in the original offering) or from an asset manager for the rated entity, or even from a hedge counterparty that is facing the rated entity but whose continued performance in that role requires—due to deteriorating credit or corporate reorganization or other intervening events—"rating agency permission".[39]

The second "sweetener" applied by the CRAs is an imprimatur of safety that is wholly inconsistent with the *legal* obligations retained by the CRA in respect of the ratings they issue. The history of the CRAs together with ubiquitous marketing by sell-side analysts reinforcing the perception that AAA instruments are extremely safe has burnished that imprimatur and aided in cementing the expectation of safety. However, in the US, the CRAs have embraced the legal environment that has developed around the publication of newsworthy *opinion*, rather than the legal requirements attaching to the statements of professional *experts* (Gaillard and Waibel 2018). The thresholds that currently apply for attaching liability to the CRAs in respect of their reasonably constructed opinions of the risk presented by widely distributed *corporate and municipal* debt issuances

---

[39] A rating affirmation letter is a letter that affirms the rating of the subject obligation as of such and such date is X. These letters may be requested in connection with a secondary market transaction or in connection with a change in control of a noteholder. A rating *confirmation* letter is akin to a "no-action" letter issued by a regulator and states that in light of some proposed action, such action "in and of itself" will not result in the reduction of the rating currently outstanding.

may be justified on public policy grounds: allocation to a centralized risk assessor is efficient and encourages a stable and liquid market. However, those same considerations are inappropriate in the context of bilateral and bespoke structured finance and complex derivative transactions. For the investors in the highly sophisticated structured derivative products, the narrow set of circumstances required for finding liability (e.g., detrimental reliance on proven *fraudulent*—not negligent—representations) begs the question: how is it that the CRAs are selling their expertise and deep experience and yet avoiding responsibility for negligent performance?[40] In fact, the *risk of error generating a loss* in the second class of opinions (i.e., ratings on structured derivative products) is significantly greater. And "opinions" given in respect of securities labelled in the highest category (AAA) have a correspondingly higher risk of error generating loss, in part because of the weight of historical performance of those opinions and in part due to a near universal misunderstanding by the investor class regarding the implied stability of such a rating. In a nutshell, the question becomes "which party is best situated to bear that risk?"

Nevertheless, the current legal regime (and perhaps the collusive efforts of the SEC in withholding enforcement of Section 939G of the Dodd-Frank Act) in which the CRAs operate in the US continues to shield them from financial responsibility for all but the most egregious and demonstrable errors. The critical point is the manifest definition of moral hazard: without having to bear the additional costs of controlling or managing financial liability for negligence, the CRAs can and will stay focused on generation of revenue, exploiting the legally acceptable volatility in the performance of their "opinions" and therefore remaining vulnerable to rating "shopping" and exposing investors to the rent-seeking activities of ratings arbitrage. Further, the relative freedom from liability facilitates the CRAs continuing to aid and abet the morally hazardous behaviour of the *customers* of the CRAs, namely, the structuring and originating banks who continue to pursue upfront fees and the front-loaded compensation of securitisation.

Other sweetening effects of CRAs are closely related to the flaws in their methodologies. For instance, Fitch, Moody's, and S&P continue to project that AAA-rated debt will be 99.995% immune to credit losses regardless of whether the issuer of that debt is party to (a) a risky swap

---

[40] One possible answer: the CRAs are *not* selling their expertise, they are selling their ratings and buying market share from their competitors. See US Senate (2010).

contract provided by a low-rated counterparty, (b) a swap contract provided by a AAA-rated counterparty, or (c) no derivative contract. More globally, mis-rated counterparties and inflated credit ratings generate an interconnectedness problem. When a bank or financial institution (as a counterparty to one or more securitisation swaps) carries an inflated rating, or a derivative product company (in the business of guaranteeing the performance of capital instruments) overstates the adequacy of its capital resources, and either one presents a misleading credit profile to both ABS issuers and other trading partners, the error in risk management multiplies (Gaillard and Harrington 2016).

A further complication derives from the way CRAs deal with express and implied government bailouts. The ratings assigned to banks are enhanced because CRAs take into account a probable bailout from their government (Moody's 2007). The problem is that, in case of a systemic crisis, a government may be unable to bail out all failing banks without jeopardizing its own credit position, and consequently increasing the ultimate costs of the bailout. However, it appears that these possible bailouts do not deflate sovereign ratings. In general terms, CRAs tend to underestimate contingent liabilities when assigning sovereign ratings (Gaillard 2017).

In addition to the underestimation of credit risk by CRAs, another factor has encouraged excessive leverage strategies and moral hazard: the lax monetary policy followed by the Federal Reserve since the 1990s.

The Federal Reserve

The Federal Reserve's duties fall into four main areas:

- Conducting the nation's monetary policy by influencing the monetary and credit conditions in the economy in pursuit of maximum employment, stable prices, and moderate long-term interest rates;
- Supervising and regulating banking institutions to ensure the safety and soundness of the nation's banking and financial system and to protect the credit rights of consumers;
- Maintaining the stability of the financial system and containing systemic risk that may arise in financial markets;
- Providing financial services to depository institutions, the U.S. government, and foreign official institutions, including playing a major role in operating the nation's payments system.[41]

---

[41] https://www.federalreserve.gov/aboutthefed/mission.htm

These duties have been imperfectly fulfilled in the past decades for several reasons.[42]

Starting in the Greenspan era,[43] the Federal Reserve's monetary policy has consisted of setting an implicit inflation target of around 2%. The focus has been on core inflation, which excludes volatile prices observed in energy and food sectors.[44] This specific inflation-targeting framework, described and advocated by Bernanke and Mishkin (1997), has shortcomings. It does not incorporate the price increase of financial and non-financial assets. Yet, there has been a striking decoupling between CPI (Consumer Price Index), on the one hand, and stock prices and real estate, on the other hand, since 1995 and 2001, respectively (Fig. 4.2). The necessity for the Federal Reserve to take these indicators into account was mentioned as early as 2000 (see Cecchetti et al. 2000) but with little success. The basic goods and services included in the CPI reflect the real economy where prices are determined by supply and demand, with no leverage. The picture is completely different regarding asset prices: homes and financial assets are often acquired through leverage strategies and, sometimes, with the view to selling them later at a higher price. In the latter case, asset bubbles are likely to appear. In the 1990s–2000s, the Federal Reserve overlooked the stock exchange rally and the boom in the real estate sector. By maintaining interest rates at excessively low levels, the central bank encouraged stock buybacks (i.e., short termism) and extravagant mergers and acquisitions (i.e., TBTF behemoths).[45]

With the advent of the subprime crisis, the Federal Reserve went several steps further: not only did it cut federal funds rates to zero, but it also launched an unconventional monetary policy: quantitative easing (QE). Starting in 2008, the US central bank purchased Treasury notes, bank

---

[42] Our critical view of the action performed by the Federal Reserve complements those developed by Laurent Dobuzinskis and Ted Cohn in this volume.

[43] Alan Greenspan served as Chairman of the Federal Reserve from 1987 to 2006. He was succeeded by Ben Bernanke.

[44] Core inflation is generally calculated using the consumer price index (CPI).

[45] Even with respect to the core inflation standard, interest rates were too low. The federal funds rate *minus* inflation differential declined from 2.3 percentage points during 1986–1995 to 1.2 percentage points during 1996–2005 and 0.9 percentage point during 2006–2015.

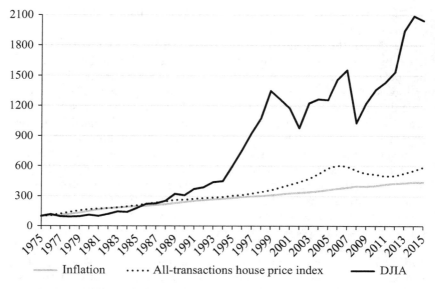

Fig. 4.2 Prices of different types of assets, 1975–2015. Note: Index 100 for 1975. Annual data. (Sources: Federal Reserve and www.measuringworth.com)

debt, and mortgage-backed securities[46] in order to increase the money supply and stimulate economic activity. The impact of the QEs is debatable. Deflation was averted. The unemployment rate fell below 5% in 2016 (for the first time since 2008), essentially because the labour force participation rate declined dramatically, reaching a 39-year low in 2016. Despite these efforts to stimulate lending, liquidity has remained trapped in banks and has fuelled asset bubbles. Direct injections of liquidity into the corporate sector would have been more efficient (Benmelech and Bergman 2012).

A second unconventional policy tool was used by Ben Bernanke and his successor Janet Yellen: "forward guidance". This communication strategy,

---

[46] Total assets of the Federal Reserve System soared from $900 billion in August 2008 (i.e., a few weeks prior to the collapse of Lehman Brothers) to $4.4 trillion in August 2014 (Federal Reserve data).

which aims to influence market expectations about future levels of interest rates, has become a "mutual anticipations game" between central bankers and institutional investors (see Yellen 2012; Holmes 2014). Month after month, "forward guidance" turned out to be as much a function of macroeconomic and microeconomic data and forecasts as it was a function of investors' beliefs and expectations. For example, in November 2016, reacting to a question on a possible interest rate hike in the very near future, Federal Reserve policy maker James Bullard replied: "Markets are currently putting a high probability on a December move by the FOMC.[47] I'm leaning toward supporting that".[48] James Bullard's statement suggests that the central bank will, if not follow, at least not disrupt what the market anticipates. This is also in line with what transpires from the minutes and transcripts of FOMC meetings released in the past years. "Forward guidance" appears less a technique promoting transparency and accountability than a guile reinforcing the primary motivations of all these "sweeteners" to not antagonize investors and trigger market disruptions. This drifting of the Federal Reserve policy was presciently described by Krippner (2007, 505): "The case of US monetary policy suggests that, under neoliberalism, the state has transferred significant aspects of policy implementation to markets, but continues to guide markets actively to achieve closely calibrated economic outcome".

POLICY RECOMMENDATIONS

The growth and increasing power of the largest financial institutions is both the reflection and the result of the encroaching tendency to disregard moral hazard. As capital flows towards the highest risk-adjusted returns, the failure to accurately assess, identify and *assign* credit risk has disproportionally benefitted those best able to exploit that failure. Once growth of the institution has enabled it to cross the threshold of too big to fail (or,

---

[47] The FOMC (Federal Open Market Committee) is the branch of the Federal Reserve Board that determines the direction of monetary policy.
[48] https://www.stlouisfed.org/from-the-president/video-appearances/2016/bullard-frankfurt-panel

more formally, to be included as a SIFI), the implicit and explicit support of taxpayer-funded "rescues" has, as shown, *lowered* the relative cost of capital for those institutions. That lower cost of capital has enabled the largest institutions to successfully take market share from the smaller (community-based) institutions, further increasing their attractiveness to investors, thereby accelerating the cycle of growth and, consequently, further encouraging the wilful blindness towards, if not actual preference for, moral hazard.

Regulatory efforts, most notably the Dodd-Frank legislation and its attendant regulations, have struggled with the increasing dichotomy of scale, and satisfying compliance requirements has only further disproportionally burdened the smaller institutions. The deregulatory efforts of the current US administration identify and use the admittedly disproportionate burden on the "community" banks as the justification for dismantling and significantly curtailing necessary regulation and prudent reforms. The populist mantra of reinvigorating small business and small banks through the wholesale removal of "burdensome" regulation serves to provide the largest source of political donations—the financial industry—with a path towards greater size, greater profits, and an even greater influence over future regulation. Regardless, since the 1980s, policy makers, de facto and de jure regulators, and senior managers within the institutions have preferred to ignore, if not tacitly encourage, morally hazardous profitable behaviour rather than risk destabilizing financial markets or jeopardize their performance-based compensation.[49] This path, which has exacerbated inequalities and impoverished the American middle class, endangers the future of *liberal capitalism*. As discussed by Helleiner (2014), the crisis of 2007–2009 and the "solutions" implemented so far have clearly preserved the *status quo*.

We believe that the implementation of a set of well-balanced reforms can limit the power of TBTF banks, stop punishing taxpayers in the event

---

[49] This fear of jeopardizing one's own short-term compensation (even when the action disproportionately threatens long-term returns) represents one critical facet of the culture steeped in moral hazard. The cognitive biases attending decisions involving immediate and future realized values, when combined with *secondary incentives* in the behaviour of sell-side analysts and traders operating in a "zero sum" trading environment, significantly contribute to less than economically optimal outcomes and amplify the swing of the regulate-deregulate pendulum.

of a severe financial crisis, and begin to restore confidence in the financial and economic system. Three areas require specific actions.

The "TBTF Banks" Era Must Be Ended

What is at stake with TBTF banks goes well beyond the relative efficiency of bail-ins and bailouts.[50] If a systemic bank is in distress, a bail-in *and* a bailout both could be required to avert a systemic crisis. The major, seminal, issue to address is undoubtedly moral hazard and how best to reverse its insidious inculcation in the culture of finance. We would echo those who argue that punitive regulations alone will inevitably fail as a solution: regulators are prone to human error, as well as susceptible to material and cultural capture (see Ted Cohn's chapter in this volume). Furthermore, innovation—itself an essential ingredient for successful competition in sophisticated markets—will always supersede and circumvent proscriptive regulation. Of course, the impossibility of perfect regulation does not imply withdrawing all regulations, as discussed in Dobuzinskis' chapter. Instead, greater incentives must also be provided—preferably through self-reinforcing market mechanisms—to both the regulators and the regulated to resist capture and reject morally hazardous behaviours.

One well-trodden suggestion deserves revisiting: enable market discipline to more effectively operate on the operations and culture of the systemically important entities by requiring those entities of sufficient size and interconnectedness to hold a substantial position of subordinated debt within their own capital structure. Poole (2010) advocates for 10% of total liabilities to be held in ten-year subordinated notes, with a requirement that the institution roll 10% of those notes each year. Should the market assess that the risk of the institution was too great, the unsold notes would be retired, requiring a concomitant reduction in liabilities. Any such reduction would further signal to equity investors an appropriate need for price compression, offering further balance sheet constraints.

We also believe that a new, redesigned, Glass-Steagall Act could be reinstated to cut the size of TBTF banks and eliminate the competitive advantages adhering to the TBTF banks solely because of size. Concretely, mega-banks should be dismantled not only horizontally (by size) but also

---

[50] A bail-in is an alternative to bailouts of failing banks where investors and in the extreme, depositors, take a loss rather than governments and taxpayers.

vertically (by line of business). With smaller and more specialized financial institutions, there is less likelihood of a taxpayer-funded bailout in case of financial distress. In April 2017, US Senators Elizabeth Warren (Democrat), Maria Cantwell (Democrat), John McCain (Republican), and Angus King (Independent) re-introduced the 21st Century Glass-Steagall Act, a modern version of the Glass-Steagall Act of 1933. This initiative represents one legislative approach to fight moral hazard efficiently and directly.[51]

A radically different solution could also be advanced. If policy makers, academic researchers, and citizens consider that restoration of the Glass-Steagall Act is not realistic and/or a sufficient majority of legislators, in exercising rational self-preservation intentions, cannot coalesce around an act that will adversely impact their principal donors, and therefore all believe that we live now in the "moral hazard era" (Summers 2007), it would be coherent to internalize the reasonably understood externalities relating to a possible bailout. Whether through contributed subscription funding or by way of a tax, the members of the TBTF class would self-insure in place of the taxpayers. The premium that a systemic firm would pay for its possible bailout would be contingent upon GDP growth and the profits posted by the TBTF entity. In no case would this self-insurance preclude financial gatekeepers from taking all necessary measures to reduce the likelihood of a bailout (see below).

The US Economy Must Be Deleveraged

The explosion of indebtedness described above has reinforced the power of TBTF banks, amplified business cycles and exacerbated the problems of income inequality. Debt, by its nature, is independent of the current value of any purchase for which it was incurred. And, by the nature of who is the creditor and who is the borrower, at the point of a crisis, debt imposes significant losses on those citizens who are the poorest. As described in Mian and Sufi (2014, 30), "[d]ebt is the anti-insurance"; instead of sharing risk, it concentrates it on those least able to bear it.

In recognition of the need for resetting leverage at *sustainable* levels, we would recommend that consideration be given to a modified "debt-reduction" programme. For example, the US Department of Education is currently employing a variety of "income-driven" repayment techniques

[51] See https://www.warren.senate.gov/?p=press_release&id=1533

to relieve some of the financial burden faced by those who have acquired student loan debt without realistic prospects of repayment at market determined interest and principal amortization levels. These programmes operate to relieve the immediate financial pain, but they somewhat permanently establish the fixed position of the debtor.[52] It is an absolute invitation for "lender moral hazard" to require the student-borrower to shoulder 100% of the unknown risk of future employment while at the same time assuring the lender no risk of repayment whatsoever. Furthermore, legislative determinations of "how much" of the earnings of the graduated student should be dedicated to loan repayment will inevitably suffer from the tyranny of the "average". Such a programme, unmodified, serves to limit and defer the consumption and entrepreneurialism of each successive generation, and in the extreme, will only increase the lenders' dependence on the government's underwriting guarantee. The government and therefore the taxpayers are subsidizing the earnings of the owners of capital, that is, TBTF banks.

We would modify the above "pay as you earn" student loan programmes to (i) require the lenders to be randomly matched with eligible borrowers (to eliminate the inefficient tendency to prefer those borrowers enrolled in programmes previously demonstrating the highest return on educational focus); (ii) reduce the government subsidy to a term of 12 years but provide a floor that ensures an IRR to the lender of at least the ten-year treasury rate[53]; and (iii) require a "shared appreciation" option, whereby the borrower would agree to pay the lender an "interest premium" above the currently scaled payments if earnings were to increase more rapidly than anticipated, if the lender would forego further government subsidy.

---

[52] Pay As You Earn, or PAYE federal student loan repayment plans adjust the monthly amount due on the loan according to the income level of the borrower, adjusted for certain necessary expenditures. The term of the plan is typically 20 or 25 years, with the federal government paying to the private lender the unpaid interest and principal otherwise coming due on the loan. However, at the end of the 25 years, any remaining balance on the loan(s) is forgiven (but, subject to contrary subsequent legislation, the forgiven amount is recognized as taxable income to the borrower in the year of forgiveness). See Federal Register. 34 CFR Parts 685. 209 and 221.

[53] IRR, or internal rate of return, is that implicit rate of return on investment from a stream of cashflows. The lender is effectively guaranteed a return of its capital at the 10-year treasury rate. The government's cost of funds, assuming some payments are made by the student-borrower, is necessarily less than the 10-year treasury rate. The lender agreeing to forego the subsidy would effectively be sharing the risk of return on the student's education.

We would also suggest using a modification of the above programmes that could apply to other forms of consumer debt. For example, in light of the extraordinary prevalence of extended term auto loans and increasing credit card balances, respective borrowers could be offered the choice of standard payment plans or modified versions of the student loan programmes. Employing generic securitisation technology and using credit scores augmented with voluntarily provided and verified asset- and income-to-debt ratios, borrowers could be pooled and classed. Participating banks could, through periodic issuances, each fund a "vertical strip" of the entire capital structure of government-supported vehicles. The government support could include supplemental equity and a guaranteed internal rate of return for each class. Borrower "migration" to a lower risk class resulting from a borrower's improved income-to-debt ratio, or when a given class has achieved a targeted IRR, would allow for payment reductions and discounted prepayment opportunities. Additional participation by banks could be incented by regulatory capital relief.

With supported lending programmes along the lines of the above, lenders may be encouraged to revisit the current forms of various consumer loan agreements with an eye towards the long-term sustainability of the indebtedness (and consequently, the long-term ability of the borrowing community to remain active customers for current and future products offered by that lender).

De Facto and De Jure Regulators Must Stop Encouraging Moral Hazard

Credit risk assessment, as performed by agents and principals both, requires further attention. CRAs could take common sense measures: for example, capping ratings at single-A for deals that contain derivative hedges (Harrington 2013) and deflating (i) all credit ratings by incorporating conservative assumptions regarding the correlation of credit risk across all sectors (Gaillard and Harrington 2016) and (ii) sovereign ratings specifically by incorporating the cost of potential bailouts (Gaillard 2017).

The official government imprimatur of NRSRO status should be cancelled, especially in light of recent legislative efforts such as those contained in the current draft of the Financial Choice Act. The safe harbours extended to the NRSROs and their senior management combine with the conflicted interests of the "issuer-pays" model of compensation to reinforce the preference for morally hazardous behaviour from all parties involved in the credit rating process. Without the market-share enhancing "NRSRO" label, CRAs will be forced to compete again on merit, and innovation in risk assessment—to the extent that it produces a better product—will return superior results. The current tendency and preference for inflating ratings and deferring risk to future taxpayers will be minimized.

Further, the misalignment of short-term rewards with long-term risk must be addressed. For so long as "issuer pays", the morally hazardous incentives for the "gatekeepers" such as the CRAs must be captured within a "shared risk" scheme of compensation. While the distribution of uncompensated opinions based on publicly available information may deserve, in our information-dependent markets, exceptional freedom, publication of opinions solicited for purposes of specific issuance and investment should be differently treated. The CRAs should face both market-based reputational risk realized over time through transparent and publicly accessible *independently generated* performance metrics, and more immediate risk through deferred compensation conditioned on the accuracy of the issued opinion sufficiently conforming to historical standards. Towards a similar end, the SEC must let Section 939G of the Dodd-Frank Act take effect and subject CRAs to meaningful liability (Gaillard and Harrington 2016).

Next, US regulators should focus more on the execution of their responsibilities and less on possible market reactions to their decisions. In what may be an unintended bias to assume greater responsibility for *macroprudential* outcomes, regulators have unwittingly opened the door to *microeconomic* misadventures, and have too often explained away, if not turned a blind eye, to morally hazardous misbehaviour.

While a quantitatively responsible analysis is beyond the scope of this chapter, it is worth considering whether the occurrence and frequency of "rogue trader" events (think Barings and most tellingly the Société Générale/Jérôme Kerviel case) are well correlated to regulator and, in particular, central bank apparent preoccupation with systemic consequences as evidenced by an overemphasis on "signaling", "guidance", and "transparency".

Transparency and accountability are not akin to benevolence or laxity. For instance, the total number of no-action letters and waivers granted each year by the SEC and the CFTC should be reduced and/or be subjected to self-extinguishing terms. Regulatory bodies should not spend their time "explicating" their decisions and smoothing out (allegedly) poor or incomplete legislation. The failure of current governance actors (including elected representatives and regulatory officials) to identify and pursue solutions beyond marginal improvements—even if structural foundations are admittedly in need of re-assessment—should not be interpreted as tacit instruction to perform gap-filling authorities at the regulatory level (including the aforementioned "no-action letters"). Extending the legislative silence has only served to increase the distance between the taxpaying citizens and their control over the use of their taxes, even as the loudest (and lobbyist-equipped) donors (e.g., the TBTF banks) have continued to insert their morally hazardous provisions into the regulatory framework. Oversight and enforcement must remain the regulatory agent's top priorities.

Lastly, the Federal Reserve should revise its implicit inflation-targeting framework and include asset price movements in its monetary policy formulation process. This measure would be adequate to cope with a capitalist system where the "financial instability hypothesis"—as suggested by Minsky (1977)—has proved right. In addition to this, the central bank's monetary policy should be coupled with macroprudential supervision and in particular with capital requirements set by regulators. These measures would have countercyclical effects and lead to higher interest rates, which is consistent with the need to deleverage the economy.

Acknowledgements Ted Cohn, Bill Harrington, and Anil Hira

References

Auletta, Ken. 1985. Power, Greed and Glory on Wall Street: The Fall of the Lehman Brothers. *New York Times*. February 17.

Bank for International Settlements (BIS). 2009. *Stocktaking on the Use of Credit Ratings*. Basel Committee on Banking Supervision, Joint Forum. June.

Barth, Mary and Wayne Landsman. 2010. How Did Financial Reporting Contribute to the Financial Crisis? *European Accounting Review*. 19(3): 399–423.

Behr, Patrick, Darren J. Kisgen, and Jérôme P. Taillard. 2018. Did Government Regulations Lead to Inflated Credit Ratings? *Management Science*. 64(3): 1034–1054.

Benmelech, Efraim and Nittai K. Bergman. 2012. Credit Traps, *American Economic Review*. 102(6): 3004–3032.

Bernanke, Ben S. and Frederic S. Mishkin. 1997. Inflation Targeting: A New Framework for Monetary Policy? *Journal of Economic Perspectives*. 11(2): 97–116.

Bernard, G. Wogan. 2009. Update on the Amendments to FAS 140 – Accounting for Transfers of Financial Assets and Repurchase Financing Transactions, available at https://www.americanbar.org/content/dam/aba/publications/rpte_ereport/2009/june/rp_g_wogan_bernard.authcheckdam.pdf

Bogle, John C. 2005. *The Battle for the Soul of Capitalism*. Yale: Yale University Press.

Bogle, John C. 2009. *Enough: True Measures of Money, Business, and Life*. New York: Wiley.

Bruce, R. Christian. 1998. Fed Approves Citicorp-Travelers Merger Creating World's Largest Bank Company. *BNA's Banking Report*. 71(449).

Carrington, Tim. 1984. U.S. Won't Let 11 Biggest Banks in Nation Fail. *Wall Street Journal*. September 20.

Cecchetti, Stephen G. and Enisse Kharroubi. 2015. Why Does Financial Sector Growth Crowd Out Real Economic Growth? *BIS Working Paper No. 490*.

Cecchetti, Stephen G., Hans Genberg, John Lipsky, and Sushil Wadhwani. 2000. *Asset Prices and Central Bank Policy*. Geneva Reports on the World Economy 2. Center for Economic Policy Research, London.

Cho, David. 2009. Banks 'Too Big to Fail' Have Grown Even Bigger. *Washington Post*. August 28.

Coffee Jr., John C. 2011. Ratings Reform: The Good, The Bad, and The Ugly, *Harvard Business Law Review*. 1(1): 795–847.

Cox, Christopher. 2008. *Chairman Cox Announces End of Consolidated Supervised Entities Program*. September 26, available at https://www.sec.gov/news/press/2008/2008-230.htm

Department of the Treasury. 2008. *The Department of the Treasury Blueprint for A Modernized Financial Regulatory Structure*. Washington, D.C. March.

Donaldson, William H. 2004. *Speech by SEC Chairman: Opening Statement at April 28, 2004 Open Meeting*. April 28, available at https://www.sec.gov/news/speech/spch042804whd.htm

Dowd, Kevin and Martin Hutchinson. 2010. *Alchemists of Loss: How Modern Finance and Government Intervention Crashed the Financial System*. Chichester: Wiley.

Dunsmuir, Lindsay and Ann Saphir. 2017. UPDATE 1 – Fed Chair Nominee Powell Sees No Too-Big-To-Fail Banks. *Reuters*. November 28, available at https://www.reuters.com/article/usa-fed-powell-banks/update-1-fed-chair-nominee-powell-sees-no-too-big-to-fail-banks-idUSL1N1NY1KY

Federal Deposit Insurance Corporation (FDIC). 1997. *History of the Eighties: Lessons for the Future*, Washington, D.C.: FDIC.

Financial Industry Regulatory Authority (FINRA). 2007. NASD and NYSE Member Regulation Combine to Form the Financial Industry Regulatory Authority – FINRA. *News Release*. July 30, available at http://www.finra.org/newsroom/2007/nasd-and-nyse-member-regulation-combine-form-financial-industry-regulatory-authority

Flores, Juan H. 2010. Competition in the Underwriting Markets of Sovereign Debt: The Baring Crisis Revisited. *Law and Contemporary Problems.* 73(4): 129–150.

Gaillard, Norbert J. 2011. *A Century of Sovereign Ratings.* New York: Springer.

Gaillard, Norbert J. 2016. Coping with Reliance on Credit Ratings. *Banking & Financial Services Policy Report.* 35(7): 12–21.

Gaillard, Norbert J. 2017. Credible Sovereign Ratings: Beyond Statistics and Regulations. *European Business Law Review.* 28(1): 5–18.

Gaillard, Norbert J. and William J. Harrington. 2016. Efficient, Commonsense Actions to Foster Accurate Credit Ratings. *Capital Markets Law Journal.* 11(1): 38–59.

Gaillard, Norbert J. and Michael W. Waibel. 2018. The Icarus Syndrome: How Credit Rating Agencies Lost their Quasi-Immunity. *Southern Methodist University Law Review.* 71(4): 1077–1116.

Gay, Gerald D. and Joanne T. Medero. 1996. The Economics of Derivatives Documentation. *Journal of Derivatives.* 3(4): 78–89. Summer.

Greenwood, Robin and David Scharfstein. 2013. The Growth of Finance. *Journal of Economic Perspectives.* 27(2): 3–28.

Hand, John R. M., Robert W. Holthausen, and Richard W. Leftwich. 1992. The Effect of Bond Rating Agency Announcements on Bond and Stock Prices. *Journal of Finance.* 47(2): 733–752.

Harries, Brenton W. 1968. Standard & Poor's Corporation New Policy on Rating Municipal Bonds. *Financial Analysts Journal.* 24(3): 68–71.

Harrington, William J. 2013. Letter to Mr. Abe Losice, Securities and Exchange Commission and Mr. Felix Flinterman, European Securities and Market Authority. September 11.

He, Jie (Jack), Jun (QJ) Qian, and Philip E. Strahan. 2012 Are All Ratings Created Equal? The Impact of Issuer Size on The Pricing of Mortgage-Backed Securities. *Journal of Finance.* 67(6): 2097–2137.

Helleiner, Eric. 2014. *The Status Quo Crisis: Global Financial Governance After the 2008 Financial Meltdown.* New York: Oxford University Press.

Holmes, Douglas R. 2014. *Economy of Words: Communicative Imperatives in Central Banks.* Chicago: Chicago University Press.

Horvitz, Paul M. 1975. Failures of Large Banks: Implications for Banking Supervision and Deposit Insurance. *Journal of Financial and Quantitative Analysis.* 10(4): 589–601.

Humphrey, Thomas M. 1975. The Classical Concept of the Lender of Last Resort. *Federal Reserve Bank of Richmond Economic Review.* 61: 2–9, January/February.

International Monetary Fund (IMF). 2009. *Global Financial Stability Report: Navigating the Financial Challenges Ahead.* Washington, D.C.

International Swaps and Derivatives Association (ISDA). 2012. *The ISDA Credit Derivatives Determinations Committees*. May.

Jiang, John (Xuefeng), Mary Harris Stanford, and Yuan Xie. 2012. Does It Matter Who Pays for Bond Ratings? Historical Evidence. *Journal of Financial Economics*. 105(3): 607–621.

JP Morgan. 1991. *1990 Annual Report*.

JP Morgan. 1992. *1991 Annual Report*.

King, Robert G. and Ross Levine. 1993. Finance and Growth: Schumpeter Might be Right. *Quarterly Journal of Economics*. 108(3): 717–737.

Krippner, Greta R. 2007. The Making of US Monetary Policy: Central Bank Transparency and the Neoliberal Dilemma. *Theory and Society*. 36(6): 477–513.

Liscio, John. 1987. No Relationship: Top Bankers' Pay Grows While Profits Lag. *Barron's National Business and Financial Weekly*. June 29.

Mason, Joseph R. 2015. *Overview and Structure of Financial Supervision and Regulation in the US*. Policy Department A: Economic and Scientific Policy, Directorate General for Internal Policies. European Parliament. Brussels, available at http://www.europarl.europa.eu/RegData/etudes/STUD/2015/492470/IPOL_STU(2015)492470_EN.pdf

Mayer, Thomas. 1975. Should Large Banks Be Allowed to Fail? *Journal of Financial and Quantitative Analysis*. 10(4): 603–610.

Mendales, Richard E. 2009. Collateralized Explosive Devices: Why Securities Regulation Failed to Prevent the CDO Meltdown, and How to Fix It. *University of Illinois Law Review*. 2009(5): 1359–1415.

Mezza, Alvaro and Kamila Sommer. 2015. A Trillion Dollar Question: What Predicts Student Loan Delinquency Risk? *FEDS Notes*. October 16.

Mian, Atif and Amir Sufi. 2014. *House of Debt: How They (and You) Caused the Great Recession, and How We Can Prevent It from Happening Again*. Chicago: University of Chicago Press.

Minsky, Hyman P. 1977. The Financial Instability Hypothesis: An Interpretation of Keynes and An Alternative to 'Standard' Theory. *Nebraska Journal of Economics and Business*. 16(1): 5–16.

Moody's Corporation. 2001. *Annual Report 2000*.

Moody's Investors Service. 2003a. *Structured Finance Rating Transitions: 1983–2002*. January.

Moody's Investors Service. 2003b. *Measuring the Performance of Corporate Bond Ratings*. April.

Moody's Investors Service. 2007. *Incorporation of Joint-Default Analysis into Moody's Bank Rating Methodology*. February.

Moody's Investors Service. 2008. *Default & Loss Rates of Structured Finance Securities: 1993–2007*. July.

Morgenson, Gretchen. 2009. The Cost of Saving These Whales. *New York Times*. October 3.

Morgenson, Gretchen and Joshua Rosner. 2011. *Reckless Endangerment: How Outsized Ambition, Greed, and Corruption Led to Economic Armageddon.* New York: Times Books.

Murdock, Charles W. 2011. The Dodd-Frank Wall Street Reform and Consumer Protection Act: What Caused the Financial Crisis and Will Dodd-Frank Prevent Future Crises? *Southern Methodist University Law Review.* 64(4): 1243–1328.

Nakamoto, Michiyo and David Wighton. 2007. Citigroup Chief Says Bullish on Buy-Outs. *Financial Times.* July 9.

O'Neal, Michael K. 2000. Summary and Analysis of the Gramm-Leach-Bliley Act. *Securities Regulation Law Journal.* 28(2): 95–126.

Oosterhuis, Paul W. 2005. Check-the-Box Planning in Cross-Border Transactions. *Taxes – The Tax Magazine.* March: 49–57.

Philippon, Thomas and Ariell Reshef. 2013. An International Look at the Growth of Modern Finance. *Journal of Economic Perspectives.* 27(2): 73–96.

Poole, William. 2010. Ending Moral Hazard. *Financial Analysts Journal.* 66(3): 17–24.

Rowell, David and Luke B. Connelly. 2012. A History of the Term "Moral Hazard". *Journal of Risk and Insurance.* 79(4): 1051–1075.

Securities and Exchange Commission. 2008. *Summary Report of Issues Identified in the Commission Staff's Examinations of Select Credit Rating Agencies.* Washington, D.C. July 8.

Securities and Exchange Commission. 2009. *The SEC's Role Regarding and Oversight of Nationally Recognized Statistical Rating Organizations (NRSROs).* Report No. 458. Washington, D.C. August 27.

Securities and Exchange Commission. 2013. *Report to Congress – Credit Rating Agency Independence Study.* Washington, D.C. November.

Sinclair, Timothy. 2005. *The New Masters of Capital.* Ithaca: Cornell University Press.

Stigler, George J. 1964. Public Regulation of the Securities Markets. *The Business Lawyer.* 19(3): 721–753.

Stigler, George J. 1971. The Theory of Economic Regulation. *Bell Journal of Economics and Management Science.* 2(1): 3–21.

Stiglitz, Joseph. 2010. *Freefall: America, Free Markets, and the Sinking of the World Economy.* New York and London: W. W. Norton.

Summers, Larry. 2007. Beware Moral Hazard Fundamentalists. *Financial Times.* September 23.

Swary, Itzhak. 1986. Stock Market Reaction to Regulatory Action in the Continental Illinois Crisis. *Journal of Business.* 59(3): 451–473.

Tett, Gillian. 2009. *Fool's Gold: The Inside Story of J.P. Morgan and How Wall St. Greed Corrupted Its Bold Dream and Created a Financial Catastrophe.* New York: Free Press.

U.S. Senate. 2009. *Hearing Before the Committee on Banking, Housing, and Urban Affairs, Oversight on the Monetary Policy Report to Congress Pursuant to the Full Employment and Balanced Growth Act of 1978.* Washington, D.C. February 24.

U.S. Senate, Permanent Subcommittee on Investigations. 2010. *Exhibits – Hearing on Wall Street and the Financial Crisis: The Role of Credit Rating Agencies.* Washington, D.C. April 23.

U.S. Senate, Permanent Subcommittee on Investigations. 2011. *Wall Street and the Financial Crisis: Anatomy of a Financial Collapse.* Washington, D.C. April 13.

Wilmarth Jr., Arthur E. 2002. The Transformation of the U.S. Financial Services Industry, 1975–2000: Competition, Consolidation, and Increased Risks. *University of Illinois Law Review.* 2002(2): 215–476.

Wilmarth Jr., Arthur E. 2009. The Dark Side of Universal Banking: Financial Conglomerates and the Origins of the Subprime Financial Crisis. *Connecticut Law Review.* 41(4): 963–1050.

Wilmarth Jr., Arthur E. 2010. Reforming Financial Regulation to Address the Too-Big-to-Fail Problem. *Brooklyn Journal of International Law.* 35(3): 707–783.

Yellen, Janet L. 2012. *Revolution and Evolution in Central Bank Communications.* Remarks by Janet L. Yellen, Vice Chair Board of Governors of the Federal Reserve System at Haas School of Business, University of California, Berkeley, California. November 13.

CHAPTER 5

Remittances, Regulation, and Financial Development in Sub-Saharan Africa

James Busumtwi-Sam

INTRODUCTION

In this chapter, I critically examine the financial regulations needed to leverage remittances into positive sustainable development outcomes in sub-Saharan Africa. Strong economic growth in the first decade of the new millennium enabled many African countries to access international financial markets. Many of them are reducing dependence on official development assistance (ODA) and seeking new sources of finance to achieve sustainable development. The African Union (AU), the United Nations (UN), and the major multilateral and bilateral ODA donors have formally recognized the importance of remittances, which have not only exceeded net ODA flows to sub-Saharan Africa but have also been the fastest growing source of private capital flows (PCF) to the region. In the wake of the 2008 financial crisis, remittances have been more stable, resilient, and reliable than other PCF to the region (Sy and Rakotondrazaka 2015; World Bank 2016). The regulation of these sources of finance globally and within sub-Saharan African countries, however, has not kept pace with their increased prominence. They are another example of a major gap in global

J. Busumtwi-Sam (✉)
Department of Political Science, Simon Fraser University, Burnaby, BC, Canada
e-mail: james_busumtwi-sam@sfu.ca

© The Author(s) 2019
A. Hira et al. (eds.), *The Failure of Financial Regulation*,
International Political Economy Series,
https://doi.org/10.1007/978-3-030-05680-3_5

and domestic financial regulations, which have not kept up with innovation, as discussed in the introductory chapter.

While remittances were not implicated in the 2008 financial crisis, and were less affected than other PCF in the aftermath of the crisis, their growing importance to the development financing needs of sub-Saharan Africa and other developing regions necessitates attention to the regulatory gaps that currently exist globally and nationally. Prior to 2008, the regulation of remittances globally focused on combating money laundering and terrorism financing, and enhancing (for balance of payments purposes) the efficiency of remittance markets. The aftermath of the 2008 crisis saw the development of regulations to manage risks and enhance consumer protection in several immigrant-receiving Global North countries. National level regulations in sub-Saharan Africa, although varying across countries, have mirrored those at the international level. However, existing national and global remittance regulations have produced unintended consequences and, in some cases, been applied disproportionately to the problem they were originally designed to address. The issue, then, is not simply the lack of financial regulation per se, but the lack of an appropriate financial regulatory *system* for remittances—one that enhances complementarities among the components of the remittance transfer chain and is designed explicitly to channel remittances in a manner that fosters development. What does this entail?

In the context of the contemporary global political economy, regulation of remittances entails interventions by public authorities via laws and other legally binding instruments, standards and guidelines, and principles, recommendations, and procedures (Bank for International Settlements and World Bank 2007). For such regulations to be effective, regulators must have relevant policy objectives, a clear idea of the failures within the remittance market that impede the realization of those objectives, and the ability to implement the necessary corrective measures. I argue that effective leveraging of remittances for sustainable development in sub-Saharan Africa requires regulations that promote financial development by deepening and broadening financial services while enhancing stability, efficiency, and consumer protection in remittance services. Evidence from the very mixed empirical record shows the development impact of remittances to be highly context-dependent. Mounting evidence also indicates a relationship between remittances, financial development, and the ability to attain a broader range of development outcomes including poverty reduction, growth, education, and health (World Bank 2015a; Misati et al. 2012; Adenutsi 2011; Aggarwal et al. 2011). This relationship does not occur automatically but requires specific regulatory and institutional measures within African countries' financial sectors and internationally that channel remittances and diaspora savings into economic and social investments.

This chapter recommends the adoption of regulations domestically and internationally to enhance capital market competition, reduce financial exclusion, and facilitate mobile and electronic financial services.[1] To that end, such regulations must address the high transaction costs of sending remittances to and within the African continent, which are currently the highest in the world and amount to a 'super tax' that discourages both senders and recipients and negatively impacts national economies by reducing the net amounts remitted. Stronger regulations are needed to curb illicit financial flows, money laundering, and the financing of terrorism, without impeding the flow of legal remittances or inadvertently creating barriers to competition in the remittance markets. Also needed are regulations to enhance the credibility of the estimates of remittances transferred through formal channels and reduce the high proportion of informal transfers. The preference for informal transfer channels reflects cumbersome and restrictive regulations in formal remittance markets, lack of competition among remittance service providers, and, as I discuss below, financial exclusion. To be clear, while the financial regulatory and institutional reforms identified in this chapter would enhance the role of remittances, such reforms are a small but important piece in the broader processes of structural and institutional transformation domestically and externally required to achieve sustainable development in Africa.

My chapter is composed as follows. First, I examine the nature and evolution of remittances compared to other types of financial flows to, within, and from sub-Saharan Africa since the early 1990s. Next, I discuss financial development as a key policy objective of remittance regulation, placing that discussion within the broader context of debates over the impact of remittances on development. Then, I identify some of the main failures in remittance markets in sub-Saharan Africa and globally that need correction. The last section outlines the contours of what a regulatory system for remittances would look like and offers specific regulatory

---

[1] A major challenge for financial regulation globally and nationally is the pace of technological change.

recommendations to correct remittance market failures. In conclusion, I advance some policy recommendations.

THE CONTEXT: REMITTANCES AND FINANCIAL FLOWS TO AND FROM AFRICA, 1990–2017

Remittances—the transfer of value between a sender and a recipient in different locations in a mutually agreed manner—are not new. They have been around for as long as people have migrated. What are new are the scale (amounts transferred), the scope, and the methods of transfer. Technological, communication, and transportation advancements in the era of liberal globalization have greatly facilitated remittance transfers and aided the ability of migrants and diaspora to stay connected with their places of 'origin' (Mohan and Zack-Williams 2002). Remittance flows do occur intra-nationally (e.g., from urban to rural areas within the same country), but the focus of this chapter is on international remittance flows—the cross-border value transfers by migrants and diaspora. Although sometimes classified within the same category, remittances differ from other types of PCF (e.g., portfolio and equity securities transfers and foreign direct investment (FDI)) and generate particular regulatory challenges in at least two significant ways. First, unlike other PCF, remittances reflect social embeddedness (i.e., enmeshed in broader social relationships). Because they mainly comprise private unrequited transfers between family, friends, and community based on empathy, solidarity, and trust (Portes and Sensenbrenner 1993), remittance flows may respond differently to economic incentives and constraints.[2] Second, the inextricable link between remittances and migration means that unlike other PCF, migration issues and policies strongly affect remittance markets and services and regulations. I discuss these in greater detail below.

The period 1990–2016 saw significant growth and changes in the composition of global financial flows—defined as the sum of gross PCF, ODA, and remittances. In 2016, PCF—comprising FDI and portfolio investment—greatly exceed ODA. FDI amounted to over US$500

---

[2] For example, the flow of remittances tends to *increase* during periods of downturn in the economies of the senders' home countries/communities, which occurs in large part because of the familial/community attachments, bonds, and obligations linking senders and recipients (World Bank 2016).

billion while ODA was around US$120 billion. Equally dramatic is the growth in remittances, amounting to about US$400 billion in 2016, second only to FDI. ODA rose at a constant rate, dipping only slightly in the late 1990s. By contrast, volatility has accompanied the steep increase in FDI and portfolio flows, with periods of rapid increase punctuated by periods of steep decline reflecting periodic failures in private capital markets (World Bank 2015a, b). Thus, the steep decline in portfolio investment in the period 1997–2001 occurred in the context of the Asian financial crisis that began in 1997. The steep decline in FDI and portfolio investment after 2007 occurred in the context of the 2008 global financial crisis. Declines in FDI and portfolio investment after 2012–2013 reflected weak economic growth in Europe and North America, the weakening of major currencies against the US dollar, and the decline in oil prices (World Bank 2017).

Such volatility has not accompanied the growth in remittances, which in the immediate aftermath of the 2008 global financial crisis declined by approximately 5% in 2009 from their 2008 peak of US$324 billion, but fully recovered by 2010. This decline was modest compared to declines of over 40% for portfolio and FDI flows between 2008 and 2009 from their 2007 peak (Mohapatra et al. 2010). In 2016, Global South states received about 80% of total remittances—that is, US$400 billion—which was almost four times the amount of ODA. The slight declines in remittances in 2015 (by 1%) and 2016 (by 2.4%) reflected weak economic growth in immigrant-receiving countries, the weakening of major currencies such as the Euro and Pound Sterling relative to the US dollar, and more restrictive immigration policies (World Bank 2017). The actual size of remittances, however, is likely to be significantly larger because official statistics do not account for 'irregular' migration and remittances sent through informal channels and because ambiguities in the definition of 'migrant' tend to downplay or overlook patterns of Global South-South migration (Kharas 2014). The volume of officially recorded Global South-South migration stood at 38% of the total migrant stock in 2015, which exceeded the 34% for Global South-North migration (World Bank 2016, XI).

Financial Flows to Africa

External financial flows to sub-Saharan Africa mirror the broader global trends. The volume of external flows to the region increased from US$20 billion in 1990 to above US$120 billion in 2012, with much of the increase attributed to the increase in PCF and the growth of remittances, especially since 2005 (Sy and Rakotondrazaka 2015). In 1990, ODA accounted for 62% of external flows to sub-Saharan Africa versus 31% for gross FDI and portfolio investment, and 7% for remittances. However, by 2012, ODA accounted for about 22% of external flows, exceeded by both remittances at 24% and by gross FDI and portfolio investment at 54% (Sy and Rakotondrazaka 2015). The change in the volume and composition of capital flows to sub-Saharan Africa has not benefitted all countries equally. Over the 2001–2012 period, PCF was concentrated in a small group of countries, with South Africa and Nigeria alone accounting for the majority. For most low-income African countries, ODA still constitutes over 50% of external capital flows compared to 23% for middle-income countries. As a share of GDP, however, private capital flows are relatively small for most African countries including middle-income countries (World Bank 2016).

Data for the 1990–2012 period show that FDI and portfolio flows to sub-Saharan Africa have been more volatile than both ODA and remittances. The effects of the 2008 financial crisis varied across countries in the region, but the overall impact on remittances was more modest in sub-Saharan Africa compared to other Global South regions. The reasons include lower levels of integration of sub-Saharan African economies into global financial markets, and the fact that for many sub-Saharan African countries receiving significant amounts of remittances, a large portion comes from intra-regional migration. With the increase in gross PCF, especially in portfolio flows, the economic vulnerabilities of sub-Saharan African countries are also likely to increase, as these flows, which strengthen the financial linkages between the sub-continent and the broader global political economy, have historically been more volatile than ODA and remittances. Remittances have been the least volatile flows, and their increase may mitigate some of the increased vulnerability to external shocks and dampen the effects of fluctuations in other financial flows into the continent.

That financial crises affect remittances less actually strengthens the case for better regulations to harness their development potential. This is underscored by the fact that, since the North Atlantic financial crisis of 2008, remittances have been the fastest growing source of private capital flows to sub-Saharan Africa, increasing from US$30 billion in 2010 to US$35 billion in 2015 (World Bank 2017). Nigeria was the largest remittance recipient by volume in the region from 1990 to 2012, but as a share of GDP,

Lesotho was the most remittance-dependent country (Sy and Rakotondrazaka 2015). The top remittance recipients in 2015 included Nigeria (US$20.8bn), Ghana (US$2bn), Senegal (US$1.6bn), Kenya ($1.6bn), and South Africa ($1bn). The relatively smaller and lower-income sub-Saharan African countries, however, show the highest remittance dependence: Eritrea (38% of GDP), Cape Verde (34%), Liberia (26%) and Burundi (23%) (World Bank 2016).[3]

It is important to stress, however, that these figures grossly underestimate the actual size of remittance flows because the predominant pattern of migration in sub-Saharan Africa is intra-regional with fluid migration within Western Africa, Southern Africa, and parts of Eastern Africa, which has an impact on remittance flows. Remittances from urban to rural areas are also important and related to intra-regional migration, particularly in Western and Southern Africa, with significant numbers of urban-based migrants remitting to rural areas in their countries of origin (International Fund for Agricultural Development (IFAD) 2009, 2016). The African Institute for Remittances (2016) and the World Bank (2016) estimate that between one-third and one-half of remittance flows to and within Africa are unrecorded because they occur through informal channels.[4] Although the formal-informal distinction is not clear-cut, formal channels generally involve transfers through banking systems and licensed money transfer and remittance service providers. Informal channels involve cash or in-kind transfers through such carriers as family members, friends, and other social networks; money or goods taken by the migrant on his/her visits to his/her homeland; and funds transmitted through unlicensed money transfer businesses.

Regulating remittances is difficult when estimates are inaccurate because of substantial informal transfers. The problem of obtaining accurate estimates of actual remittance flows to and within Africa, however, also extends to funds transferred through formal channels due to differences and inconsistencies among countries in what to measure as a 'remittance', ambiguities in the definition of 'migrant' (e.g., 'seasonal' v.

---

[3] Such dependence constitutes a major challenge for the credit position of these countries. For a study of the impact of remittances on the sovereign ratings of low- and middle-income economies, refer to Avendano et al. (2011) and Ratha et al. (2011).

[4] The African Union Commission (AUC), the European Commission (EC), the World Bank, the African Development Bank (AfDB), and the International Organization for Migration (IOM) collaborated to create the African Institute for Remittances (AIR).

'permanent', 'documented v. undocumented'), and distinguishing between 'migrants' and 'residents' (even among documented migrants). In 2010, the International Monetary Fund (IMF) introduced a new method for calculating and reporting remittances in countries' annual balance of payments. Remittances are said to comprise 'compensation of employees' and 'personal transfers' including 'capital transfers between households'. If people have lived in a country less than a year, they are considered 'migrants' and their entire annual income is included in the 'compensation of employees' category; if they have been there for more than a year, they are considered 'residents' regardless of their immigration status, and their transferred funds fall under the 'personal transfers' category (World Bank 2016).

The distinctions among these categories, however, and between these categories and other types of PCF are somewhat arbitrary with a great deal of variation across countries in their application. Because of difficulties in obtaining data on 'capital transfers between households', for example, many countries do not report this category; and because 'personal transfers' are not restricted to family members but can include any recipient in the home country, they can be reported as FDI or portfolio investments (World Bank 2016). Central banks are responsible for reporting remittances in African countries' annual balance of payments but some only report data from commercial banks and underreport data from non-bank entities (e.g., post offices) involved in remittance transfers (World Bank 2016). As shown below, measures to decrease informal transfers, increase remittance flows through formal channels, and improve the accuracy and credibility of estimates of flows through formal channels are key components of the kind of financial regulations that, in the context of financial development, will leverage remittances as a tool for sustainable development in Africa.

In addition to remittances, the issuing of 'diaspora bonds' and 'remittance-backed securities' represent other sources of private capital that provide African governments an alternative to borrowing on international capital markets, or from multilateral and bilateral donors.[5] The

[5] A bond is a debt security instrument with a maturity of more than one year and is usually tradable in financial markets. A diaspora bond is one issued by a country specifically targeting its own diaspora to tap into the latter's assets in their host countries (African Development Bank 2010a). A 'remittance-backed security' or 'securitized remittance' is a bond backed by the future flow of remittances into a trust account held by a banking institution or money transfer organization.

African diaspora, according to some estimates, holds over US$400 billion in savings in their host countries of residence, which many African countries are eager to tap for investment (African Development Bank 2010a, 2012). While familial and/or community ties underpin remittances, diaspora bonds are a direct investment by migrants/diaspora members residing abroad in the economy of their home country at the national level and have been used successfully in countries such as China, India, and Israel to finance large infrastructural projects.[6] Ethiopia was the first African country to issue a diaspora bond in 2008–2009, and since then, several African countries including Kenya, Nigeria, and Ghana have announced their intention to issue such bonds. Several African countries, including Ghana and Nigeria, have used remittance-backed securities to negotiate loans from commercial banks. The African Development Bank estimates that African countries could raise US$17 billion a year by using remittance-backed securities (and the future flows of other receivables) as collateral (African Development Bank 2012).

Financial Flows Out of Africa

Outflows of capital resulting from 'capital flight' also increase significantly Africa's vulnerabilities. Capital flight includes a licit and an illicit component, although in practice the distinction is blurred. The African High-Level Panel on Illicit Financial Flows (AHPIFF), established in 2012 by the Economic Commission for Africa (ECA) and the African Union Commission (AUC), has adopted a definition of illicit financial flows that focuses on how the funds are *earned* (e.g., proceeds of crime), *transferred* (e.g., tax evasion, money laundering), or *utilized* (e.g., financing terrorism) (ECA 2012, 2014). This represents a break from the erstwhile dominant views on capital flight, which emphasized domestic economic and political conditions as the main drivers of capital outflows and placed the blame for and burden of resolving the problem on Global South states rather than promoting shared responsibility between Global North and South.

Estimates reveal that from 1970 to 2008, Africa lost between US$854 billion and US$1.8 trillion in illicit financial flows. The 2013 AHPIFF

---

[6] The practice of issuing diaspora bonds goes back to the early 1930s when Japan and China first issued them followed in the 1950s by Israel and later by India.

progress report estimated that the annual average was between US$50 billion and US$148 billion (ECA 2014), which meant that Africa was a net creditor to the world rather than a net debtor. Offshore tax havens have played a significant role in the outflow of unrecorded capital from Africa (see Hira et al. in this volume). Sub-Saharan Africa's assets held in tax havens grew at an annualized rate of over 20% from 2005 to 2011, a faster rate than any other region. Commercial illicit financial flows including tax evasion, trade and services mispricing, and transfer pricing by multinational corporations account for a large proportion of Africa's illicit financial flows, followed by proceeds from criminal activities and corruption (Global Financial Integrity 2010, 2015). The UN's 2030 Agenda recognizes illicit financial flows as a major impediment to sustainable development, and the AU's Agenda 2063 highlights the importance of controlling such flows as central to increasing domestic resource mobilization.

Illicit financial flows have important implications for remittance transfers to and within Africa. Concerns over money laundering and financing terrorism led most African countries to pass an anti-money laundering legislation in response to increased international attention to countering terrorist financing in the wake of the attacks in the USA on September 11, 2001. They also limited the amount of money that remittance senders could transfer, the methods of payments to remittance receivers, and the types of entities authorized to make remittance payments. Next sections discuss these issues, which are central to financial regulation and financial development.

POLICY OBJECTIVE: PROMOTING FINANCIAL DEVELOPMENT

In January 2015, the AU adopted *Agenda 2063*, which sets a framework for Africa's long-term political and socio-economic transformation, and September that same year saw the adoption of the 17 Sustainable Development Goals (SDGs) of the UN's 2030 Agenda. The AU's Agenda 2063 and the UN's 2030 SDG Agenda converge in several areas, including the recognition of the need for substantial and reliable sources of finance. According to some estimates, achieving the SDGs in Africa will require investments of at least US$600 billion per year (United Nations Conference on Trade and Development (UNCTAD) 2016). While ODA remains important, it falls far short of the required amounts and needs supplementation by alternative sources of finance. Remittances could help close this large financing gap. Both the AU's Agenda 2063 and the UN's 2030 SDG Agenda formally recognize the potential of remittances and the broader contributions of African migrants and diaspora to achieving sustainable development on the continent.

A key argument of this chapter is that effective leveraging of remittances for sustainable development in sub-Saharan Africa requires regulations designed to promote financial development as a policy objective, which will entail the deepening and broadening of financial services. In this section, I discuss this issue within the broader context of debates over the so-called 'migration and development nexus' and the impact of remittances on development. The interested parties can be roughly divided into 'optimists', who view remittances in a positive light, and 'pessimists', who view them negatively. While some optimists are guilty of 'romanticizing' remittances as a spontaneous 'bottom-up' source of development finance that bypasses inefficient and corrupt political-economic structures, some pessimists dismiss them as little more than the 'human face of neoliberalism' and discount the contributions remittances make in improving well-being and living standards in the receiving countries (de Haas 2010, 2012).

This divide is partly rooted in intellectual/ideological differences, with some of the strongest remittance optimists situated within the neoclassical/neoliberal camp (including the major multilateral financial institutions such as the IMF and World Bank), and pessimists within the historical structuralism/dependency and the more recent 'critical' and 'postcolonial' camps (Skeldon 2008; de Haas 2012). The divide also reflects the mixed empirical record of remittances, which stems from differences in the development dimension being measured (e.g., achieving economic growth, poverty reduction, reducing inequality, enhancing human capabilities, improving health, education, etc.); the ways they are measured; and the scale at which they are measured (e.g., individuals, families and households, local communities, regional, national).

Reconciling the diverging opinions is beyond the scope of this chapter, which takes the view that the development outcomes of remittances, positive and negative, are highly context-dependent. The discussion begins with a summary of some of the main arguments and evidence provided by remittance pessimists and optimists and then proceeds to focus on the impact of remittances on the development of the domestic financial sector. I argue that the development potential of remittances depends on broadening and deepening domestic financial services, necessitating their prioritization as a policy objective in remittance regulations.

Remittance Pessimists

The standard pessimistic view of remittances is that they primarily finance consumption. While acknowledging that remittances augment incomes of receiving households, which may contribute to poverty reduction, critics contend that remittances provide only a temporary, unreliable external source of income; it is rarely invested productively by recipients and does not play an important role in facilitating longer-term investments that generate economic growth (de Haas 2012; Giuliano and Ruiz-Arranz 2009). Others contend that because remittances are private transfers that occur in the context of information asymmetry, the remitter lacks control of how the recipient uses funds transferred. Thus, even where funds are remitted for investment, the recipient may not use the funds as originally intended (Misati et al. 2012).

Some pessimists also suggest that remittances produce adverse effects through the 'Dutch disease' and 'moral hazard' problems.[7] The Dutch disease argument suggests that like other financial flows, large remittance flows into a country could result in an appreciation of the real exchange rate and loss of international competitiveness by making the production of cost-sensitive tradables, including cash crops and manufactured goods, less profitable (Acosta et al. 2009). Because remittances are non-market private transfers, an increase in remittance flows produces moral hazard by reducing recipients' motivation to work, manifesting in a decline in the recipient's labour market and civic participation and an increase in consumption demand biased towards non-tradables such as housing. This creates permanent financial dependency and slows economic growth (Chami et al. 2003, 2008).

Other critics contend that not only does migration produce a 'brain drain' (i.e., the loss of the 'best' and 'brightest') that systematically undermines national development efforts and especially educational investments, they also contend that because international migrants are rarely among the poorest in their communities, remittances tend to reinforce

[7] For a broader analysis on how moral hazard has distorted liberal capitalism and financial rules, see Gaillard and Michalek in this volume.

income inequality in origin communities/countries (de Haas 2012). Some studies suggest that poorer and lower-skilled households get marginal benefits from remittances because of prohibitive costs of migration and the stringent immigration policies in wealthier immigrant-receiving economies that tend to favour skilled workers (Carling 2004). Thus, it is argued, while remittances may improve per capita incomes and thereby reduce poverty in receiving countries, they may worsen income inequality. This may exacerbate urban-rural inequality as remittances mainly finance consumption in urban areas. A similar argument extends to the global scale—that international remittance flows may sustain international inequalities and particularly the gap between low- and middle-income countries (de Haas 2012). As shown in the previous section, the bulk of gross remittance flows to sub-Saharan Africa goes to middle- and lower middle-income countries, respectively, while low-income countries receive a much smaller portion.

Remittance Optimists

Remittance optimists counter these criticisms with the following observations. They reject the argument that remittances encourage consumption by noting how increased consumption in the form of increased household expenditures may directly or indirectly lead to increased production through 'multiplier' and 'stimulus' effects if goods and services are bought locally/domestically. This puts a positive spin on the benefits of the kinds of remittance-financed 'consumption' that critics dismiss as 'non-productive investments' such as housing. Investment in housing by remittance receivers, they argue, improves well-being, health and safety, and the investment in construction creates significant employment and income (de Haas 2012). A study focusing on Nigeria and Kenya, for example, showed more than 50% of total remittance spending invested in home-building, land purchases, and farm improvements (World Bank 2011).

Furthermore, at the microeconomic level, remittances are said to have a direct effect on food consumption, and remittance-receiving households are better able to withstand food-related shocks, such as sudden increases in food prices (Athanasoulis and van Wincoop 2000; Pallage and Robe 2003). Others contend that remittances contribute to poverty reduction by loosening borrowing constraints faced by households and by giving financially constrained households access to credit. Remittances may also contribute to an increase in aggregate investment and savings. Yet others have shown how remittances affect marginal spending behaviour of households. Households receiving remittances spend less at the margin on food by as much as 14% and more at the margin on education by as much as 33% (World Bank 2011). According to a 2011 study of 77 countries by the UNCTAD between 1970 and 2008, holding all else equal, a 10% increase in remittances reduced the poverty gap by about 3–5%, depending on how the poverty gap is measured (US$1.25 or US$2.00 a day) (UNCTAD 2011).

Other studies support the findings of the positive effects of remittances on the marginal spending of households by examining an often-overlooked dimension of migration within and out of Africa—because most migrants are male, a significantly higher number of female-headed households emerge in the home country. In Ghana, for example, 52% of households with migrant workers were female headed, compared with only 25% for households with no migrant workers. The significance of this is that female-headed households in Africa have a considerably higher inclination to invest remittances received in health care and education as well as a higher propensity to save (African Institute for Remittances 2016). Other studies have pointed out how the effects of remittances revert to the whole community, where investments in education and healthcare, among others, translate into lower maternal and infant mortality rates and increased literacy rates, all of which affect productivity, employment, and ultimately growth and development (Anton 2010; Woodruff 2007).

At the macroeconomic level, optimists contend that remittances do have a positive impact on economic growth (Adams and Page 2005; Gupta et al. 2007a, b). They also claim that remittances have the capacity to reduce macroeconomic volatility (Chami et al. 2009). Other economists suggest that for many African countries, because empathy towards family/community motivates migrants, remittances can serve as automatic stabilizers, as they tend to increase when the recipient economy undergoes negative macroeconomic shocks from natural disasters, financial crises, or conflicts (Gupta et al. 2007a; Mohapatra and Ratha 2011). Some studies also claim that remittances contribute to macroeconomic stability by lowering the probability of current account reversals, especially in countries where they exceed 3% of GDP, and contribute to stabilizing the current account by reducing the volatility of overall capital flows (Bugamelli and Paterno 2009; Chami et al. 2008; IMF 2009).

The literature also points to the benefits of 'social remittances'—the circulation and exchange of ideas, norms, practices, and knowledge through migration (Levitt and Lamba-Nieves 2011). These studies transform the pessimist's negative notion of 'brain drain' into positive notions of 'brain gain' and 'brain circulation'. Studies on social remittances also stressed its positive impacts on social mobility, health, gender roles, intrafamilial relations, and household structures, and they contend that social remittances at the household level 'scale up' to effect national changes (Carling 2014; Rahman 2013).

Remittances and Financial Sector Development

As this brief review shows, the literature provides a very mixed picture on the role of remittances (and migration more broadly) in development. A purported positive effect counters every purported negative effect. What both optimists and pessimists may agree on is that remittances on their own cannot foster the processes of economic, social, and political transformation that make up 'development'. This chapter takes the view that the role of remittances in development is highly context-dependent and that financial development is a key condition that facilitates the development potential of remittances. I suggest that promoting financial development, as a key policy objective of remittance regulation, would address several of the criticisms of remittance pessimists. Financial sector development is about overcoming costs and constraints in the financial system by deepening and broadening financial services. It occurs when financial regulations, institutions, instruments, markets, and intermediaries ease constraints on access to financial services and markets, promote financial inclusion and literacy, increase competition and the range of products, alleviate credit constraints, ease the effects of information asymmetries and enforcement, and reduce transaction costs (World Bank 2015b).

A well-established body of literature indicates that financial sector development plays a significant role in achieving positive development outcomes. It promotes economic growth through capital accumulation by increasing the savings rate, mobilizing and pooling savings, producing information about investment, and facilitating the inflows of foreign capital.[8] Some studies suggest that low-income countries tend to grow faster than high-income countries through financial sector development

---

[8] Early theoretical arguments supporting the role of financial development in promoting growth include Schumpeter (1911) and Hicks (1969).

(Easterly and Levine 1997; Sachs and Warner 1997). Financial development is also said to reduce poverty and inequality by broadening access of poor, vulnerable, and excluded groups to financial services, reducing their vulnerability to shocks, and increasing investment and productivity that result in higher income generation (Adenutsi 2011; Mundaca 2009; Misati and Nyamongo 2011, 2012). Recent studies indicate an important relationship between remittances, financial sector development, and the ability to achieve a broad range of development outcomes including poverty reduction, growth, education, and health (World Bank 2015b; Misati et al. 2012; Adenutsi 2011; Aggarwal et al. 2011).

The relationship between remittances and financial development runs in both directions. For example, studies have shown that remittances may influence financial development in recipient countries if recipients convert their remittances channelled through banks and other licensed institutions into deposits with those financial institutions. This may result in more funds becoming available for lending and investment to achieve a range of development objectives (Aggarwal et al. 2011; Misati and Nyamongo 2011). Other studies have shown that financial sector development allows migrants to send money more cheaply, quickly, and safely, with some suggesting a complementary relationship between increased remittances, financial development, and positive development outcomes. Here, an increase in remittances stimulates a higher level of financial development that allows migrants to send even more money through cost-effective financial institutions. This helps channel remittances towards investment projects (Terry and Wilson 2005). The literature also suggests that remittances promote financial development in African states and alleviate credit constraints by increasing the level and stability of foreign exchange receipts (Ratha 2007; Ratha et al. 2011). As noted, several sub-Saharan African countries have raised international financing at lower interest rates and longer maturities through remittance-backed securities (Gupta et al. 2007a). Remittances, therefore, are not only a direct source of funds; they can also be used as collateral for access to more funding on international capital markets at lower costs for African states (Ketkar and Ratha 2001).

The relationship between remittances and financial sector development is complementary and reciprocal, not causal. Increases in remittance flows stimulate financial development, and financial development facilitates increases in remittance flows (Misati et al. 2012). This, however, does not necessarily occur automatically; and the kinds of remittance market failures and other impediments discussed below impede the emergence of the complementarity and reciprocity. And although increased remittances stimulate financial sector development and create conditions for positive development outcomes, this is more likely to occur through the implementation of specific regulatory and institutional measures within African countries' financial sectors. Such a framework would channel remittances and diaspora savings into economic and social investments (see the discussion below).

REMITTANCE MARKET FAILURES AND REGULATORY CHALLENGES

Although African governments and the AU have recognized the contributions of remittances, these resources remain underutilized and public policies to engage African migrants and diaspora are lacking when compared with other Global South regions such as Latin America and Asia. To realize the benefits of remittances in Africa, regulations addressing market failures and the challenges stemming from weak financial sectors are needed.[9] Among the most pressing issues are limited market access and financial exclusion, market competition and transaction costs, illicit financial flows and money laundering, and the challenges of informal transfers and technological change.

Market Access and Financial Exclusion

Regulatory reform regarding remittance service providers (RSPs) is necessary to expand financial access for remittance senders and recipients. Many African countries treat remittances as foreign exchange transactions, reserved for banks and foreign exchange bureaux. However, a range of institutions including micro-finance institutions, credit unions, cooperatives, post offices, and specified retail locations have the operational and financial capacity—but not the legal authority—to conduct remittance transfers. Of 50 African countries reviewed in a recent study (IFAD 2009), 8 authorized only banks to pay remittances, and 32 authorized banks and foreign exchange bureaus. Six countries allowed banks, foreign exchange bureaus, and micro-finance institutions to pay money directly, and four allowed the above plus retail locations to pay remittances. Because African

---

[9] For a specific focus on market failures, refer to Dobuzinskis in this volume.

countries generally have a small number of banks usually concentrated in urban areas, this unnecessarily restricts access to remittance payments and creates an incentive for the use of informal channels for remittance transfers.

High levels of financial exclusion and low levels of financial literacy in many parts of sub-Saharan Africa underscore the importance of increasing financial access by expanding the kinds of institutions that can participate as RSPs. Financial inclusion/exclusion addresses the public's access to and use of financial services and products (Refera et al. 2016). Financial literacy entails knowledge about the range of financial services and the ability to make informed financial decisions (Refera et al. 2016). Around 80% of adults in sub-Saharan Africa (excluding South Africa) lack an account with a formal banking institution (African Development Bank 2010a; World Bank 2011). Since African banks generally do not cater to lower-income individuals and households, financial access among senders and recipients in Africa is relatively low. This situation is compounded for migrants in some countries (e.g., South Africa), where access to financial services is based on the migrant's legal status, which tends to disenfranchise large numbers of 'undocumented' migrants. Regulatory environments that prevent or limit non-bank financial institutions from making transfers or restrict outbound transfers hamper physical access to RSPs. African countries have a small number of remittance payout locations compared to countries in other Global South regions. Mexico, for example, has almost as many payout locations as the entire African continent, despite having only one-tenth of Africa's population. Bringing non-bank RSPs into the remittance transfer market would greatly increase the number of payout locations and increase competition among RSPs.

While commercial banks are largely inaccessible to the poorest in many countries, far more people are connected to micro-finance institutions. However, most countries either prohibit micro-finance institutions from making money transfers or restrict their ability to do so (IFAD 2009, 2016). The Democratic Republic of Congo, Ghana, and Kenya are among the few countries that allow micro-finance institutions to carry out international money transfers. In these countries, however, the relatively low capitalization and the lack of technical capacity to enable them to function effectively as payers limit the participation of such institutions. As a result, banks present themselves as the only entities capable of handling foreign cash transfers. In countries where micro-finance institutions do pay remittances, they often operate as subagents of banks (e.g., Uganda).

This situation curtails their independence and limits the revenues they receive from the services they provide (IFAD 2016).

Post offices also have more extensive coverage than banks. One survey estimates that more than 80% of post offices in sub-Saharan Africa are located outside the three largest cities in the region (IFAD 2016). This provides postal networks a unique opportunity to become a link in the remittance transfer chain. However, in total, only about 20% of all post offices in Africa are authorized to pay remittances. The International Fund for Agricultural Development and the Universal Postal Union have supported the creation of post-office remittance services in West Africa, spanning Benin, Burkina Faso, Mali, and Senegal. While relatively small in scale, the project has reportedly reduced the cost and time of remittance transfers (IFAD 2016).

Informal Transfers, Illicit Financial Flows, Technological Innovation

When compared with other Global South regions, a high portion of remittance transfers to and within sub-Saharan Africa occurs through informal channels, in part the result of the problems of market access and financial exclusion discussed above. Many migrants find informal money transfer systems attractive because they are: (i) more accessible, since no bank account is required and no cumbersome procedures are needed; (ii) anonymous, as no proof of identity is required; (iii) cheaper than official channels; and (iv) swift and reliable because they are based on embedded social ties and networks. High levels of financial exclusion and low levels of financial literacy among remittance recipients are also contributing factors, as is the lack of trust in official institutions (Maimbo and Passas 2004; de Haas 2012).

The use and popularity of informal channels generates uncertainty about the volume of remittances to and within Africa, to which governments have responded by developing regulations to protect against illicit financial flows including limits on, and requirements for, money transferred. At the international level, the Financial Action Task Force (FATF), the Bank for International Settlements (BIS), and the World Bank have set standards and principles governing remittances.[10] The FATF developed its recommendations in response to concerns linking terrorism and informal remittance transfers in the aftermath of the September 11, 2001 attacks in the USA. These often restrictive regulations, however, can hinder African migrants and diaspora from transferring funds to their home countries. The application of regulations to combat money laundering, the financing of terrorism, and illicit financial flows, while necessary, should not be arbitrary nor should they erect barriers to the entry of new remittance service providers and the introduction of innovative technology.

Most African countries place fewer restrictions on inbound transfers compared to outbound transfers. However, restrictions on outbound money transfers coupled with high intra-regional migration also generates demand for informal transfers (Jowell and Ratha 2015). Anti-illicit financial flow regulations may also act as a barrier to the entry of non-bank RSPs because compliance and monitoring costs (record keeping, staff hiring and training, etc.) are high relative to the amounts transferred. Many small micro-finance institutions, for example, generally lack the ability and funds to develop such capacities. To grant micro-finance institutions and other non-bank RSPs greater market access, it is important that governments establish basic requirements regarding (i) compliance with standard regulations on financial crime prevention, (ii) the training of staff, (iii) access to technological innovations, and (iv) cash flow and the maintenance of necessary liquidity to cover payments.

Most formal remittance transfers from destination countries outside Africa are sent as cash through money transfer operators (MTOs) or through banks that are acting as agents of money transfer companies, rather than potentially cheaper account-to-account and cash-to-account transfers, reflecting the problems of market access and financial exclusion noted above. This creates a related set of problems, which are discussed in the next section below. Stringent anti-money laundering protocols and the measures combating the financing of terrorism hinder the transfer of remittances through such formal channels. Although such measures are necessary for security reasons, they should not make it inordinately difficult for MTOs to do business with correspondent banks. In 2013, for

[10] The FATF is an inter-governmental body established in 1989 comprising 35 countries and 2 regional organizations, which develops and promotes policies and standards to combat money laundering and terrorist financing. See Financial Action Task Force (2012).

example, several banks in the USA and the UK closed the accounts of money services businesses serving Somalia, fearing penalties for non-compliance with anti-money laundering regulations. Sending remittances from the USA and UK to Somalia became more difficult and expensive (World Bank 2014).

Innovative technologies could help ease the problems of financial exclusion and dampen the use of informal channels (Mohapatra and Ratha 2011). Some African countries have taken innovative steps to ease financial access by leveraging remittance transfers through mobile telephony. For example, Kenya has the M-Pesa mobile banking services, and Orange Money Transfer International, launched in 2012, has linked up with MFS Africa—a company that operates across the region—to enable customers to make payments to mobile accounts. Such mobile technologies could be adapted for use by post offices and micro-finance institutions. While such technological innovations are important to reducing the problems of informal transfers, financial exclusion, and restricted market access, introducing new technologies into uncompetitive markets will not automatically generate price-reducing benefits for consumers. When mobile banking operators in Africa enter remittance markets, they commonly do so through partnerships with the major global money transfer operators that have oligopolistic control of the market. Moreover, African financial regulators have shown little inclination to promote the use of mobile banking for remittances because of concerns over money laundering, illicit flows, and their ability to manage foreign currency risks (UNCTAD 2016).

Market Competition and the Cost of Sending Remittances: The Super Tax

In addition to expanding market access and reducing the use of informal channels, regulations should also aim to increase market competition among the major international money transfer operators (MTOs) and reduce the transaction costs of sending and receiving remittances. Market entry is difficult when a small number of MTOs have effective control of the available banks paying remittances. In countries that only authorize banks to pay remittances, the combination of exclusivity agreements and restrictive regulation leads to the concentration of payments in a few

MTOs.[11] Of these MTOs, Western Union and MoneyGram are, by far, the most significant market players. They have a combined 50% or more of the market in three-quarters of sub-Saharan countries (using number of pay-out locations as a proxy for market share). In Zambia, Zimbabwe, Angola, Mali, and Liberia, among others, they have over 90%. These two firms account for two-thirds of all transfers to the region from Europe and North America. In some countries where both are present, they effectively operate local monopolies, with Western Union dominant or the sole operator in some parts of the country and MoneyGram dominant in others. In all of West Africa, for example, one MTO handles 70% of official payments, and demands exclusivity from the banks in money transfers. In Nigeria, one MTO handles nearly 80% of transfers, expects exclusivity, and prevents other MTOs from contracting agreements with those banks that are the sole remittance payers in the country (IFAD 2009). Since banks are the only entities paying money transfers, a small group of remittance service providers and MTOs handle most formal remittance flows.

The cost of sending remittances to and within Africa is well above global average levels. A recent report (Overseas Development Institute (ODI) 2014) found that Africa's diaspora and migrants paid an average of 12.3% to MTOs to send US$200 home, compared with a global average of 7.8%. Typically, Africa's migrants and diaspora paid twice as much as their South Asian counterparts. Remittance corridors within Africa have some of the highest charges in the world. For example, migrants from Mozambique sending money home from South Africa, or Ghanaians remitting money from Nigeria can pay charges well above 20% (Jowell and Ratha 2015). While fees for financial transactions by MTOs are expected, the evidence suggests that the current costs are excessive and restrict the ability of African migrants/diaspora and African people and governments to leverage the benefits of remittances (Economist 2014; ODI 2014; Jowell and Ratha 2015). The ODI estimates that Africa is losing between US$1.4 billion and US$2.3 billion annually because of high remittance charges, implying a mid-range loss estimate of US$1.8 billion annually,

[11] In fact, the inordinate power of MTOs may suggest that there is a substantial 'regulatory capture' problem in many sub-Saharan countries. For a thorough study of regulatory capture, see Cohn's chapter in this volume.

which they refer to as a 'super tax' (ODI 2014, 20–21).[12] This 'remittance super tax' is effectively a levy on the resources Africa needs to achieve the SDGs and the AU's Agenda 2063. Indeed, to the extent that the AU considers the African diaspora to be the continent's sixth region, the 'remittance super tax' is a form of capital outflow that hurts not only African remittance senders and recipients but also national economies by effectively reducing the amounts remitted.

Why does Africa face such high remittance charges? The highly opaque nature of remittance markets, mechanisms and transfer interfaces, and the complex range of products available make it difficult to provide a precise answer. As far as transfers within the African continent are concerned, the need to convert local currency of the source country to the US dollar or the euro and back again to the local currency of the beneficiary's country nearly doubles the foreign exchange commission, thus contributing to higher remittance fees. The arbitrariness in applying regulations proscribing money laundering and terrorism financing also acts as a barrier to the entry of new market players and the introduction of new technology, thus preventing remittance fees from falling further (World Bank 2014). The lack of competition among the major international MTOs is also a major reason.

The MTOs argue that higher costs reflect currency risk in volatile markets. Western Union and MoneyGram, as pioneers, were instrumental in creating the international network and infrastructure that has facilitated the growth in remittance transfers. Both companies, however, have protected the returns on their initial investment by requiring that agents sign exclusivity agreements. They defend exclusivity agreements with local RSPs claiming they are necessary to prevent competitors from free riding on the training of local agents and the networks in which they have invested heavily (Economist 2014). These agreements effectively 'lock in' more than half of all available payout locations. Because they apply to all local RSPs—banks, foreign exchange bureaus, post offices, and so on—they also control the authorized payout market. Entities wishing to partner with these companies must sign exclusivity agreements. This prevents

[12] They estimate the 'super tax' transfer by reference to two benchmarks. The first lower-bound estimate is the gap between charges for Africa and global average charges. The second benchmark follows a method used by the World Bank and others that estimate the gain that would accrue if charges were lowered to the 5% international target level.

other competitors from expanding their network to institutions that are not agents of the two largest companies or are not in the market, which is the case with most micro-finance institutions and other non-bank RSPs (IFAD 2009).

In 2009, the G8 pledged to pursue the '5×5 goal' of reducing the global average fee for remittances to 5% within 5 years (ODI 2014). Although some reduction has occurred since 2010, according to the data collected by the African Institute for Remittances (AIR), during the second quarter of 2016, the cost of sending remittances to and within Africa was still the highest in the world (AIR 2016; World Bank 2017). The top ten most expensive corridors in the world are all intra-African. The average cost of sending money to and within Africa, in the second quarter of 2016, was between 8.5% and 9%, which was 1.4% more expensive than the global average transfer costs for the same period, and 6% above the 3% target (by 2030) set by the UN's SDGs (AIR 2016).

Diaspora Bonds

As noted at the beginning of this chapter, African governments are looking to leverage diaspora bonds as sources of finance. Ethiopia issued Africa's first Diaspora bond in 2008 (the 'Millennium Corporate Bond') to finance the Ethiopian Electric Power Corporation's hydroelectric power project, the Gilgel Gibe III dam. This bond failed to meet revenue expectations, and the reasons are indicative of the challenges facing African countries in general, including the lack of trust in the ability to service the debt, the quality of the credit guarantee of the government, and uncertainty about the overall political climate in Ethiopia (African Development Bank 2012). A major challenge for African governments in issuing such bonds, therefore, will be to secure credit enhancement from creditworthy lenders and/or guarantors to mitigate the perceived risks and low levels of trust.

However, there are political and legal problems as well. For diaspora bonds to work in sub-Saharan Africa, a major shift among migrant and diaspora communities must occur: from remitting cash/goods, which is a minimal risk private transaction for which communities and social networks of empathy, solidarity, trust, and accountability exist, to actively partnering with home country governments to invest in major development projects. The so-called 'patriotic bond' upon which diaspora bonds have traditionally depended to entice diaspora investors is insufficient. Authoritarian and repressive governance coupled with weak and arbitrary legal institutions in parts of sub-Saharan Africa are not conducive to generating the kind of trust needed for diaspora bonds to work.

A Regulatory System for Remittances

The market failures and other challenges plaguing remittance transfers to and within sub-Saharan Africa identified in the previous section are not due to a lack of financial regulations, but to the lack of an adequate financial regulatory system for remittances that enhances complementarities among the components or phases of the remittance transfer chain. This typically involves a sender in the host country, a recipient in the home country, and intermediaries in both countries employing specific transfer mechanisms/interfaces to make payments. Understanding this transfer chain as a *system* comprising three interconnected phases—origination, operation, and distribution—is necessary to the development and implementation of effective regulations. Although depicted as separate categories in Fig. 5.1, the origination, operation, and distribution phases are closely interconnected and mutually reinforcing—the choices made by senders at the origination phase are strongly influenced by the payment options available to recipients at the distribution phase, and together they strongly influence the transfer mechanism/interface at the operation phase.

The intermediaries through which remittances are channelled in host and home countries are not identified as, and separated into, 'formal' and 'informal' in Fig. 5.1 for several reasons. First, different classifications of a particular intermediary/channel may exist, depending on the regulations in different countries. For example, micro-finance institutions would be 'formal' in those African countries where they are licensed as RSPs and 'informal' in countries where they are not. Second, because of the rapid pace of innovation among RSPs and the difficulty in obtaining accurate information (especially on informal transfers), the inventory of home and host country intermediaries and transfer mechanisms to and within sub-Saharan Africa depicted in Fig. 5.1 is necessarily incomplete. Third, there is a tendency to associate informal remittance flows with illegality and criminality. This presumed association should be broken. A remittance channel is 'informal' because it occurs outside official

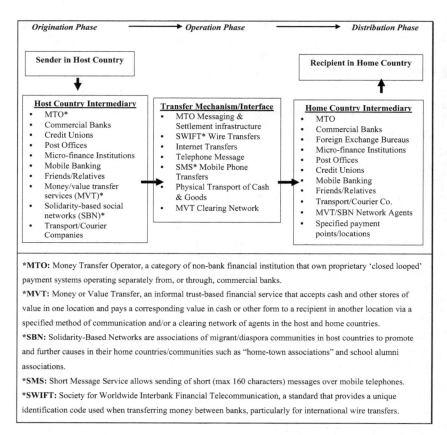

Fig. 5.1 Remittance channels to and within sub-Saharan Africa. (Sources: Author's adaptation from IMF 2009, 7; Weiss 2016; Maimbo 2004)

financial regulation and supervision. As noted above, the choice between formal and informal transfer channels is influenced by a range of factors that underscore the importance of crafting financial regulation with a goal of promoting the financial deepening and broadening associated with financial development. The discussion below summarizes the kinds of financial regulations needed in each of the phases of the remittance transfer chain within the context of promoting financial development as a policy objective.

Origination Phase

The main goals of financial regulations at the origination phase are to facilitate and expand remittance senders' access to lower-cost and reliable remittance services and to enhance competition among remittance service providers in host countries. These goals can best be accomplished by licensing and/or registering a wider range of intermediaries authorized to transfer remittances.[13] In addition, clearer customer identification guidelines, higher record keeping standards, and better transaction reporting procedures at the point of transfer are also needed. Such regulations would also help separate legal from illegal remittance service providers. However, the application of these measures will differ across sending countries, depending on their financial development. This is because expanding licensing, registration, identification, and reporting requires a careful balancing act to bring more remittance service providers into the formal system without placing additional barriers in the way of remittance senders.

In sub-Saharan African countries, where informal remittance channels are substantial, regulations would seek to bring the informal remittance systems closer to the formal financial sector without altering the specific nature of the former, while simultaneously addressing the weaknesses in the latter (Maimbo 2004). The formal and informal financial systems each have deficiencies. Cumbersome bureaucratic policies and procedures for simple money transfers, high transaction costs, delays in effecting transfers, and restrictive exchange controls are major reasons for the existence of informal transfers. Commercial banks especially have not traditionally offered remittance services, and the international money transfer services they do offer (such as SWIFT wire transfers) are comparatively expensive, and have thus tended to serve clients transferring larger amounts of money than the typical migrant remitter (Weiss 2016).

---

[13] In the broadest terms, 'registration' requires RSPs to identify themselves to the authorities and provide information about their services, with few or no conditions applied to the ability of the RSP to provide its service, while 'licensing' attaches substantive conditions. In practice, however, the distinction between registration and licensing is blurred (Bank for International Settlements and World Bank 2007, 22). The requirement of registration/licensing is in line with the FATF Special Recommendation VI, which called on countries to license or register informal remittance services and to subject them to all FATF recommendations that apply to banks and non-bank entities (FATF 2012).

Within sending countries, additional measures are required to increase the attractiveness of regulated (formal) payment systems to all migrants irrespective of their legal status. Some of the largest immigrant-receiving Global North countries, including the USA and Canada, currently do not require remitters to provide documented evidence of their legal status in the country. However, pressures to tighten immigration regulations may lead to regulations that require senders to present certain types of identification issued only to 'documented' migrants and residents, thereby excluding 'undocumented' migrants and leaving them no option but to use informal channels. As noted in a 2017 World Bank report, several high-income countries that are host to many migrants are also considering imposing a tax on outward remittances, partly to discourage undocumented migration and partly to raise revenue. This is the opposite of the kind of regulation needed. If implemented, it is more likely to drive remittance flows to informal or illegal channels (World Bank 2017). It is also unjust because it amounts to double taxation in that the remitter, in principle, has already paid taxes on the income earned in the host country.

Operation Phase

Regulations at the operation phase of the remittance transfer system aim to increase transparency and accountability, reduce transaction costs, increase the speed and security of funds transferred, expand the remittance transfer options available to senders, and facilitate accurate monitoring and reporting of remittance flows. Internationally, the World Bank and the BIS have sought to improve the operational aspects of remittance transfers. They issued a joint statement of principles in 2007, which noted that to achieve the objectives of safe and efficient international remittance transfers, markets for remittance services had to be 'contestable, transparent, accessible and sound' (Bank for International Settlements and World Bank 2007, 19).[14] Effective regulation and monitoring of remittance operations includes understanding their size, corridors, transfer mechanisms, and costs.

---

[14] A 'contestable' market is one in which there are low barriers to entry and where potential entrants therefore exert competitive pressure on incumbents, forcing the latter to be efficient to maintain their market position.

At the national level, regulations to increase transparency and accountability would mandate the compilation and publication (in easily accessed venues) of remittance price comparisons across different intermediaries and their transfer mechanisms/interfaces (as listed in Fig. 5.1). Regulations would also mandate the disclosure of the range of products available, the fees/commissions earned, and the information on foreign exchange conversion charges. Of particular relevance is transparency about the total price of the service because, in addition to the direct fee charged to the sender by the RSP, the total price of the transaction is affected by the exchange rate applied and by any fee charged to the receiver by the disbursing RSP or its agent. National regulatory authorities should also facilitate and closely monitor changes in the transfer mechanism/interface for remittance payments, including new payment technologies, platforms, or instruments such as mobile phones or internet-based remittance instruments. Regulations would also govern and monitor access of remittance agents to clearing and settlement systems, and mandate the disclosure of fees attached to these operations. Section 1073 of the Dodd-Frank Act of 2010 is an example. It requires remittance transfer operators to disclose upfront consistently and reliably the price of a transfer, the amount the recipient will receive, and the date of availability (Weiss 2016). It also requires remittance providers to investigate disputes and remedy errors related to the transaction.

With respect to reducing transaction costs, regulations in sending countries would limit the fee charged for a remittance transfer to no more than 5% of the amount transferred, which is in line with the 2009 G8 recommendations. Additional measures may also be necessary to reduce costs, including investigations of the major global MTOs by anti-trust authorities in North America and Europe, to identify areas where market concentration and commercial practices are artificially inflating charges. Requiring greater consistency in calculating what counts as a remittance and in reporting by national authorities would enhance the accuracy and credibility of estimates of remittances flowing through formal channels.

Distribution Phase

Regulations at the distribution phase should be developed and implemented within a broader framework that aims to improve financial literacy and reduce financial exclusion by expanding the types and numbers of distribution points through which remittance payments are received. This approach recognizes that the choice of remittance transfer channel is essentially a payment systems (distribution) issue, and that a remittance payment system simply represents a transfer of value between a sender and a recipient in an agreed upon manner (Maimbo 2004). Given the high levels of financial exclusion and financial illiteracy in sub-Saharan Africa, direct transfers of value by cash (or goods) between sender and recipient is often the only choice available. Regulations are therefore needed that will encourage and allow the number and types of distribution points of the payment network to grow by permitting a range of bank and non-bank entities, including postal services and micro-finance institutions, to make remittance payments. Such expansion is particularly needed in rural areas. For this to work, African governments should revoke, or at least renegotiate, the 'exclusivity agreements' signed between the major global MTOs and African commercial banks and promote the use of non-bank institutions such as micro-finance institutions and post offices as remittance payout agencies.

While financial intermediaries such as banks can help with remittance payments, for reasons outlined earlier, they are largely inaccessible to the poorest in many sub-Saharan African countries, especially in rural areas. Establishing and regulating rural banks or credit unions should thus be a key priority. These banks would then offer remittance and other financial services such as insurance that attract new customers and encourage savings.[15] Enabling regulation would also expand and consolidate innovative technologies, such as mobile banking that are rapidly transforming the financial landscape in sub-Saharan Africa.

Africa is at the forefront globally in the development and application of mobile telephony as a platform for financial services, aided by the rapid expansion of mobile phone services and infrastructure throughout the continent (African Development Bank 2010b). Mobile financial services, which began with simple payments and transfers, have progressed to offering 'virtual' accounts, consumer credit loans, and more recently into insurance services. Subscribers can now open accounts, check balances, pay bills, send and receive money transfers, and so on (African Development

---

[15] Evidence shows lower rates of savings for cash remittances than bank deposits and for many of the poorest households in sub-Saharan Africa, remittances are the only point of contact with the formal financial sector (Mohapatra et al. 2010).

REMITTANCES, REGULATION, AND FINANCIAL DEVELOPMENT... 183

Bank 2010b; Global Economic Governance 2016).[16] In this context, such new technology-based financial services could substantially reduce financial exclusion by making financial services available in remote areas where conventional banks have been physically absent. However, the expansion of financial services, whether through conventional banks, non-bank entities such as micro-finance institutions, or non-conventional digital technologies, generates risks and regulatory challenges. For example, while promoting financial inclusion by expanding access to credit brings important benefits, it could also increase the risk of default. Regulatory challenges include keeping abreast with the pace of technological change, and 'unbundling' the range of financial services offered (money transfers, accounts, credit, insurance, etc.) so that they can be regulated according to the level of risk they generate (Global Economic Governance 2016).

Concerns regarding the regulatory challenges raised by the entry of non-bank entities into the domain of traditional banking are valid, for telecommunications companies and other non-bank RSPs should not necessarily be subject to the same regulations as banks. Regulations in this context must be non-discriminatory; that is, the regulatory framework should apply equally to different types of RSPs insofar as they are providing equivalent services (Bank for International Settlements and World Bank 2007). Such regulations, therefore, are functional rather than institutional. Non-bank RSPs, therefore, would not be subject to the same regulations and requirements as banks, except to the extent that the remittance services they provide are functionally equivalent to that provided by banks. In this way, different sets of rules and guidelines within an established regulatory framework would govern bank and non-bank RSPs. This will promote a level playing field between different RSPs and encourage competition.

---

[16] Kenya's M-Pesa digital financial service, with about nine million subscribers, is the best known, but similar initiatives are underway in many other sub-Saharan African countries including Tanzania, Rwanda, South Africa, Nigeria, Ghana, and Côte d'Ivoire.

Summary of Recommended Regulations

Origination Phase

1. Registration and/or licensing of a wider range of RSPs.
2. Clearer customer identification guidelines, but verification of identity independent of immigration status.

Operation Phase

1. Increase transparency.
2. Reduce transaction costs.
3. Increase speed and security of transactions.
4. Increase remittance transfer options, including new transfer technologies.
5. Facilitate accurate recording, monitoring, and reporting of remittance transfers.
6. Increase consumer protections.
7. Limit remittance sending fees to no more than 5% of the total amount transferred.
8. Enhance accuracy of remittance estimates and greater consistency in reporting by national authorities.

Distribution Phase

1. Expand distribution points for remittance payments, including the use of non-bank entities as RSPs.
2. Establish more rural banks/credit unions.
3. Revoke/renegotiate exclusivity agreements with the major global MTOs.
4. Consolidate innovative technologies including mobile banking.
5. Establish non-discriminatory regulatory framework for bank and non-bank RSPs.

CONCLUSION

This chapter identifies some of the major challenges to establishing an adequate financial regulatory system for remittances in sub-Saharan Africa and outlines some of the key financial regulations needed. Taking into consideration the context-dependent nature of the remittance-development relationship, the focus was on financial development—specifically, how the deepening and broadening of financial services and instruments may facilitate positive development outcomes from remittances. Accordingly, regulatory changes need to consider and accommodate the remittance/financial development nexus and its contribution to fostering development generally. Although the relationship between remittances and financial development is complementary, the attainment of positive outcomes across different development dimensions does not occur automatically but requires specific financial regulatory and institutional measures within sub-Saharan African countries in order to channel remittances and diaspora savings into economic and social investments.

The challenges to establishing an effective regulatory system for remittances in sub-Saharan Africa should not be underestimated. A remittance involves at least two jurisdictions—the sending and the receiving countries—and may involve other jurisdictions where the RSP or its agents operate in third countries. To be successful, therefore, the kinds of financial regulations outlined in this chapter would require coordination and harmonization across sub-Saharan African countries, as well as between sub-Saharan African countries and the major immigrant-receiving countries outside the region. In addition, regulatory frameworks at the national level have to meet internationally agreed standards and principles, especially those set by the FAFT, the BIS, and the World Bank. Questions regarding regulatory capacity must be addressed, as well as the potential risks that accompany financial deepening and broadening.

The 2008 global financial crisis raised questions about the limits and trade-offs of financial development, particularly in relation to negative impacts on economic stability and growth. These concerns are underscored by the fact that the crisis originated in the wealthiest Global North countries that are supposed to have high levels of financial development (IMF 2015). The relative stability of remittance flows to and within Africa compared to other private flows in the aftermath of the 2008 financial crisis, and their continued growth since then, reinforce the need for better financial regulations to leverage remittances into positive sustainable development outcomes.

Acknowledgements Ted Cohn, Norbert Gaillard, and Anil Hira

REFERENCES

Acosta, Pablo, Emmanuel Lartey, and Federico Mandelman. 2009. Remittances and the Dutch Disease. *Journal of International Economics.* 79(1): 102–116.

Adams, Richard and John Page. 2005. Do International Migration and Remittances Reduce Poverty in Developing Countries? *World Development.* 33(10): 1645–1669.

Adenutsi, Deodat E. 2011. Financial Development, International Migrant Remittances and Endogenous Growth in Ghana. *Studies in Economics and Finance.* 28(1): 68–89.

African Development Bank. 2010a. Diaspora Bonds and Securitization of Remittances for Africa's Development. *Africa Economic Brief.* 1(7): December.

African Development Bank. 2010b. Mobile Banking in Africa: Taking the Bank to the People. *Africa Economic Brief.* 1(8): December.

African Development Bank. 2012. Diaspora Bonds: Some Lessons for African Countries. *Africa Economic Brief.* 3(13): December.

African Institute for Remittances (AIR). 2016. Diaspora/Migrant Remittances and the African Institute for Remittances. Potsdam Spring Dialogue 2016. April 7–8, available at http://www.sef-bonn.org/fileadmin/Die_SEF/Veranstaltungen/PFG/2016_pfg_bune_en.pdf

Aggarwal, Reena, Asli Demirguc-Kunt, and Maria Soledad Martinez Peria. 2011. Do Remittances Promote Financial Development? *Journal of Development Economics.* 96(2): 255–264.

Anton, José-Ignacio. 2010. The Impact of Remittances on Nutritional Status of Children in Ecuador. *International Migration Review.* 44(2): 269–299.

Athanasoulis, Stefano and Eric van Wincoop. 2000. Growth Uncertainty and Risk Sharing. *Journal of Monetary Economics.* 45(3): 477–505.

Avendano, Rolando, Norbert Gaillard, and Sebastian Nieto-Parra. 2011. Are Workers' Remittances Relevant for Credit Rating Agencies? *Review of Development Finance.* 1(1): 57–78.

Bank for International Settlements and World Bank. 2007. *General Principles for International Remittance Services.* January.

Bugamelli, Matteo and Francesco Paterno. 2009. Do Workers' Remittances Reduce the Probability of Current Account Reversals? *World Development.* 37(12): 1821–1838.

Carling, Jorgen. 2004. Emigration, Return and Development in Cape Verde: The Impact of Closing Borders. *Population, Space, and Place.* 10(2): 113–132.

Carling, Jorgen. 2014. Scripting Remittances: Making Sense of Money Transfers in Transnational Relationships. *International Migration Review.* 48(Golden Anniversary Issue): S218–S262.

Chami, Ralph, Connel Fullenkamp, and Samir Jahjah. 2003. Are Immigrant Remittance Flows a Source of Capital for Development? *IMF Working Paper No. 03/189.*

Chami, Ralph, Adolfo Barajas, Thomas F. Cosimano, Connel Fullenkamp, Michael T. Gapen and Peter J. Montiel. 2008. Macroeconomic Consequences of Remittances. *IMF Occasional Paper No. 259.*

Chami, Ralph, Dalia S. Hakura, and Peter J. Montiel. 2009. Remittances: An Automatic Output Stabilizer? *IMF Working Paper No. 09/91.*

De Haas, Hein. 2010. Migration and Development: A Theoretical Perspective. *International Migration Review.* 44(1): 227–264.

De Haas, Hein. 2012. The Migration and Development Pendulum: A Critical View on Research and Policy. *International Migration.* 50(3): 8–25.

Easterly, William and Ross Levine. 1997. Africa's Growth Tragedy: Policies and Ethnic Divisions. *Quarterly Journal of Economics.* 112(4): 1203–1250.

Economic Commission for Africa (ECA). 2012. *Illicit Financial Flows from Africa: Scale and Development Challenges.* Background Paper by the High-level Panel on Illicit Financial Flows from Africa.

Economic Commission for Africa (ECA). 2014. *Progress Report of the High-level Panel on Illicit Financial Flows from Africa.*

Economist (The). 2014. Remittances to Africa: Do the Middlemen Deserve their Cut? April 17, available at http://www.economist.com/blogs/bao-bab/2014/04/remittances-africa

Financial Action Task Force (FATF). 2012. *FATF Recommendations: International Standards on Combating Money Laundering and the Financing of Terrorism and Proliferation.*

Giuliano, Paola and Marta Ruiz-Arranz. 2009. Remittances, Financial Development, and Growth. *Journal of Development Economics.* 90(1): 144–152.

Global Economic Governance. 2016. *Consolidating Africa's Mobile Banking Revolution.* Global Economic Governance Program. Oxford: Oxford University.

Global Financial Integrity. 2010. *Illicit Financial Flows from Africa: Hidden Resource for Development.*

Global Financial Integrity. 2015. *Financial Flows and Tax Havens: Combining to Limit the Lives of billions of People.*

Gupta, Sanjeev, Catherine A. Pattillo, and Smita Wagh. 2007a. Impact of Remittances on Poverty and Financial Development in Sub-Saharan Africa. *IMF Working Paper No. 07/38.*

Gupta, Sanjeev, Catherine A. Pattillo, and Smita Wagh. 2007b. Making Remittances Work for Africa. *Finance and Development.* 44(2).

Hicks, John. 1969. *A Theory of Economic History.* Oxford: Clarendon Press.

International Fund for Agricultural Development (IFAD). 2009. *Sending Money Home to Africa: Remittance Markets, Enabling Environment and Prospects.* Rome: IFAD-FAO.

International Fund for Agricultural Development (IFAD). 2016. *Remittances at the Post Office in Africa: Serving the Financial Needs of Migrants and their Families in Rural Areas.* Rome: IFAD FAO.

International Monetary Fund (IMF). 2009. *International Transactions in Remittances: Guide for Compilers and Users.* Washington, DC: IMF.

International Monetary Fund (IMF). 2015. Rethinking Financial Deepening: Stability and Growth in Emerging Markets. *IMF Staff Discussion Note No. 15/08.*

Jowell, Dame Tessa and Dilip Ratha. 2015. It's Time to Repeal the Remittance 'Super-Tax' on Africa. *World Bank blog.* March 3, available at http://blogs.worldbank.org/peoplemove/it-s-time-repeal-remittances-super-tax-africa

Ketkar, Suhas and Dilip Ratha. 2001. Securitization of Future Flow Receivables: A Useful Tool for Developing Countries. *Finance and Development.* 38(1).

Kharas, Homi. 2014. *Financing for Development: International Financial Flows after 2015.* Washington, DC: Brookings Institution.

Levitt, Peggy and Deepak Lamba-Nieves. 2011. Social Remittances Revisited. *Journal of Ethnic and Migration Studies.* 37(1): 1–22.

Maimbo, Samuel Munzele. 2004. The Regulation and Supervision of Informal Remittance Systems: Emerging Oversight Strategies. *IMF Seminar on Current Developments in Monetary and Financial Law.* November 24.

Maimbo, Samuel Munzele and Nikos Passas. 2004. The Regulation and Supervision of Informal Remittance Systems. *Small Enterprise Development.* 15(1): 53–62.

Misati, Roseline Nyakerario and Esman Morekwa Nyamongo. 2011. Financial Development and Private Investment in Sub-Saharan Africa. *Journal of Economics and Business.* 63(2): 139–151.

Misati, Roseline Nyakerario and Esman Morekwa Nyamongo. 2012. Financial Liberalisation, Financial Fragility and Economic Growth in Sub-Saharan Africa. *Journal of Financial Stability.* 8(3): 150–160.

Misati, Roseline Nyakerario, Esman Morekwa Nyamongo, Leonard Kipyegon, and Lydia Ndirangu. 2012. Remittances, Financial Development and Economic Growth in Africa. *Journal of Economics and Business.* 64(3): 240–260.

Mohan, Giles and A. B. Zack-Williams. 2002. Globalisation From Below: Conceptualising the Role of the African Diasporas in Africa's Development. *Review of African Political Economy.* 29(92): 211–236.

Mohapatra, Sanket, Dilip Ratha, and Ani Silwal. 2010. Outlook for Remittance Flows 2011–12: Recovery After the Crisis, But Risks Lie Ahead. *Migration and Development Brief No.13.*

Mohapatra, Sanket and Dilip Ratha. 2011. *Remittances Markets in Africa.* World Bank, Washington, DC: World Bank, 3–88.

Mundaca, B. Gabriela. 2009. Remittances, Financial Market Development, and Economic Growth: The Case of Latin America and the Caribbean. *Review of Development Economics.* 13(2): 288–303.

Overseas Development Institute (ODI). 2014. *Lost in Intermediation: How Excessive Charges Undermine the Benefits of Remittances for Africa.* London: ODI.

Pallage, Stéphane and Michel A. Robe. 2003. On the Welfare Cost of Economic Fluctuations in Developing Countries. *International Economic Review.* 44(2): 677–698.

Portes, Alejandro and Julia Sensenbrenner. 1993. Embeddedness and Immigration: Notes on the Social Determinants of Economic Action. *American Journal of Sociology.* 98(6): 1320–1350.

Rahman, Md Mizanur. 2013. Gendering Migrant Remittances: Evidence from Bangladesh and the United Arab Emirates. *International Migration.* 51(s1): e159–e178.

Ratha, Dilip. 2007. Leveraging Remittances for Development. *Policy Brief.* Washington, DC: Migration Policy Institute. June.

Ratha, Dilip, Prabal K. De, and Sanket Mohapatra. 2011. Shadow Sovereign Ratings for Unrated Developing Countries. *World Development.* 39(3): 295–307.

Refera, Matewos Kebede, Navkiranjit Kaur Dhaliwal, and Jasmindeep Kaur. 2016. Financial Literacy for Developing Countries in Africa: A Review of Concept, Significance and Research Opportunities. *Journal of African Studies and Development.* 8(1): 1–12.

Sachs, Jeffrey and Andrew M. Warner. 1997. Fundamental Sources of Long-Run Growth. *American Economic Review.* 87(2): 184–188.

Schumpeter, Joseph A. [1911] 1961. *The Theory of Economic Development: An Inquiry into Profits, Capital, Credit, Interest, and the Business Cycle.* Oxford and New York: Oxford University Press.

Skeldon, Ronald. 2008. International Migration as a Tool in Development Policy: A Passing Phase? *Population and Development Review.* 34(1): 1–18.

Sy, Amadou and Fenohasina Maret Rakotondrazaka. 2015. *Private Capital Flows, Official Development Assistance, and Remittances to Africa: Who Gets What?* Washington, DC: Brookings Institution. May 19.

Terry, Donald F. and Steven R. Wilson (Eds.). 2005. *Beyond Small Change: Making Migrant Remittances Count.* Washington, DC: Inter-American Development Bank.

United Nations Conference on Trade and Development (UNCTAD). 2011. *Impact of Remittances on Poverty in Developing Countries.* New York: United Nations.

United Nations Conference on Trade and Development (UNCTAD). 2016. *Economic Development in Africa Report 2016: Debt Dynamics and Development Finance in Africa.* New York: United Nations.

Weiss, Martin A. 2016. *Remittances: Background Issues for Congress.* Washington DC: Congressional Research Service. May 9.

Woodruff, Christopher. 2007. Mexican Microenterprise Investment and Employment: The Role of Remittances. *INTAL-ITD Working Paper No. 26.* Buenos Aires: Institute for the Integration of Latin America and the Caribbean and Inter-American Development Bank.

World Bank. 2011. *Migration and Remittances Factbook 2011.* Washington, DC: World Bank.

World Bank. 2014. Migration and Remittances: Recent Developments and Outlook. *Migration and Development Brief 22.* April.

World Bank. 2015a. *Global Economic Prospects.* Washington, DC: World Bank.

World Bank. 2015b. *Global Financial Development Report 2015–2016: Long-Term Finance.* Washington, DC: World Bank.

World Bank. 2016. *Migration and Remittances Factbook 2016.* Washington, DC: World Bank.

World Bank. 2017. Migration and Remittances: Recent Developments and Outlook. *Migration and Development Brief 27.* April.

CHAPTER 6

Regulatory Mayhem in Offshore Finance: What the Panama Papers Reveal

Anil Hira, Brian Murata, and Shea Monson

INTRODUCTION

Susan Strange offered these prophetic words in 1986 (1), "The Western financial system is rapidly coming to resemble nothing as much as a vast casino." In April 2016, the International Consortium of Investigative Journalists (ICIJ) announced the release of 11.5 million leaked documents from the Panamanian law firm Mossack Fonseca dating back to the 1970s. The documents were leaked originally to the German newspaper Süddeutsche Zeitung, who then contacted the ICIJ for help. In 2017, another trove of documents, called the Paradise Papers, was released, further demonstrating widespread global tax evasion and connections through offshore financial holding companies, such as those revealed between US Commerce Secretary Wilbur Ross and Russian President Vladimir Putin. The Panama and Paradise Papers help to shed light on how wealthy individuals and corporations around the world use offshore financial centres to hide wealth and evade taxes. News that prominent leaders such as former UK Prime Minister (PM) David Cameron and Icelandic PM Gunnlaugsson had such accounts created public awareness

A. Hira (✉) • B. Murata • S. Monson
Department of Political Science, Simon Fraser University, Burnaby, BC, Canada
e-mail: ahira@sfu.ca; shea_monson@sfu.ca

© The Author(s) 2019
A. Hira et al. (eds.), *The Failure of Financial Regulation*,
International Political Economy Series,
https://doi.org/10.1007/978-3-030-05680-3_6

about how widespread such practices are. Offshore finance is a growing area of concern reflecting lax or absent regulation for global financial flows. While there has been great journalism, there is very little in the way of deep analysis for what the hacks reveal about the nature of the global financial system.

In line with the theme of this volume, we demonstrate in this chapter that offshore financial tax evasion is nothing new; it is a persistent problem that has been effectively tolerated for decades, and its increasing scope portends a role in future crashes. In examining the issues, we demonstrate elements of regulatory complexity, as discussed by Dobuzinskis in this volume. Regarding the evasive nature of offshore finance, in which even when crackdowns occur—such as recent EU actions to increase transparency within their jurisdiction or US requirements to force citizens to declare assets abroad—there is a "whack a mole" quality to evasion. We further touch on the issue of regulatory capture, elucidated in Cohn's chapter, in the sense of the ability of corporations to compromise reform efforts, through watering down enforcement and preserving loopholes, and potential conflicts of interest where wealthy individuals who are able to influence or directly in charge of regulation—such as Wilbur Ross, US Commerce Secretary—have assets overseas. We also point to moral hazard, as explored by Gaillard and Michalek, where significant proportions of the Western financial system are in some way tied to offshore havens, allowing for corporations and individuals to not only evade taxes but incur risks that can rebound into more soundly regulated financial institutions. Offshore finance is similar in these ways to remittances, as discussed in Busumtwi-Sam's chapter, a large and growing area of global financial transactions that is only weakly regulated and is subject to continual evolution and change, particularly from the point of view of technology. While important, for example, it is outside our scope to cover the emerging topic of cryptocurrencies (e.g., Bitcoin), but these certainly provide avenues for further evasion.

The issue *dates back to the 1960s* when offshore centres were set up. Like remittances, it is a persistent issue in that it is very poorly regulated. While there are no good data, for obvious reasons, as we discuss below, the leaks reveal a problem that is growing over time. By 1998, the Organisation for Economic Co-operation and Development (OECD) published a report about "harmful tax competition" from offshore centres. The Panama Papers reinforce the perceptions of widespread injustice in the financial and taxation systems, which feeds into a wider discourse centred around global and national inequality. As Susan Strange pointed out in 1996 (63), the social and political consequences of the failure of governments to harmonise taxes are "almost entirely overlooked" in the political economy literature. Moreover, there are few academic overviews of the topic *from the perspective of regulation*; most writing is descriptive and alarmist in nature (e.g., Brittain-Catlin 2005). The literature that does exist in regard to regulation is mostly from international organisations such as the OECD. It is highly technical in nature, avoiding the larger and more controversial consequences of this parallel financial system. The neglected consequences are substantial, including an increasingly disproportionate burden on individual taxpayers, exacerbating inequality, and excessive resort to debt by governments. We examine issues around global tax evasion, including obstacles to reform and possible paths forward. Our goal is to provide a fairly comprehensive guide to readers about how offshore finance works from a regulatory perspective, setting up an analysis of reform efforts and why they come up short. Our suggestions for reform focus on the core persistent principles touched on throughout the volume, namely a lack of consensus, transparency, coordination, harmonisation, and enforcement in global financial regulation.

GROWING CONCERNS ABOUT OFFSHORE FINANCE AMIDST INCREASINGLY COMPLEX STATE-CORPORATE RELATIONS

What is clear is that the Western state is fiscally constrained on a number of fronts. For example, the increasing size and scope of transactions through the internet, including via e-commerce, make taxation ever more challenging. Moreover, financial transactions are now global, often taking place through intra- or inter-corporate exchanges rather than through traditional currency transactions. The greying of Western populations while life spans increase puts an unfair burden on smaller cohorts of young workers. Automation and loss of jobs to cheaper labour abroad accent a widening gap in income inequality and perennial unemployment that threaten the ability to tax as well as income mobility. Meanwhile, large government deficits twinned with trade deficits in most countries, especially the US, constrain the possibilities for a large Keynesian stimulus programme to shift economies out of recession and create new jobs. Low commodity prices, along with an attempt to shift away from fossil fuels, in turn, create an accelerating fragility in the developing world which has long depended upon Western consumers for growth. This era of doldrums has led to the rise of far-right alternatives across the West. All of this suggests the need for greater tax cooperation.

An international regime for taxation cooperation does formally exist, primarily functioning through the OECD Model Income Tax Convention, passed in 1963. The convention seeks to avoid double taxation, that is, two or more states taxing the same sources of income. The regime is built on the foundation of taxation by geographic origin of the entity. However, there is no enforcement, the focus is exclusively on income taxes, and it is a collection of bilateral rather than multilateral agreements (Paris 2003). Despite the international tax regime, empirical studies suggest strongly that there is corporate tax competition, leading to a lowering of rates over time (Genschel 2002; Overesch and Rincke 2011). Corporate taxes, in particular, declined markedly upon the adoption of neoliberal policies in the 1980s related to competition for "mobile assets" and the re-prioritisation of efficiency over redistribution (Swank 2006).

As alluded to in the introductory chapter, technology has played a significant role in enabling offshore finance. Needless to say, large portions of financial transactions are now conducted through electronic transfers, at the interbank, corporate, and individual levels, confounding efforts by states to monitor them. Beyond reducing transaction costs and allowing transfers of capital within seconds, such developments also have eased the way in for non-banking financial intermediaries to develop, such as PayPal, the ubiquitous online payment system. New developments such as Apple's digital wallet service will further erode traditional banking services. Recent developments in cyber security have led to the creation of private currencies, traded over electronic platforms. Sometimes called "cryptocurrencies," these devices allow for peer-to-peer transfer of a given number of units between two or more parties with the use of any financial institution (Lam and Lee 2015, 8–9). There are over 400 different types of cryptocurrencies, the most well-known of these being *Bitcoin*, a peer-to-peer electronic cash system founded in 2008, by an unknown individual or group (Lam and Lee 2015, 11 and 13). To verify proof of payment, one merely needs to know the alphanumeric identification of two parties as well as the transaction number. Each transaction is automatically checked against the previous recorded transactions. Thus, Bitcoin offers both security and anonymity.

The existence of a parallel offshore financial system is alarming for a number of reasons beyond loss of tax receipts. It undermines faith in national financial systems and, indirectly, political legitimacy based on fairness in democracies. Moreover, the parallel system abets a wide range of illegal activities, from terrorism to narco-trafficking. The issue is fraught as it is currently impossible to reliably track global financial flows. In fact, the OECD estimates that some 60% of world trade actually takes place *within* MNCs (Love 2012).

International financial evasion can therefore be seen as a two-level game (Putnam 1988). Simply put, states have, through changes in domestic political interests, moved to support financial globalisation, as reflected in the accompanying chapter on regulatory capture (see Cohn's chapter in this volume). The trend fits generally with Mancur Olson's prescient suggestions in *The Rise and Decline of Nations* (1982) about the rise of private special interests who are able to crowd out public collective goods at the national, and by extension, global level. Olson's perspective explains the weakness of state enforcement of international tax evasion norms, which share broad acceptance between Washington and the EU. This fact is reflected in the important lobbying power of Wall Street and London financial interests in their domestic politics. It remains to be seen if the growing power of financial over productive interests will continue or be challenged as reflected in the most recent swings to the right, including both anti- big finance and anti-globalisation/trade candidates such as Trump and Le Pen.

Nonetheless, it is important to point out that state and corporate interests are often intertwined, even if they are contradictory in formal terms. The steady mergers and acquisitions which gained pace in the 1990s also suggest that corporations clearly have common interests in regard to maintaining financial havens. The possibility of states uniting against them seems slim when there is competition to capture production for local multiplier effects. In short, states and corporations are complex collections of different actors with shifting and often conflicting interests. For these reasons, this chapter will approach tax evasion as a policy issue that can be tackled, understanding that if erosion of the tax base continues, states and the companies that depend upon a stable regulatory environment and demand will eventually build a political consensus to ramp up reform past the initial efforts described below.

How Offshore Finance Works and Some
of the Consequences

In 2010–2011, Findley et al. (2014, 182) conducted a very interesting experiment. They contacted 3771 firms around the world that specialise in incorporation service by e-mail, requesting assistance in setting up shell corporations. Over a fifth (22.1%) were willing to provide services without any photo identification and almost half (48%) did not request proper identification (61 and 169). Even more sobering is the result that signals of corrupt origins of money in e-mails or knowledge of international standards of transparency yielded no significant response from potential providers (171).

The OECD uses the term base erosion and profit shifting in its research on offshore tax havens. It estimates that tax evasion results in the loss of $100–240 billion annually for 4–10% of global corporate tax income revenues (http://www.oecd.org/tax/oecd-presents-outputs-of-oecd-g20-beps-project-for-discussion-at-g20-finance-ministers-meeting.htm). Zucman (2015, 3–4, 36, 47) gives some alarming estimates about the amount of wealth held in offshore tax havens. Considered globally, 8% of the financial wealth of households or $7.6 trillion is held offshore. $5.3 trillion is held in offshore havens and $2.3 trillion (30%) by foreigners in Switzerland alone. In terms of corporations, 55% of all foreign profits, totalling at least $130 billion annually are kept in tax havens by US companies alone. This results in a loss of at least $200 billion in taxes every year to governments around the world. Other authors estimate even higher levels of hidden wealth. Palan et al. (2010, 5) put the figure at $12 trillion in 2007, equivalent to the entire US annual GNP. Developing country companies and individuals are as, if not more, involved in offshore financial havens. Buckley et al. (2015) estimate that at least $74.7 billion of FDI were funnelled from China through the Caymans, the British Virgin Islands, and Hong Kong, and another $116 billion from them into China. Moreover, "the vast majority" of Chinese firms listed in the US are incorporated offshore. One of the largest and most admired global companies, Apple, created a subsidiary, Apple Operations International, that had income of $30 billion from 2009 to 2012, but "filed no corporate tax anywhere" (Cobham et al. 2015).

It is a common and increasingly reported occurrence that large multinationals pay little to no taxes in major countries where they operate. Haberly and Wójcik (2015) note that the US Bureau of Economic Analysis

(BEA) data from 2012 suggest that more than half of the FDI stock of US non-financial firms ($1.9 trillion) is attributed to overseas holding companies rather than functional subsidiaries. Nearly a third of the total FDI stock of US firms is held in 3 jurisdictions: the Netherlands, Luxembourg, and Bermuda. They conclude that at least 30% and possibly 50% of all FDI is related to offshore havens.

As an illustration, according to a report by the UK Parliament (http://www.publications.parliament.uk/pa/cm201213/cmselect/cmpubacc/716/71605.htm) in 2013, Starbucks reported that it had lost money in 2014/2015 of the years it operated in the UK, despite managing a 31% market share. It paid 4.7% of its profits to its Dutch affiliate for intellectual property but did not provide details on what this constituted. In turn, the Dutch company paid a Swiss affiliate for coffee with a 20% mark-up, which was then passed on to the UK company. In addition, a loan between the US and UK Starbucks businesses was set at a "higher rate than any similar loan we have seen." The end result was that Starbucks paid no corporate taxes in the UK. By the same token, despite sales of £207 million in the UK by Amazon, the firm paid only £1.8 million in taxes. After enquiry, the commission found that Amazon's European holding company had a profit of €301.8 million, but paid no taxes. Yet, 25% of all of Amazon's international sales took place in the UK, including inventory warehouses with 15,000 employees there. Google keeps its non-US corporate headquarters in Ireland. It had £396 million in revenues in 2011, but paid taxes of only £6 million, despite having 1300 employees there. Google keeps an entity in Bermuda to manage its intellectual property royalties.

Besides tax avoidance for the wealthy and corporations in the West, offshore financial havens serve all customers, from narco-traffickers to terrorists to corrupt officials and dictators. In fact, it was the 9/11 destruction of the World Trade Centre that spurred new action. As Brittain-Catlin (2005, 211) states:

> Post-9/11 scrutiny showed Bin Laden to be, among other things, a grand master of offshore economics. His use of established offshore networks, with their protected freedoms and secrecy setups, had bewitched investigators and was still no less impenetrable. To this he had added private banks, in Africa and elsewhere, where supervision barely existed, and a network of charities, many with legal status in Western countries....There was the *hawala* system, an international money transfer system that bypassed banks

and allowed payments to be made in one place in return for cash being provided in another, with no record of the transaction....There were the tens of thousands of "money service" businesses in the United States alone that offered easy and unsupervised check cashing, wire transfer, and currency exchange facilities, not to mention transfer points for gold, diamonds, and other precious commodities.

The results for developing countries are devastating, leading to a significant loss of revenues and helping to fuel and facilitate widespread corruption. An estimated $600 billion has left Africa since 1975, with 90% remaining abroad, making Africa a net creditor to the world (see Busumtwi-Sam's chapter in this volume). Ironically, therefore, Northern states that are relatively efficient are integral to corruption in the South (Christensen 2012, 334–335). The infamous cases of US-based Riggs Bank knowingly taking millions from Chilean dictator Pinochet and Equatorial Guinea dictator Obiang and hiding it in secret accounts in 2002–2004 are symptomatic of how the financial system abets corruption in the developing world. Widespread reports of cash payments for real estate in major cities around the world reveal the global extent of capital flight and money laundering. Corruption is one of the central obstacles to development, undermining public trust and accountability and haemorrhaging finances as well as facilitating tax evasion. New accountability arms in developing countries are thus stymied in their efforts to create transparency among public officials (Hira 2016). The Panama Papers name a number of prominent officials from the developing world, including Presidents Macri of Argentina and Correa of Ecuador.

General Measures of Offshore Finance

The revelations of the Panama Papers highlighted a series of stories around offshore financial havens that have picked up steam since the 2008 financial crisis, such as the 2008 leak about the Swiss bank UBS aiding US citizens to evade taxes and the Luxembourg Leaks of 2014 in which the ICIJ revealed corporate tax avoidance schemes leaked from consulting firm PriceWaterhouse Coopers. An emerging part of that discussion is the fact that offshore tax havens are not limited to small palm-fringed islands. The Tax Justice Network (TJN) created a financial secrecy index (http://www.financialsecrecyindex.com) to rank the lack of transparency by tax havens that begins to examine the ways to measure the activity of numerous havens. While Switzerland takes the top spot, the rest of the list is somewhat surprising. The US ranks 3rd, Germany 8th, Japan 12th, and the UK 15th.

One of the most interesting aspects of international economic analysis is the inability to trace FDI, a key financial flow for the global economy and supposedly vital to economic growth. The following graph reflects the fact that tax havens and shell corporations are used in small economies to redirect investment flows, making their origins impossible to determine with any confidence. We have ranked the top 9 economies in terms of FDI flows as a percent of gross domestic product (GDP). Notice how much larger the stocks are in the three haven countries of Ireland, Switzerland, and Luxembourg (Fig. 6.1).

We also looked at FDI inflows in total amounts for 2015. The following table shows that among the largest economies (with Russia curiously absent) are several offshore havens, including Hong Kong, Ireland, Switzerland, Singapore, British Virgin Islands, and Luxembourg who are the top recipients of FDI in total amounts. It is notable that Cayman Islands ranks three places below the bottom of this list (Table 6.1).

Why is so much of global finance going to relatively small and sometimes obscure destinations like the Cook Islands? To answer that question, we examine the basic parameters of the offshore finance world.

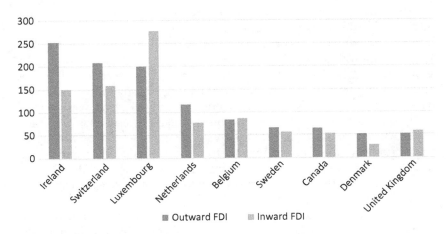

Fig. 6.1 FDI stocks, top 9 countries in 2014 (in % of GDP). (Source: Authors from OECD data)

Table 6.1   FDI flows by country, top 18 in 2015 (in $ millions)

US	379,894	Canada	48,643
Hong Kong, China	174,892	India	44,208
China	135,610	France	42,883
Ireland	100,542	UK	39,533
Netherlands	72,649	Germany	31,719
Switzerland	68,838	Belgium	31,029
Singapore	65,262	Mexico	30,285
Brazil	64,648	**Luxembourg**	24,596
British Virgin Islands	51,606	Australia	22,264

Sources: Authors from UNCTAD *World Investment Report 2016*

BASICS: HOW OFFSHORE HAVENS WORK

Underlying the issue of offshore finance is the fact that the historical basis of taxation for individuals is citizenship, but for companies it is based on where their command and control activities take place. Global taxation follows some established principles. One is that double taxation (taxing the same income twice) should be avoided. This means countries depend on citizens to report their taxes elsewhere and give them credit for doing so. Naturally, it sets up competition for lower taxation, in order to attract business and investment. A second principle is that business (active) income should be taxed primarily by the country of source and investment (passive) income by the country of residence. These two principles are increasingly difficult to put into practice and to reconcile.

Mossack Fonseca, whose e-mails were hacked to create the Panama Papers, demonstrates a rather routine set of procedures for tax evasion. In simple terms, the law firm would set up a shell corporation (formally known as an international business corporation) registered in an offshore haven such as the British Virgin Islands. There are several variations of shell companies. For example, the limited liability partnership (LLP), under which companies can set up a separate company for ownership of assets from the one creating income from those assets, again separating taxable income into a tax haven-protected entity. A protected cell company (PCC) sets up separate companies with a shared management structure. This allows for an additional layer of obfuscation of income and assets, whereby the relations and activities among the companies are unclear. One company's activities therefore, cannot lead to liability for another one. Another common practice is called an "inversion." In this case, a subsidiary is established in a tax haven and then inverts the situation by reversing roles and becoming the parent company. This allows the company to move income to no or low tax havens. The practice is widespread. Virgin Corporation licences its logo to all operations from its company based in the British Virgin Islands; Microsoft holds its copyright in its company in Ireland, where it faces lower taxes: 12.5% vs. 35% in the US (Palan et al. 2010, 88–90).

Offshore havens guarantee financial secrecy and low or non-existent tax rates for non-residents, generally in exchange for annual registration fees of a few hundred dollars. In fact, the registration requirements for companies are simplistic, meaning that little to no information about the company exists. The main loophole is based on the fact that countries tax companies based on their "tax domicile," that is, where their central management and control is located. Though companies setting up subsidiaries or headquarters in havens are prevented from focusing on local operations, as a way to prevent local companies from taking advantage of the rules, there are often requirements that locals be appointed on the board of directors and a certain number of board meetings take place there. As a result, locals frequently "rent out" their names to companies. For example, in 2012, the British Virgin Islands (BVI) had 830,000 companies registered but just 31,000 residents, as compared to Norway with 270,000 and a population of 5 million. A BVI resident had on average 27 directorships as opposed to 0.05 for Norwegians (Schjelderup 2016). In fact, in a World Bank study of offshore jurisdictions as part of its Stolen Asset Recovery programme, only one—Jersey—required a government body to record the "beneficial" owner (Van der Does de Willebois et al. 2011, 71).

Purchases of assets through company, foundation, or trust accounts are often wired through several different global accounts, sometimes with different shells, making detection by tax authorities extremely difficult. The legal fees are minimal considering the size of the assets hidden, often less than $10,000, and the accounts can be set up in a matter of hours (Gates 2016; Lipton and Creswell 2016; Christensen 2012, 333).

Individual Strategies

Offshore financial centres serve a similar role in terms of wealthy individuals seeking to avoid inheritance taxes. Individuals can set up shell corporations in which their salaries or other income is paid. They make themselves employees of the companies and then receive minimal salaries to lower income taxes. In addition, the companies can be used to re-categorise income into capital gains or dividend income to lower taxes and avoid social security payments (Palan et al. 2010, 91). An Integrated Estate Plan (IEP) is intended to protect the wealth of an individual through mitigating estate taxes and providing increased protections and control for the individual (Engel 2002, 7). As with corporations, personal trusts set up in offshore centres are not taxed, which allows wealthy individuals to avoid having their assets subjected to estate taxes. The privacy afforded by offshore trusts allows for individuals to keep the extent of the wealth private as well as to protect the estate from claims against it (Metaxatos 2008, 173–175; Engel 2002, 7–8). Any challenge or deposition of the estate must be conducted in the jurisdiction where the offshore trust operates, which typically involves significant standards of proof that fall on the challenger, thus protecting the settlor by limiting their exposure to liability. Wealth transferred to an offshore trust as part of an IEP can also be distributed in any manner the settlor of the estate chooses, allowing wealthy individuals to circumvent forced heirship laws which exist in many jurisdictions to stipulate how the estate's assets are to be distributed.

Trusts and Foundations

Trusts and foundations are popular vehicles used in offshore finance. In addition to shell companies, trusts and foundations are typically used to control offshore financial assets, such as equities and bonds, as well as tangible assets such as real estate, gold, or even yachts (Palan et al. 2010). Both entities benefit in practice from the secrecy surrounding their founders, beneficiaries, and other parties associated with their operations.

Trusts

Trusts are contractual agreements between two private individuals that create a barrier between the legal owner of an asset and its beneficiary, and this arrangement allows for the transfer of legal ownership of property or financial assets to another person on behalf of a third party (Palan et al. 2010, 92). In short, trusts are agreements whereby a third party (the trustee) manages the assets of an individual (the settlor) for the future benefit of another individual (the beneficiary). Trusts require their creators to forgo any interest from income arising from them. However, in practice, the offshore finance industry enables individuals to evade tax obligations by creating arrangements that appear like trusts; in these cases, trusts are often run by 'nominee' trustees who are residents of a tax haven (Palan et al. 2010, 92). Trustees are liable for tax on income they receive from trust assets unless that income must be paid to another person under the terms of the trust. In cases of offshore trusts, the trustees are usually professionals who ensure that trusts earn and accumulate income tax-free. Because such trusts are located offshore, they do not have to declare to tax authorities the payment of income to beneficiaries that do not live in the tax haven where the trusts are located—income is paid into beneficiaries' offshore accounts without the knowledge of home jurisdictions. Once assets are transferred to an offshore trust, it is difficult to trace them back to their owners, which is compounded by the widespread absence of registration procedures (Palan et al. 2010, 93).

Van der Does de Willebois et al. (2011) claim that the majority of trusts are used for legitimate purposes, such as estate planning, managing charitable donations, and corporate functions such as isolating funding for an employee pension plan from a business' assets. However, Christensen (2012) notes that charitable trusts are regularly established for the purpose of owning 'special purpose vehicles' used for international tax planning and hiding assets and liabilities off balance sheets. With a few exceptions, no jurisdiction currently requires trusts to register in a publicly accessible register and many, such as Panama, have enacted strict confidentiality laws, prohibiting the disclosure of information regarding trusts (van der Does de Willebois et al. 2011, Tax Justice Network 2009). In regard to Panama, only trusts holding property in Panama must be registered, and the agent must be a Panamanian lawyer (van der Does de Willebois et al. 2011).

Trusts are effective for evading/avoiding taxes due to two main reasons: the separation of parties involved in their establishment, and the secrecy surrounding them. Once a trust is formed, its assets legally do not belong to the settlor or to beneficiary parties, though the trustee has a fiduciary duty to manage the assets (van der Does de Willebois et al. 2011). With the separation of legal and beneficial ownership, it is often difficult for private or public parties to enforce claims against these assets unless it can be demonstrated that the trust was specifically established to evade claimants such as creditors (van der Does de Willebois et al. 2011). The separation between parties also complicates how to tax the trust, and authorities cannot easily find the assets to tax them due to secrecy (Tax Justice Network 2009). Further, even if a trustee can be discovered, the trustee may be bound by a confidentiality agreement not to reveal who the settlors or beneficiaries are, and oftentimes in a jurisdiction with secrecy, the trustee will be an anonymous trust company that specialises in being a trustee for many trusts, with no clue to suggest who the settlor or beneficiaries are (Tax Justice Network 2009).

Foundations

Foundations can be best described as a form of trust recognised as having a separate legal existence similar to a limited company (Palan et al. 2010, 93). Foundations are a form of 'unowned' economic entity, whereby contributors cede rights of ownership, control, and beneficial interest from donated assets to the foundation, and in many jurisdictions, foundations are simply corporate vehicles intended to benefit a cause rather than to provide a return on investment (van der Does de Willebois et al. 2011). Foundations traditionally require that property from donors be dedicated to a particular purpose, and income derived from assets is used to fulfil the intended purpose (van der Does de Willebois et al. 2011). Among the principal tax havens, the Netherlands Antilles, Austria, Denmark, Panama, the Netherlands, Liechtenstein, and Switzerland allow the creation of private foundations, and many tax havens demand only minimal disclosure; in an extreme case, no approval is needed to create one in Panama (Palan et al. 2010). In terms of registration, Panama only requires that a foundation's charter be filed with the Public Registry Office (van der Does de Willebois et al. 2011). The success of foundations is due to their combination of secrecy with a legal existence separating them from the lawyer that manages them and from the settlor, and their non-taxable status (Palan et al. 2010).

Tax Abuse of Charities

Based on results from its 2008 survey, the OECD (2009) identified numerous methods by which charities' tax-exempt status is abused for tax evasion and money laundering. Tax authorities across 19 countries identified many general methods and schemes, including, among many others:

- An organisation poses as a registered charity to perpetrate tax fraud;
- A charity wilfully participates in a tax evasion scheme to benefit its organisers or directors, which can occur with or without an intermediary's assistance;

- A charity is unknowingly abused by a taxpayer or third party, such as a tax return preparer who prepared and submitted false charitable receipts;
- Issuing receipts for payments that are not true donations;
- Misuse of charity funds by charities;
- Criminals using charity names to collect money;
- Terrorist organisations using charities to raise or transfer funds to support terrorist organisations; and
- Manipulation of the value of donated assets.

The most prevalent scheme identified involves charities selling donation receipts for a commission. Under this scheme, a donor may receive amounts such as $10,000 in donation receipts for a $1000 cash payment to a charity. The OECD estimates that a government may end up paying 40% for each $1 in false donations, and very little (if any) of the donation money ends up supporting a charitable purpose. The Canada Revenue Agency noticed that charities and tax return preparers who had previously been identified as being involved in false receipting continue to issue false receipts.

Tax authorities use several indicators to detect possible cases of tax evasion and/or money laundering involving the abuse of charities. These include taxpayers who report low or moderate income abruptly changing their donation patterns; taxpayers with no donation history suddenly making donations in varying ranges; high ratios of donation amounts to net incomes; multiple charitable causes with no apparent connection; donors with the same community/cultural backgrounds and relationships; donors working together in similar work or for the same large company; donors providing insufficient documentation or information when approached by tax authorities; and loopholes around donations, such as taxpayers making donations under $500.

Examples of Corporate Strategies Including Transfer Pricing

A practice that has received a great deal of attention is "transfer pricing." Generally, businesses buy and sell services at prices dictated by the market, a price usually considered to be at "arms length"—for example, when two unrelated parties have made an arrangement that reflects current market valuations in relation to the provision of such services. When the parties to the transaction are related, the price is not considered to be a fair market price, but a "transfer price." A multinational corporation can benefit from such practices due to differential tax rates (McCann 2006, 115). Such tax rates provide incentives for a corporate entity to establish decentralised autonomous entities in tax haven jurisdictions, which are nevertheless vertically integrated within the entire structure of the multinational corporation (Cecchini et al. 2013, 32).

The general approach is to create an associated corporate entity operating in a jurisdiction with a lower tax rate than that of the parent company. Under this strategy, the company raises the price of purchases and lowers the price of goods and services sold by branches in high tax jurisdictions to other branches in lower tax ones. It is difficult to detect this strategy as there may not be readily available prices for comparable items. Profits can be shifted to holding companies in tax havens such as the Caymans where there is no tax. Typically, such international or offshore business companies pay no tax if their revenue did not originate in the offshore financial centre (McCann 2006, 61–62). The result of such transfer pricing is to effectively transfer profits into low- or no- tax jurisdictions.

A 2015 Congressional Research Service report (Gravelle 2015, 9–14) offers a useful overview of how US corporations use offshore finance to avoid tax through common practices, including transfer pricing. Income earned by foreign subsidiaries is not taxed by the US until it is repatriated to the US parent as dividends, with some exceptions related to passive income (Subpart F). Credit for foreign income taxes is also given upon repatriation to avoid double taxation, excluding domestic income. Furthermore, companies use the practice of "earnings stripping" whereby the borrowing is done by related firms or through foreign borrowers who are not subject to US taxation. Firms use "inversion," by which they move the parent company abroad, or merge with a smaller foreign company, so that US operations become a subsidiary. Companies may also prefer to use contracts with a company in a high tax area to avoid reporting profits earned in that country. Under cross crediting, firms can use foreign tax credits to reduce their US taxes once they repatriate profits. The practices of corporate tax mitigation are an industry for consultants and lawyers seeking to find opportunities in the global financial system and emerging technological and geographic markets (Gilligan 2004, 22).

A related practice is to use interest payments to dodge taxes. For example, capital is borrowed in a high tax area, where interest payments are deductible, and shifted to a low tax area where expenditures take place. Similarly, interest payments can be received in a low/no tax area. Moreover, lending charges to subsidiaries can be inflated to move funds to low tax jurisdictions. Companies avoid payroll taxes by placing employees under a foreign subsidiary, even when they are working in the home country. Hybrid mismatch arrangements are when a company reports an income payment for deduction purposes in one entity but does not report the income in the jurisdiction of the receiver. Even more common is to use trademarks, copyrights, and patents to shift valuation, as it is exceedingly hard to put a valuation on them (Beer and Loeprick 2015; Karkinsky and Riedel 2012). Detection can be particularly difficult in MNEs (multinational enterprises, aka MNCs) that cross multiple sectors. As Palan et al. (2010, 91) conclude: "The offshore operations of many MNCs are a charade."

Multinationals also profit from offshore centres through specialised mechanisms to manage corporate debt (McCann 2006, 60). Specialised debt management entities are known as special purpose vehicles (SPVs), which involve the pooling of the debt of the parent company and transferring it to an associated or subsidiary entity. This is done in order to shield investors of the originating institution from the credit risk associated with the debt (Stowell 2010, 48). SPVs can take a number of forms, all of which involve securitisation, through the transferring of assets and debt to a separate legal entity (456–457). Collateralised debt obligations (CDOs) are securities where the debt in question is backed by other assets in various tranches which compensate the purchaser for the risk of default (49), or as a similar security where the backing assets are high-yield bonds (collateralised bond obligations, or CBOs). Securitisation of debt can also occur through credit default swaps, where the party purchasing the security is paid if the underlying debt results in a default, (106), and in structured investment vehicles (SIVs), which generate returns through credit spreads between the assets and liabilities (185). SIVs operating offshore or with other offshore subsidiaries serve a dual role in both mitigating credit risk as well as generating profits that are taxed at a much lower level (if taxed at all) than they would be if the SIV was operated domestically. As Gaillard and Harrington (2016) note, SPVs and SIVs are often used to ostensibly mitigate risk from balance sheets and avoid downgrading of corporate debt (see also Gaillard and Michalek's chapter in this volume).

These debt management systems and other complex, dynamic tax avoidance schemes are notoriously difficult for regulators to monitor, as demonstrated by their role in the 2008 financial crisis (Hetzel 2012, 181–183). The overall effect of offshore havens, in relation to multinational transfer pricing and SIVs, is to create a system where the investments and structures of multinational corporations become virtually untraceable.

Last but not least, MNEs set up "captive insurance companies." They are created in tax havens to manage risk and minimise taxes. They allow companies to reduce reserve and capital requirements and manage catastrophic risk through reinsurance systems, whereby the reinsurer agrees to pay out some of the claims of the original insurer. Palan et al. (2010, 96–97) estimate that at least 5000 such companies existed as of 2007, with Bermuda, the Cayman Islands, Vermont, the British Virgin Islands, and Guernsey heading the list.

Money Laundering

The same mechanisms that allow for tax mitigation for corporations and individuals can be used for money laundering. The goal of money laundering is to integrate funds garnered through illegal activities into the legitimate finances of the launderer though disguising/"anonymising" the source of the funds and conferring an appearance of legitimacy.

Money laundering takes place in three main steps: placement, layering, and integration. Placement is the step where the funds that are to be laundered are placed in a financial institution, through depositing cash, the use of wire transfers or checks, or the transfer of gold or other luxury goods (Turner 2011, 8–9, 73). Layering: this step involves stratifying the financial transaction—other transactions are conducted with, and around, the capital that is to be laundered. This can involve moving funds from one account to another, from institution to institution, shifting the money from one asset type to another through various accounts related to shell companies. The layering process can also include various financial accounts associated with the purchase of high-value items, currency equipment sales, as well as the purchase of legitimate business or real estate (9). Integration, the final step, involves returning the laundered capital back to the perpetrator. The goal would be to use mechanisms that will withstand ordinary scrutiny and hence will give the sought legitimacy. This often takes the form of loans from the layered transactions or holding/front companies back to the perpetrator (9–10, 74, 89–90).

The banks themselves also play a role in the integration stage, where the laundered funds are reincorporated into the finances of the launderer. As noted above, the goal of money laundering is to achieve the appearance of legitimacy of the funds at this stage. In order to accomplish this, money laundering uses the participation or inclusion of otherwise law-abiding citizens or entities (Turner 2011, 7). Banks can either directly or inadvertently facilitate money laundering by providing launderers with the ability to move and layer their funds. Banks are already involved with the movement of large sums of money, which aids in disguising the origin and destination of proceeds from illegal activities (15–16). When the funds are sent back to the launderer, either as a transfer or as a loan, they appear to be coming from corporate entities through legitimate banks operating in foreign countries, thus conveying a sense of legitimacy of the source of the funds. One can readily see, then, how the offshore financial systems of obfuscation, including shell companies, can readily lend themselves to money laundering.

Reform Efforts

The problems of offshore finance have been known for decades, resulting in a series of reform efforts. Some of the efforts are oriented towards greater transparency of legitimate flows for taxation purposes, while others target illicit flows. Below we discuss the major efforts and their shortcomings.

TIEAs and the FATF

In 2002, the OECD developed the Model Agreement on Exchange of Information in Tax Matters (TIEAs, or Tax Information Exchange Agreements). This derived from concerns related to the loss of revenues to money laundering. These concerns led to the creation of the Financial Action Task Force (FATF, www.fatf-gafi.org/about), an intergovernmental group that came out of the G-7 meeting in Paris in 1989. The FATF sets out guidelines for measures to counter money laundering and terrorist financing. It includes self- and peer assessments of reporting and, from 2000, a list of non-cooperative countries that could be sanctioned. It has regional offices around the world (Jakobi 2015). Such efforts pushed the OECD to release its 1998 report *Harmful Tax Competition: An Emerging Global Issue*. The OECD set up model agreements that could be signed bilaterally for the disclosure of financial information. While not binding, peer pressure placed on offshore havens led to a large number of them signing the agreements, through the threat of blacklisting. The 1998 report was the start of a wave of policy innovation aimed to deal with off-shore evasion, but, as we discuss below, with very limited effectiveness.

According to Deneault (2015, 49), TIEAs are full of loopholes. For example, Canada uses them to attract capital from Caribbean countries into its financial system to avoid local taxes, as under the agreement they are not taxed in Canada. Under its TIEA with Switzerland, if the government wanted information on a Canadian's supposed assets there, it would have to provide details on the individual's banking operations, information which it does not have because the TIEA does not allow for the free flow of information! (127) Moreover, there are no time limits for responding to requests for information from Canadian authorities (Kerzner and Chodikoff 2016, 404). Deneault therefore concludes that Canada's apparent moves to fight against tax evasion are nothing more than "smoke and mirrors" (190). His conclusion is reinforced by a study commissioned by the Norwegian Government, which concludes that tax treaties do nothing to improve transparency or the transfer of funds back to the country where companies are domiciled (Government of Norway 2009, 13).

US FATCA (Foreign Account Tax Compliance Act)

Earnest reform in the US came after the release of secret documents in 2007 by Bradley Birkenfeld of UBS bank revealing that many US citizens were evading taxes by placing money in secret accounts in Switzerland. The subsequent indictments helped to bring down Switzerland's oldest (270 years) bank Wegelin in 2013. In 2010, the US enacted Foreign Account Tax Compliance Act (FATCA) in order to force overseas banks to disclose information about Americans holding accounts abroad. FATCA also applies to other financial entities, such as foundations. It imposes a 30% withholding tax against non-compliant financial institutions. In 2012, France, Germany, Italy, Spain, and the UK issued a joint statement in support of FATCA (Rahimi-Laridjani and Hauser 2016, 10). FATCA is to be extended to a number of Caribbean havens from 2017 (Snyder 2015). Unfortunately, as we discuss below, the US has refused to extend reciprocity.

OECD-CRS

In response to FATCA, in 2014, the OECD developed a similar provision called the Common Reporting Standard (CRS). The CRS Handbook with guidelines for information sharing was published in 2015. As of 2016, 96 jurisdictions had signed onto CRS, with the first exchanges of information to take place in 2017 (Rahimi-Laridjani and Hauser 2016, 10). The CRS is one part of the GATCA, or Global FATCA, which seeks to extend FATCA rules overseas. There are many jurisdictions that fall outside of CRS.

In April 2016, the OECD joined with the IMF, the UN, and the World Bank to announce "the Platform for Collaboration on Tax," to coordinate their research efforts in response to states' concerns about tax evasion. The OECD's Base Erosion and Profit Shifting Package (BEPS) (https://www.oecd.org/tax/beps/beps-about.htm) is an effort to address the loss of tax revenue from the use of offshore financial centres, dating from 2013. It estimates that between $100 and 240 billion are lost annually. It suggests diplomatically that "gaps and mismatches" in tax rules lead to profit shifting to low or no tax havens. BEPS includes developing countries. BEPS has four main initiatives (background brief). The first is "model provisions" for treaties between countries that impede the use of "conduit" (shell) companies to channel investments to lower tax jurisdictions. It refers here to treaties between states in regard to tax provisions. The second is "country-by-country reporting" on MNE profits, tax and other activities to assist auditors. The third is "a revitalised peer review process to address harmful tax practices" including patent boxes and a commitment to transparency, referring to the sharing of information. Patent boxes refers to preferential tax treatment for income deriving from an innovation. Companies sometimes park a patent in a country even if innovation activity is not taking place there to take advantage of such provisions. The final one is "an agreement to secure progress on dispute resolution" through "the mutual agreement procedure" (MAP). The challenges here beyond compliance include how to value intangible goods often used in transfer pricing, such as royalties for intellectual property, including trademarks.

The EU Savings Taxation Directive and Directive on Administrative Cooperation

The European Union (EU) has been at the forefront in the development of mechanisms for automatic information exchange (Christensen III and Tirard 2016). On July 1, 2005, the EU's Savings Taxation Directive (the Directive)—formally Council Directive 2003/48/EC—came into force.

Politically, the Directive's fruition was dependent upon the cooperation of non-member jurisdictions (Sharman 2008). The Directive's goal was to allow EU member states to tax the foreign interest income of their residents (Hemmelgarn and Nicodème 2009), who were deemed "beneficial owners" as they were interest income recipients. Originally, the Directive utilised automatic information exchange but allowed Austria, Belgium, and Luxembourg to levy a 35% withholding tax for a transitional period. Under this arrangement, the three member states did not share information but shared 75% of the revenue from the withholding tax with the member state of the beneficial owner's residence. However, this arrangement was transitional as there was to be full disclosure once secrecy laws were revised by January 1, 2015 (Christensen III and Tirard 2016). Various member state-dependent territories, including several Caribbean jurisdictions, and Lichtenstein, Switzerland, Andorra, Monaco, and San Marino, also maintained a withholding tax regime (Michaels et al. 2007).

The Directive's limitations included that only individuals (natural persons) were to be taxed. This led to evasion through routing of interest payments via intermediaries so that final payment is made by an agent outside the EU. There is also a lack of clarity on its application regarding innovative financial products (Michaels et al. 2007). In regard to the entities liable for taxation, Swiss tax authorities issued a memo stating legal entities that did not fall under the Directive's scope included companies in the Cayman and Virgin Islands, trusts and companies in the Bahamas, companies and foundations in Panama, and trusts, holdings, and foundations in Liechtenstein, among others (Zucman 2015, 71). However, Sharman (2008) notes that despite the predictions of capital flight, major financial centres among EU member states and dependent territories enjoyed steady growth, and regulatory arbitrage and capital flight failed to emerge. Though there was some movement of funds to Singapore, Hong Kong, and other non-participating countries, the magnitude of outward capital flows was far lower than would be needed to explain the low tax revenue totals (Sharman 2008). Sharman concludes it is not so much the power of capital flight that frustrated the European Commission's ambitions, but rather the loopholes created during the negotiation process, especially those pushed by the UK and Luxembourg including the exemption of companies, trusts, many kinds of bonds, and innovative financial products.

The Directive's lukewarm effectiveness was echoed by the EU's own research. Deposits from non-bank depositors did shift to third countries outside the Directive's scope, but this was a trend before the Directive came into force, though its anticipation could have induced some investors to shift their deposits. Hemmelgarn and Nicodème (2009) further found that while there was a shift from interest to dividend income, the Directive did not lead to major changes in European households' savings income. The weakness was attributed to the Directive's loopholes, including its narrow geographical scope, its definition of beneficial owner that did not include entities such as companies, and its narrow definition of interest that did not capture more innovative financial products and life insurance products (Hemmelgarn and Nicodème 2009). More recent research found that the main effect of the Directive was encouraging more Europeans to transfer wealth to shell corporations, trusts, and foundations, with the most visible case being Switzerland. In 2005, six months after the withholding tax's introduction, the accounts in Switzerland owned by shell companies increased by 10% over 2004 levels (Zucman 2015, 72).

Major Obstacles to Resolution

The following section reviews issues that stand in the way of creating a more transparent, accountable, and stable global financial system. While technical in nature, behind them as discussed earlier is the strength of financial lobbies. Undoubtedly, the pressure is present on both sides of the Atlantic, as the financial sector in the UK has also chafed against greater EU-based regulations.

Continuing Lack of Transparency

What constitutes transparency in financial markets? In introducing their financial secrecy index, Cobham et al. (2015) suggest three main factors, whether (i) relevant information is on public record and accessible; (ii) access to certain private financial data is available to relevant public authorities, such as tax administrations and police; and (iii) information is shared effectively with foreign counterparts. To a large extent, the modern system, which relies upon bank reporting of suspicious activity (suspicious activity reports, or SARS, in the US) under the guise of "customer due diligence" or "know your customer" guidelines, falls far short of such principles. There are reasons to be doubtful about the effectiveness of SARS based on the lack of correlation with prosecutions. Non-currency transactions are even harder to track; banks are rarely required to report on wire transfers (Cuéllar 2003, 425 and 432). Even if frequent wire transfers take place, criminals use "smurfing," breaking cash up into smaller pieces and using proxies so that the connections among them are very hard to establish.

In terms of transfer pricing, Article 9 of the OECD's Model Tax Convention suggests that MNCs should use the "arm's length principle," whereby transactions between associated units should be seen as though one were selling to a separate entity. Thus, each transaction should be comparable to what would occur with a third party. However, multiple research papers show that such principles are ignored in practice, though it is difficult to separate out transfers in estimations (Hunter et al. 2015, 76).

OECD and other efforts have fallen short in terms of information exchange, leading some to question basic principles about taxation. For example, some scholars are now arguing for a "limitation on benefits" principle to avoid double non-taxation. That is, where the preferred jurisdiction, such as an offshore haven that is the home of a company, does not tax, the secondary jurisdiction, such as the US where a company operates, should (Avi-Yonah 2015, 310). The OECD places emphasis on transfer pricing guidelines in regard to intangibles, a generic category used by companies in financial reporting. Intangibles can be anything from intellectual property to trademarks to software use. There is no question that intangibles are growing in importance in economic activity; however, there is limited knowledge about how to harness or develop them productively. The OECD uses the term "value creation" as a way to locate where taxation should take place, that is, where substantive economic activities are located vs. where they are reported. There is also concern with base erosion through interest expense deductions, which can be abused through intra-group or third party loans that are used specifically for the purpose of reducing revenue reporting. The OECD seeks to avoid "hybrid mismatch arrangements" through greater tax coordination. Examples given are: "costly multiple deductions for a single expense, deductions in one country without corresponding taxation in another, and the generation of multiple foreign tax credits for one amount of foreign tax paid" (OECD 2015, 13).

The US and the EU have reached several impasses in regard to information exchange. In general, a lack of harmonisation and fragmentation of institutional reporting across jurisdictions inhibit information flow (Takáts 2007, 235–236). Moreover, many banks see third party software and training as sufficient to check for money laundering (Liss and Sharman 2015). Levi (2007, 275) concludes that the software currently being used depends upon "the automated checking of multiple lists (where name spellings themselves generate many false positives and opportunities for evasion through slight spelling changes)," and "there are no clear models available to predict which funds are likely to be used for criminal or terrorist purposes and which are not."

Ineffective Action on Terrorist Financing

The US, for example, has initiated the Terrorist Finance Tracking Program (TFTP) whereby it shares with Europe SWIFT (Society for World Interbank Financial Telecommunications) data related to interbank transfers. However, the European Parliament has raised objections to the TFTP including not agreeing with the list of terrorist groups and privacy concerns (Kingah and Zwartjes 2015). The dispute over TFTP appears to have been worked out, partly through maintaining data in Europe and allowing Europol to refuse requests for data by the US Treasury. However, terrorists have effectively responded to these efforts through several adjustments. They may not launder money at all, using legitimate businesses to send money to individuals, or using the *hawala* informal networks common in the Islamic world and involving person to person lending. Some estimate *hawala* flows to be at least $200 billion annually. While cash may be given in one country after a signal from an informal *hawaladar* network agent, payment may be received in a variety of ways, from payment through other transactions to the receipt of goods or favours (Razavy and Haggerty 2009). Because *hawala* is a response, in part, to Islamic proscriptions against usury, and in part based upon informal networks of trust, it is highly unlikely that any formal regulatory process will be able to monitor it (Razavy 2005). Beyond this, terror groups and the financiers (reportedly some with indirect ties to the Saudi royal family) have used religious non-profit organisations as conduits for financial flows and investments, sometime using shell corporations and couriers to cover their tracks (Raphaeli 2003). The general granting of tax-free status to religious organisations in the West helps to obscure their activities.

If non-profit organisations are used, the chances of detection are slim as this sector is poorly regulated. Furthermore, the shift to low-cost tactics such as lone wolf attacks in Nice and San Bernardino in 2015–2016 means that financing can be done by the individuals themselves. In fact, terror groups have diversified their funding sources so that if one stream is detected several others take its place (Shillito 2015). Last but not least, the shift from the use of wire transfers to mobile money or bitcoin transfers creates even more challenges for tracking (Vlcek 2012). We should point out that the costs for most terrorist activities are quite small. The estimates for the costs of the 9/11 attacks are put at $500,000 and for the bombings in Bali, London, and Madrid at 1/10th of that (Sharman 2011, 31).

By contrast, for the most egregious cases, there appears to be some effort to crack down on the purchases of assets by corrupt strongmen from the developing world. For example, in 2016, under the new Kleptocracy Initiative and requirements to reveal cash buyers of high-end real estate in 2016, the US Department of Justice prosecuted several cases of corruption of public funds used to purchase assets in the US, including cases against the ruler of Equatorial Guinea, the sovereign wealth manager of Malaysia, with direct ties to the Prime Minister, and the daughter of the President of Uzbekistan. Reports noted that most of the transactions took place through shell corporations.[1]

However, given that the vast majority of financial transactions in the developing world are outside the banking system, and that the banks there lack management and information capacity, it seems difficult to create adequate information flows for many transactions. Indeed, Eckert and Biersteker (2010, 253, 257, and 263) note that despite the US government's self-assessed grade of "A-" on efforts to combat terrorist financing, some US government officials themselves admit that most metrics to monitor the assets of terrorists are seriously flawed, and that it is "impossible" to stop financial flows to terrorists. The best that can be hoped for is to "constrict" the environment. They conclude that "terrorist financing remains a little understood and inadequately researched topic (263)."

Lack of Enforcement Tools

Even if information exchange is established, it will be insufficient to prevent evasion and money laundering. The FATF process of mutual

---

[1] See, for example, http://www.nytimes.com/2016/02/17/business/wanted-by-the-us-the-stolen-millions-of-despots-and-crooked-elites.html   and   http://www.nytimes.com/news-event/shell-company-towers-of-secrecy-real-estate

evaluations focuses on legislation and the existence of a financial intelligence unit (FIU) but largely ignores the effectiveness of ongoing monitoring, implementation, and enforcement activities (Biersteker et al. 2007, 241). Tsingou (2010, 623–624) concludes that efforts to combat terrorist financing and money laundering have been ineffective. Membership in FATF has been too limited; for example, the United Arab Emirates (UAE, an emerging financial hub) is not included. Moreover, removal from the non-compliant "blacklist" has been perfunctory following legislative changes to the banking system. Even within nations, such as the US, there is a lack of clarity over regulatory oversight roles. She therefore concludes (629) about the anti-money laundering/counter financing of terrorism regimes that both do "not rely on provable effectiveness but rather, (are) is mostly symbolic; the more honest aim of the regime is to serve wide ranging policy goals without actually threatening the core of the financial system."

The OECD highlights the particularly vexing issues of how to establish the presence of a "permanent entity," meaning even if a company has a nominal headquarters elsewhere, it has an effective (and taxable) presence in a particular area. The second issue is how to evaluate transfer pricing so that it is reasonable. A third is to try to avoid both zero and double taxation, requiring considerably improved coordination of both codes and reporting (OECD 2015, 13). After an extensive review, Sharman (2011, 43 and 50) concludes that the FATF, while improving information recording and accountability, has made no discernible impact on money laundering. At the same time, it has vastly increased the costs for compliance. Even when anti-money laundering cases are found, as was the case with Lloyds, Credit Suisse, and Barclays in 2009, there is little in terms of consequences beyond "transitory embarrassment."

The think tank/NGO Tax Justice Network (TJN) (http://www.taxjustice.net/2015/10/05/press-release-oecds-beps-proposals-will-not-be-the-end-of-tax-avoidance-by-multinationals/) criticised the OECD for not going far enough in its proposals. While lauding the OECD's requirement that companies provide "country-by-country" reporting of profit, activity, employment, and sales in each country where they operate, they note such reports will only be filed with home country tax authorities, not made public (or available to other countries). Under its FAQ section, the OECD's BEPS project notes that efforts are "soft" legal instruments, meaning that they are not binding. The main tangible outcomes seem to be increasing pressure on disclosure of account holders, which has already put pressure on the Swiss banking system. However, whether such efforts will be effective in the multitude of other offshore havens is dubitable.

In sum, as with most other global issues, transparency and enforcement are lacking. In regard to TIEAs (Tax Information Exchange Agreements), the state requesting information must provide "significant accurate information" regarding "a specific person, transaction, account, trust or company," along with evidence about "why it believes the requested jurisdiction holds the information in question and demonstrate that it has exhausted all other means of information" (within reason). Trusts are considered private agreements and are not subject to public disclosure rules. Even where company registries exist in offshore havens, they tend to have scant information. In fact, the FATF has been largely ignored in practice. There is very little to no reporting of important financial transactions used by money launderers through non-financial agents, such as casinos; real estate agents; precious metals/stones or high-value goods (such as art or antiques) dealers; lawyers, accountants, and consultants; and trust companies (Choo 2014). Common practices include exchanging cash for chips and then getting clean money at casinos; hiring third parties who are clean to send money transfers; purchasing insurance and then recouping money through false claims with kickbacks to the insurance companies; falsifying invoices to hide higher revenues; purchasing gems or precious metals, such as gold; and using prepaid credit or gift or phone cards (Unger 2007, 133, 139, 144, and 147). Problems extend to sea transport, where flags of convenience allow vessels to avoid fishing licences or abide by environmental or labour standards. Similarly, many airline companies use leased planes from companies registered in offshore havens (Shillito 2015; Schjelderup 2016). Ultimately, illicit cash flows are intricately intertwined with legal ones, making detection exceedingly difficult.

Lack of US Reciprocity

In line with FATCA, the IRS (Internal Revenue Service) of the US offered citizens offshore voluntary disclosure programmes from 2009 whereby criminal penalties would be waived if overseas accounts designed for tax evasion were disclosed within a grace period, subject to payment of modest penalties. The IRS also used information from the efforts to track down other citizens who had not reported. The programme was considered a major success bringing in an estimated $5.5 billion from 2009 to 2012. However, a 2013 GAO (Government Accountability Office) report concluded that billions more were offshore and that data existed to find them. Moreover, the IRS was inadequately publicising its programmes to US citizens living abroad.

Despite serious efforts by the US under FATCA to obtain more information about Americans holding money overseas, it does not provide nearly the same level of information to other countries about their citizens' holdings in the US. While it promised reciprocity in principle, it has not provided any timetable for achieving it. The US has not complied with CRS reporting requirements (Knobel 2015). In fact, there are many ways that non-US citizens can avoid reporting requirements for deposits held in the US. This raises the spectre that US citizens will find non-citizens to act as trustees for them while keeping their holdings in the US without reporting them (Cotorceanu 2015). There are also loopholes in CRS reporting requirements. Moreover, CRS does not impose penalties; these are left up to individual jurisdictions to decide. More problematic still is the lack of a global registration process for determining whether a financial institution is consistently compliant. There are naturally serious concerns within the banking community about these new reporting requirements (Rahimi-Laridjani and Hauser 2016, 13–14; Knobel and Meinzer 2014). By one estimate, the US is the destination for 18.9% of all global money laundering or $538.1 billion, more than four times the amount going to the next destination, Cayman Islands (Schneider 2013, 691).

US efforts to promote global tax reform appear duplicitous in light of the emerging facts. In the aforementioned Findley study sending out e-mail incorporation requests to legal firms around the world, the differences in level of compliance with international standards between international providers and US providers were remarkable. Only 16.4% of those in the international pool did not require any photo identification to open a shell corporation, while a staggering 41.5% in the US pool were similarly negligent. In fact, only 9 of the 1772 US providers contacted required full, certified identification disclosure (Findley et al. 2014, 170). A World Bank report notes the following numbers of international business corporations: 500,000 (40%) in the British Virgin Islands, with around 70,000 new companies formed each year; Panama with 320,000; and Belize, the Seychelles, the Bahamas, and the Caymans with approximately 50,000–70,000 companies each. In the UK, around 362,000 companies were formed in 2009–2010. By contrast, there are a total of 18 million corporations in the US, and approximately 2 million new ones per year (Van der Does de Willebois et al. 2011, 136–137). A 2016 USA Today investigation of the Panama Papers revealed that more than 1000 shell companies were set up in US states including Nevada, Wyoming, Delaware, and Florida. Only 100 of these had officers based in the US. More than 600 of the remaining had addresses in Panama or the Seychelles. Nevada- and Wyoming-based corporations have been tied to scandals in Argentina, the Operation Car Wash involving the Brazilian state oil company, Petrobras, and a corruption scandal at FIFA, the global soccer federation.[2] In fact, states are free to write their own trust laws, allowing for individuals to shield their assets. This has led to states such as Nevada to become havens for secret trusts, followed more recently by others, such as New Hampshire, in a race to the bottom.[3] States such as Delaware act as nominal headquarters for companies, allowing them to avoid paying state taxes where activity takes place. An estimated $9.5 billion in taxes from 2002 to 2012 was saved that way. Before WorldCom collapsed in 2002, it shifted $19.4 billion in intellectual property to a holding company in Delaware to reduce taxes. Corrupt figures from Viktor Bout, the Russian arms dealer known as the "merchant of death" to Jack Abramoff use the remarkably easy procedures to set up sham "shell" corporations.[4] As a result, Delaware is the state of incorporation for many of the largest US corporations, including Wal-Mart, Exxon Mobil, Chevron, Berkshire Hathaway, Apple, GM, GE, and Ford. It is the legal home, in fact, of 54% of all public companies. Fees from companies constitute 26% of the state budget or $1 billion in 2015.[5] Nevada had 307,210 corporate entities listed in the state as of August 2016, 22,060 of which had addresses from outside the US. In 2015–2016, the state collected nearly $144 million from corporate registrations, filings, and associated charges. Its history as a tax shelter

[2] http://www.usatoday.com/story/news/2016/04/07/1000-secret-nevada-firms-and-most-trace-2-overseas-addresses/82760186

[3] Patricia Cohen. 2016. States Vie to Shield the Wealth of the 1 Percent. August 8. *New York Times*. http://www.nytimes.com/2016/08/09/business/states-vie-to-protect-the-wealth-of-the-1-percent.html [accessed October 6, 2016].

[4] Leslie Wayne. 2012. How Delaware Thrives as a Corporate Tax Haven. June 30. *Washington Post*. http://www.nytimes.com/2012/07/01/business/how-delaware-thrives-as-a-corporate-tax-haven.html [accessed October 6, 2016] and Lynnley Browning. 2009. Critics Call Delaware a Tax Haven. May 30. *New York Times*. http://www.nytimes.com/2009/05/30/business/30delaware.html [accessed October 6, 2016].

[5] Liz Hoffman. 2015. Dole and Other Companies Sour on Delaware as Corporate Tax Haven. August 2. *Wall Street Journal*. http://www.wsj.com/articles/dole-and-other-companies-sour-on-delaware-as-corporate-haven-1438569507 [accessed October 6, 2016].

dates back to 1991, when lawmakers decided to compete with Delaware as a centre for incorporation. In 1996, they passed a law that any tax increase would require a 2/3 vote in both the Senate and Assembly. In 2001, they went further by limiting corporate liability. You can register a corporation or partnership online in ten minutes in Nevada *without providing any identification*.[6] A World Bank study suggests that US jurisdictions are among the worst in terms of the amount of information required for company/trust registration (Van der Does de Willebois et al. 2011, 92).

Companies use their Delaware/Nevada incorporations to avoid paying taxes in part through transfer pricing. In the WorldCom case, royalty payments were made by entities in other states to the Delaware incorporation. These payments are not subject to tax, and reduce the earnings and thereby tax payments elsewhere. Another dodge involves using a Real Estate Investment Trust (REIT), which, once incorporated into Delaware, can receive rent payments from subsidiaries. These are tax-free since Delaware does not have corporate taxes on investment income. Estimates by *The Wall Street Journal* are that Walmart avoided paying $230 million in state taxes this way from 1998 to 2001. Similar schemes are used around intellectual property payments. However, there are new arguments by other states that "economic nexus" or where economic activity takes place requires some payment of local taxes (Dyreng et al. 2013).

Based on reporting by the CBC and Toronto Star, Canada is increasingly being used a tax haven as well, which they call "snow washing." Canada does not require companies at either the federal or provincial level to list the name of real owners or operators. Limited partnerships do not have to pay taxes in Canada if owners do not live there. The Panama Papers revealed that Mossack Fonseca used Canada regularly to launder money from South America, wiring transactions through Canadian shell companies and reporting to the Canada Revenue Agency that "no activity to report" meant that no tax was due. Equally invidious is the use of TIEA agreement countries to hide Canadian money. Reports reveal that Canadian corporations and individuals have parked at $80 billion in Barbados. More than 1000 Canadian companies including stalwarts such

---

[6] McClatchy Washington Bureau. 2016. Nevada shelters offshore shell companies. *Times Record*. August 14. http://www.swtimes.com/news/20160814/nevada-shelters-offshore-shell-companies [accessed October 6, 2016].

as Petro-Canada and Loblaws have subsidiaries there. The *Toronto Star*, in addition, reported on several individuals who had hired out their names as corporate directors to hundreds of Canadian companies, when they had nothing to do with them (Dubinsky 2016a, b; Oved and Cribb 2017; and Seglins et al. 2017). A September 2016 assessment of Canada, while generally positive, states that there is "a high risk of misuse" of nominee ownership because of a lack of meaningful beneficial ownership requirements (FATF and AMG 2016, 7–8). Moreover, a recent report by Transparency International Canada (2016) sardonically notes that it is "harder to get a library card" than to register a company in regard to identification requirements. It also points to the fact that Canada still allows bearer shares, which are physical documents similar to bonds that companies pay out to whomever holds them. Meanwhile, there are millions of trusts in Canada, but only 210,000 report to the Canada Revenue Agency because they are treated as private contracts, subject to attorney-client privilege. While banks are supposed to identify beneficial ownership for new accounts (after 2014), no such obligation exists for real estate brokers, precious metals/gems dealers, or accountants. Transparency International Canada's investigation of the luxury real estate market in Vancouver revealed that shell companies were the owners of 30% of titles from 2006 to 2016.

Possible Steps Forward

In this final section, we suggest several directions for regulatory reform. Much depends on the political will to make meaningful reform. As we have seen, reform efforts have been at best haphazard and at worst disingenuous and negligent. We believe the rush of attention to the issue from the Panama and Paradise Papers creates a window of opportunity for meaningful reform to take place.

Though there is temporary attention from the Panama Papers, we should be concerned that attention will wane, as it has in the past. We are not yet at the moment where the conflicts of interest or domestic angst of the middle class from tax evasion has created a large enough push for regulatory reform at the global level. Part of this, of course, is based on the complexity of the issue creating barriers to understanding. Moreover, from a political perspective, the attrition of fiscal capacity has not yet reached crisis proportions that would begin to arrest its marked deterioration from its post-war Keynesian heyday. Even the reforms in the wake of the 2008 recession, such as Dodd-Frank, became heavily watered down by financial lobbies. However, the Brexit and Trump successes, along with the general rise of reactionary globalisation suggest that such a day may in fact come. As Strange pointed out in 1998 (139), both greed and fear abound in financial trading. Too much of these elements can undermine the very foundations of confidence in financial systems. Financial systems are thus a classic collective action problem, with risk-taking by individual traders and banks having the potential to tear asunder the very systems by which they make their livelihoods.

In order for genuine reform to happen, the US must open itself up to regulatory harmonisation with the EU, starting with giving up its own tax havens and creating transparency for those who hold assets. The fact remains that US leadership is essential for progress on tax evasion and reducing global financial risk. It is still the closest thing we have to a lender and currency provider of last resort (Strange 1986, 176), and thus wields leadership power in terms of regulatory norms. Absent US leadership, it is therefore unlikely for now that the OECD or any of the other efforts will establish what would be needed to wipe out tax avoidance, namely a global tax administration (not necessarily in the form of a central entity). Until the US accepts the principle of revealing who owns assets in its own tax havens, no progress can be made.

The answer, as suggested by US Republicans via the 2017 tax reform, is not simply to lower taxes across the board to minimal levels. It takes easy reflection to realise that growth and high taxation are compatible, and tax evasion can be minimised, if one only looks at the Scandinavian economies. For Kleven (2014), there are three key policy lessons from these cases. First, Scandinavian countries have a broad tax base (particularly VAT) with very few deductions or loopholes. Second, information reporting is quite thorough. Third, and perhaps most importantly, there is a broad consensus around progressive taxation since redistribution is not just about safety nets but also about tangible support to businesses, such as retraining programmes. Some form of fiscal tax harmonisation may, in the long run therefore be feasible, albeit still remote under current conditions. Such efforts would be highly complex, requiring considerations of flexibility for local conditions and perhaps equity among regions with different sizes and types of fiscal base (ability to tax and sources of revenue) (Gaigné and Riou 2007).

In the longer term, we need a fundamental shift across the world in regard to taxation principles, from taxation based on corporate headquarters to where business activity—and particularly sales—takes place. In August 2016, the European Commission ordered Apple to pay Ireland

and other members of the EU $14.5 billion in back taxes. The ruling suggested that Apple had created a shell that received finances but without much real activity in Ireland, thus diverting revenues from across Europe because of special deals created by the Irish government. The commission viewed such deals as one off special treatment that created unfairness to European competitors. It followed similar cases against Starbucks in the Netherlands and Anheuser-Busch InBev in Belgium. Luxembourg is also home to many holding companies for multinationals seeking to avoid tax, including PepsiCo, FedEx, Ikea, and Amazon. Even the Canadian federal pension board set up Luxembourg companies to reduce taxes on German properties. The US reaction has been strongly negative, suggesting that such "clawbacks" harm its own ability to collect taxes on multinationals.[7] It is interesting to note that the 2017 Republican tax debate contains, as of this writing anyway, the principle of a minimum corporate taxation, regardless of where revenues are accrued. This would be an important step forward to move away from fear of double taxation towards ensuring that all corporations and wealthy individuals pay some tax somewhere.

TJN offers two useful proposals to move forward in regard to transparency (http://www.taxjustice.net/topics/corporate-tax/taxing-corporations). The first is transparent country-by-country reporting of corporate activities, as discussed above. The second is unitary taxation, where a company's taxes would be allocated to the different jurisdictions where it does business on the basis of variables such as "sales, payroll, and physical assets." TNCs would be treated as a whole, rather than as separate subsidiaries, ignoring transfer pricing.

The United Nations' Practical Manual on Transfer Pricing (2013) furthermore offers a number of suggestions for monitoring for transfer pricing. Under the Comparable Uncontrolled Price Method, transfer prices would be "compared" to comparable transactions (196). Under the safe harbour rules, if a company reports profits below a certain threshold, a country may choose alternative methods for establishing tax burdens (73). This and the arm's length rules bring up, of course, the question of what is really "comparable." A study of French company transfer payments for 1999 concluded that French tax authorities had lost at least €390 billion

[7] http://www.nytimes.com/2016/08/31/technology/apple-tax-eu-ireland.html   and https://www.icij.org/project/luxembourg-leaks/leaked-documents-expose-global-companies-secret-tax-deals-luxembourg

due to under-reporting. However, 450 of the 2495 firms sampled accounted for 90% of the exports to ten tax havens, including Switzerland, Ireland, and Singapore. Just 25 firms accounted for 50% of all intra-firm exports to the tax havens (Davies et al. 2015, 21). Therefore, concentration on the leading firms makes reform seem much more feasible. A study by Marques and Pinho (2016) of the behaviour of 27,278 foreign subsidiaries in Europe found that increasing the strictness of transfer pricing rules (using the aforementioned arm's length principle) in fact appears to reduce profit-sharing between host companies and subsidiaries.

We summarise this discussion with a priority "to do" list for beginning to regulate offshore financial tax evasion.

- The first would be steps towards increased transparency and accountability. The foundations of the financial system's auditing and accountability systems, including corporate statements, need serious attention. Transparency extends to the local level, such as New York, Los Angeles, and Vancouver, where new regulations require disclosures of the citizenship of purchasers of real estate in certain instances, for example. Transparency, as demonstrated by the US FATCA efforts, can be enforced in offshore havens if there is consensus and regulatory harmonisation among the largest Western economies. Along with that, we need to build regulatory capacity at the global level to monitor and manage the incredibly fast technological evolution of global financial transactions.

- Of second urgency is the desperate need to convince Washington to adopt the same levels of transparency for its onshore havens. Until there is a willingness to share information about asset holders, real estate purchasers, and who is on boards of companies, there will be no sense of responsibility or shame for tax evasion. We cannot rely upon hackers to do this job. Similarly, the EU and the UK need to move to close the loopholes still clearly present in its own efforts, as discussed above. Clearly parts of Europe are still havens for tax evasion.

- This could go hand-in-hand with wider discussions around a third priority, which is to change tax principles to place of activity rather than state domicile. Such a step, while intuitive and foundational, would require extensive policy investigation, for metrics of how to measure and assign tax responsibility for certain types and levels of activities.

- We need a movement towards global tax harmonisation, so that the developing world can be brought on board with the same principles. The benefits of harmonisation are immeasurable and could lead to a greater fiscal policy revolution and improvement of state capacity than has been considered so far. We would no longer have to engage in debilitating tax competition, which leads to subsidies and loop-holes that are, in the end, most likely to be counter-productive to the giving state. We can no longer, in good conscience, allow our wealthy, along with terrorists, narco-traffickers, arms dealers, and the like to use the offshore financial system to create chaos, leaving the middle class to pay for all public services benefiting corporations and the wealth as much or more as anyone else.
- All of these measures should be accompanied by meaningful enforcement. Washington, London, and Brussels have a lot more power than they acknowledge in this issue. This is the power to close off their markets to countries who don't follow the principles above. The flow of investment capital from offshore in the West is important, but it should follow proper channels for productive investment, rather than propping up real estate bubbles and other dodgy schemes set up through shell corporations. Until there is transparency and enforcement in the West's own financial systems, no global system can be put into place.

In a time of growing inequality, political volatility and extremism, con-sternation about jobs, and an eroding faith in the financial and labour markets, restoring fiscal capacity and, even more importantly, a sense of fairness and rule of law, upon which democracy rests, could not be more important.

Acknowledgements Norbert Gaillard, Patty Hira, James Busumtwi-Sam, Ted Cohn, Michael Webb

References

Avi-Yonah, Reuven S. 2015. Who Invented the Single Tax Principle? An Essay on the History of U.S. Treaty Policy. *New York Law School Law Review*. 59(2): 305–315.

Beer, Sebastian and Jan Loeprick. 2015. Profit Shifting: Drivers of Transfer (Mis) pricing and the Potential of Countermeasures. *International Tax Public Finance*. 22(3): 426–451.

Biersteker, Thomas J., Sue E. Eckert, and Peter Romaniuk. 2007. International Initiatives to Combat the Financing of Terrorism. 234–259. In Thomas J. Biersteker and Sue E. Eckert (Eds.). *Countering the Financing of Terrorism*. New York: Routledge.

Brittain-Catlin, William. 2005. *Offshore: The Dark Side of the Global Economy*. New York: Farrar, Straus and Giroux.

Buckley, Peter J., Dylan Sutherland, Hinrich Voss, and Ahmad El-Gohari. 2015. The Economic Geography of Offshore Incorporation in Tax Havens and Offshore Financial Centers: The Case of Chinese MNEs. *Journal of Economic Geography*. 15(1): 103–128.

Cecchini, Mark, Robert Leitch, and Caroline Strobel. 2013. Multinational Transfer Pricing: A Transaction Cost and Resource Review. *Journal of Accounting Literature*. 31(1): 31–48.

Choo, Kim-Kwang Raymond. 2014. Designated Non-Financial Businesses and Professionals: A Review and Analysis of Recent Financial Action Task Force on Money Laundering Mutual Evaluation Reports. *Security Journal*. 27(1): 1–26.

Christensen, John. 2012. The Hidden Trillions: Secrecy, Corruption, and the Offshore Interface. *Crime, Law and Social Change*. 57(3): 325–343.

Christensen III, Henry and Jean-Marc Tirard. 2016. The Amazing Development of Exchange of Information in Tax Matters: From Double Tax Treaties to FATCA and the CRS. *Trusts & Trustees*. 22(8): 898–922.

Cobham, Alex, Petr Jansky, and Markus Meinzer. 2015. The Financial Secrecy Index: Shedding New Light on the Geography of Secrecy. *Economic Geography*. 91(3): 281–303.

Cotorceanu, Peter A. 2015. Hiding in Plain Sight: How Non-US Persons Can *Legally* Avoid Reporting under Both FATCA and GATCA. *Trusts and Trustees*. 21(10): 1050–1063.

Cuéllar, Mariano-Florentino. 2003. The Tenuous Relationship between the Fight against Money Laundering and the Disruption of Criminal Finance. *Journal of Criminal Law and Criminology*. 93(2): 311–466.

Davies, Ronald B., Julien Martin, Mathieu Parenti, and Farid Toubal. 2015. Knocking on Tax Haven's Door: Multinational Firms and Transfer Pricing. *Oxford University Centre for Business Taxation. Working Paper*. Oxford: Oxford Business School.

Deneault, Alain. 2015. *Canada: A New Tax Haven – How the Country that Shaped Caribbean Tax Havens is Becoming One Itself*. Trans. Catherine Browne. Vancouver: Talonbooks.

Dubinsky, Zach. 2016a. Deals Canada Signed to Catch Tax Cheats Allow Billions in Taxes to Escape. June 17. CBC. Available at http://www.cbc.ca/news/business/canada-offshore-tax-avoidance-corporations-tiea-1.3639597 [accessed March 16, 2017].

Dubinsky, Zach. 2016b. How Canada Got into Bed with Tax Havens. June 18. CBC. Available at http://www.cbc.ca/news/business/canada-offshore-treaties-barbados-tax-avoidance-1.3641278 [accessed March 16, 2017].

Dyreng, Scott D., Bradley P. Lindsey, and Jacob R. Thornock. 2013. Exploring the Role Delaware Plays as a Domestic Tax Haven. *Journal of Financial Economics.* 108(3): 751–772.

Eckert, Sue E. and Thomas J. Biersteker. 2010. (Mis)Measuring Success in Countering the Financing of Terrorism. 247–263. In Peter Andreas and Kelly M. Greenhill (Eds.). *Sex, Drugs, and Body Counts: The Politics of Numbers in Global Crime and Conflict.* Ithaca: Cornell University Press.

Engel, Barry S. 2002. The Integrated Estate Planning Trust as an All-Perils Insurance Policy. *Trust & Trustees.* 8(4): 7–15.

Financial Action Task Force (FATF) and Asia/Pacific Group on Money Laundering (AMG). 2016. *Anti-Money Laundering and Counter-Terrorist Financing Measures: Canada.* September. Paris: FATF and AMG.

Findley, Michael G., Daniel L. Nielson, and J.C. Sharman. 2014. *Global Shell Games: Experiments in Transnational Relations, Crime, and Terrorism.* New York: Cambridge University Press.

Gaigné, Carl and Stéphane Riou. 2007. Globalization, Asymmetric Tax Competition, and Fiscal Equalization. *Journal of Public Economic Theory.* 9(5): 901–925.

Gaillard, Norbert J. and William J. Harrington. 2016. Efficient, Commonsense Actions to Foster Accurate Credit Ratings. *Capital Markets Law Journal.* 11(1): 38–59.

GAO (US Government Accountability Office). 2013. *Offshore Tax Evasion: IRS Has Collected Billions of Dollars, but May be Missing Continued Evasion.* GAO-13-318. Washington: GAO.

Gates, Guilbert. 2016. How Mossack Fonseca Helped Clients Skirt or Break U.S. Tax Laws With Offshore Accounts. *New York Times.* June 5.

Genschel, Phillipp. 2002. Globalization, Tax Competition, and the Welfare State. *Politics and Society.* 30(2): 245–275.

Gilligan, George Peter. 2004. Overview: Markets, Offshore Sovereignty and Onshore Legitimacy. In Donato Masciandaro (Ed.). *Global Financial Crime: Terrorism, Money Laundering and Offshore Centres,* 7–59. Aldershot: Ashgate Publishing Limited.

Government of Norway. 2009. *Tax Havens and Development: Status, Analyses and Measures.* Report from Government Commission on Capital Flight from Poor Countries. Oslo: Government Administration Services.

Gravelle, Jane G. 2015. *Tax Havens: International Tax Avoidance and Evasion.* Congressional Research Service (CRS). Washington: CRS.

Haberly, Daniel and Dariusz Wójcik. 2015. Regional Blocks and Imperial Legacies: Mapping the Global Offshore FDI Network. *Economic Geography*. 91(3): 251–280.

Hemmelgarn, Thomas and Gaetan Nicodème. 2009. Tax Co-ordination in Europe: Assessing the First Years of the EU-Savings Taxation Directive. Taxation Paper No. 18. Brussels, Belgium: European Commission Taxation and Customs Union. Available at http://ec.europa.eu/taxation_customs/resources/documents/taxation/gen_info/economic_analysis/tax_papers/taxation_paper_18.pdf

Hetzel, Robert L. 2012. *The Great Recession: Market Failure or Policy Failure?* New York: Cambridge University Press.

Hira, Anil (Ed.). 2016. Culture and Corruption in Developing States – Parts I & II. *Journal of Developing Societies*. 32(1/2). March/June.

Hunter, Constance L., Thomas Herr and Marcus Heyland. 2015. Transfer Pricing for the Rest of Us. *Business Economics*. 50(2): 75–79.

Jakobi, Anja P. 2015. Global Networks Against Crime: Using the Financial Action Task Force as A Model? *International Journal*. 70(3): 391–407.

Karkinsky, Tom and Nadine Riedel. 2012. Corporate Taxation and the Choice of Patent Location within Multinational Firms. *Journal of International Economics*. 88(1): 176–185.

Kerzner, David S. and David W. Chodikoff. 2016. *International Tax Evasion in the Global Information Age*. New York: Palgrave Macmillan.

Kingah, Stephen and Marieke Zwartjes. 2015. Regulating Money Laundering for Terrorism Financing: EU–US Transnational Policy Networks and the Financial Action Task Force. *Contemporary Politics*. 21(3): 341–353.

Kleven, Henrik Jacobsen. 2014. How Can Scandinavians Tax So Much? *Journal of Economic Perspectives*. 28(4): 77–98.

Knobel, Andres. 2015. The Next Rising Tax Haven. *World Policy Journal*. 32(1): 43–52.

Knobel, Andres and Markus Meinzer. 2014. 'The End of Bank Secrecy'? Bridging the Gap to Effective Automatic Information Exchange. Evaluation of OECD's Common Reporting Standard (CRS) and its Alternatives. Available at www.taxjustice.net [accessed May 31, 2017].

Lam, Pak Nian, and David Lee Kuo Chuen. 2015. Introduction to Bitcoin, 3–30. In David Lee Kuo Chuen. *Handbook of Digital Currency: Financial Innovation, Financial Instruments and Big Data*. London: Elsevier Press.

Levi, Michael. 2007. Lessons for Countering Terrorist Financing from the War on Serious and Organized Crime. 260–288. In Thomas J. Biersteker and Sue E. Eckert (Eds.). *Countering the Financing of Terrorism*. London: Routledge.

Lipton, Eric, and Julie Creswell. 2016. Panama Papers Show How Rich United States Clients Hid Millions Abroad. *New York Times*. June 5.

Liss, Carolin and J.C. Sharman. 2015. Global Corporate Crime-Fighters: Private Transnational Responses to Piracy and Money Laundering. *Review of International Political Economy.* 22(4): 693–718.

Love, Patrick. 2012. Price Fixing. *OECD Insights.* Available at: http://oecdinsights.org/2012/03/26/price-fixing [accessed October 17, 2016].

Marques, Mário and Carlos Pinho. 2016. Is Transfer Pricing Strictness Deterring Profit Shifting within Multinationals? Empirical Evidence from Europe. *Accounting and Business Research.* 46(7): 703–730.

McCann, Hilton. 2006. *Offshore Finance.* Cambridge: Cambridge University Press.

Metaxatos, Evan. 2008. Thunder in Paradise: The Interplay of Broadening United States Anti-Money Laundering Legislation and Jurisprudence with the Caribbean Law Governing Offshore Asset Preservation Trusts. *University of Miami Inter-American Law Review.* 40(1): 169–195.

Michaels, Marnin, Marie-Thérèse Yates, and Katherine Price. 2007. The Implications for Trustees of the Possible EU Savings Directive Reforms. Trusts & Trustees. 13(9): 558–560.

OECD. 2009. *Report on Abuse of Charities for Money-Laundering and Tax Evasion.* Paris: OECD.

OECD. 2015. *OECD/G20 Base Erosion and Profit Shifting Project: Explanatory Statement. 2015 Final Reports.* Paris: OECD.

Olson, Mancur. 1982. *The Rise and Decline of Nations: Economic Growth, Stagflation, and Social Rigidities.* New Haven: Yale University Press.

Oved, Marco Chown and Robert Cribb. 2017. Signatures for Sale: Paid to Sign Corporate Documents, Nominee Directors Serve to Hide Companies' Real Owners. January 26. *Toronto Star.* Available at http://projects.thestar.com/panama-papers/canada-signatures-for-sale [accessed March 17, 2017].

Overesch, Michael and Johannes Rincke. 2011. What Drives Corporate Tax Rates Down? A Reassessment of Globalisation, Tax Competition, and Dynamic Adjustment to Shocks. *Scandinavian Journal of Economics.* 113(3): 579–602.

Palan, Ronen, Richard Murphy, and Christian Chavagneux. 2010. *Tax Havens: How Globalisation Really Works.* Ithaca: Cornell University Press.

Paris, Roland. 2003. The Globalisation of Taxation? Electronic Commerce and the Transformation of the State. *International Studies Quarterly.* 47(2): 153–182.

Putnam, Robert. 1988. Diplomacy and Domestic Politics: The Logic of Two-Level Games. *International Organization.* 42(3): 427–460.

Rahimi-Laridjani, Eschrat, and Erika Hauser. 2016. The New Global FATCA: An Overview of the OECD's Common Reporting Standard in Relation to FATCA. *Journal of Taxation of Financial Products.* 13(3): 9–14.

Raphaeli, Nimrod. 2003. Financing of Terrorism: Sources, Methods and Channels. *Terrorism and Political Violence.* 15(4): 59–82.

Razavy, Maryam. 2005. Hawala: An Underground Haven for Terrorists or Social Phenomenon? *Crime, Law and Social Change*. 44(3): 277–299.

Razavy, Maryam, and Kevin D. Haggerty. 2009. Hawala Under Scrutiny: Documentation, Surveillance and Trust. *International Political Sociology*. 3(2): 139–155.

Schjelderup, Guttorm. 2016. Secrecy Jurisdictions. *International Tax and Public Finance*. 23(1): 168–189.

Schneider, Friedrich. 2013. The Financial Flows of Transnational Crime and Tax Fraud in OECD Countries: What Do We (Not) Know? *Public Finance Review*. 41(5): 677–707.

Seglins, Dave, Rachel Houlihan, and Zach Dubinsky. 2017. 'Tax Haven' Canada Being Used by Offshore Cheats, Panama Papers Show. January 25. CBC. Available at http://www.cbc.ca/news/investigates/panama-papers-canada-tax-haven-1.3950552 [accessed March 17, 2017].

Sharman, J.C. 2008. Regional Deals and the Global Imperative: The External Dimension of the European Union Savings Tax Directive. *Journal of Common Market Studies*. 46(5): 1049–1069.

Sharman, J.C. 2011. *The Money Laundry: Regulating Criminal Finance in the Global Economy*. Ithaca, NY: Cornell University Press.

Shillito, Matthew R. 2015. Countering Terrorist Financing via Non-Profit Organisations: Assessing Why Few States Comply with the International Recommendations. *Nonprofit Policy Forum*. 6(3): 325–352.

Snyder, Eric J. 2015. FATCA and the Broader Tax Crackdown. *Trusts and Trustees*. 21(6): 596–604.

Stowell, David. 2010. *An Introduction to Investment Banks, Hedge Funds and Private Equity*. London: Elsevier.

Strange, Susan. 1986. *Casino Capitalism*. New York: Basil Blackwell.

Strange, Susan. 1996. *The Retreat of the State: The Diffusion of Power in the World Economy*. New York: Cambridge University Press.

Strange, Susan. 1998. *Mad Money*. Manchester: Manchester University Press.

Swank, Duane. 2006. Tax Policy in an Era of Internationalization: Explaining the Spread of Neoliberalism. *International Organization*. 60(4): 847–882.

Takáts, Elöd. 2007. International Enforcement Issues. 225–241. In Donato Masciandaro, Elöd Takáts, and Brigitte Unger. *Black Finance: The Economics of Money Laundering*. Northampton, MA: Edward Elgar.

Tax Justice Network. 2009. In trusts we trust [blog post]. July 22. Available at http://taxjustice.blogspot.ca/2009/07/in-trusts-we-trust.html [accessed August 4, 2016].

Transparency International Canada. 2016. *No Reason to Hide: Unmasking the Anonymous Owners of Canadian Companies and Trusts*. Toronto: Transparency International Canada.

Tsingou, Eleni. 2010. Global Financial Governance and the Developing Anti-Money Laundering Regime: What Lessons for International Political Economy? *International Politics.* 47(6): 617–637.

Turner, Jonathan E. 2011. *Money Laundering Prevention: Deterring, Detecting and Resolving Financial Fraud.* Hoboken: John Wiley & Sons.

Unger, Brigitte. 2007. The Impact of Money Laundering. 103–148. In Donato Masciandaro, Elöd Takáts, and Brigitte Unger. *Black Finance: The Economics of Money Laundering.* Northampton, MA: Edward Elgar.

United Nations (UN). 2013. *Practical Manual on Transfer Pricing for Developing Countries.* UN Department of Economic and Social Affairs. ST/ESA/347. New York: United Nations.

Van der Does de Willebois, Emile, Emily Marie Halter, Robert Mansour Harrison, Ji Won Park, and Jason Campbell Sharman. 2011. *The Puppet Masters: How the Corrupt Use Legal Structures to Hide Stolen Assets and What to Do About It.* Washington: The World Bank.

Vlcek, William. 2012. Power and the Practice of Security to Govern Global Finance. *Review of International Political Economy.* 19(4): 639–662.

Zucman, Gabriel. 2015. *The Hidden Wealth of Nations: The Scourge of Tax Havens.* Chicago: University of Chicago Press.

CHAPTER 7

Concluding Remarks

Anil Hira, Norbert Gaillard, and Theodore H. Cohn

This edited volume has shown that the 2008 financial crisis stemmed from a wide range of long-standing regulatory problems that were not adequately confronted. It is even more concerning that economists, leading politicians, and regulators have not clearly identified the persistent flaws embedded within the current system of *finance* capitalism (see Lo 2012). As a result, regulatory problems persist at the domestic and international levels, and we have not seen the last of major financial crises (Reinhart and Rogoff 2009). Several reasons might be advanced to explain such blindness.

First, too many policymakers remain convinced that the 2008 crisis was primarily driven by bad decisions and poor timing; for example, the lack of regulation of the real estate sector in the 1990s–2000s; the excessively high ratings granted to CDOs, RMBS, and CMBS until 2007; and the failure to bail out Lehman Brothers in September 2008.

Second, in the aftermath of the Lehman Brothers collapse, dogmatic, monolithic, and intellectually "convenient" solutions flourished. They

A. Hira (✉) • T. H. Cohn
Department of Political Science, Simon Fraser University, Burnaby, BC, Canada
e-mail: ahira@sfu.ca; cohn@sfu.ca

N. Gaillard
NG Consulting, Paris, France
e-mail: gaillard@alumni.princeton.edu

© The Author(s) 2019
A. Hira et al. (eds.), *The Failure of Financial Regulation*,
International Political Economy Series,
https://doi.org/10.1007/978-3-030-05680-3_7

tended to satisfy policymakers who were eager to find people to blame, and measures aimed at stimulating economic recovery. The persistent debate between neoliberal and post-Keynesian economists about how to promote growth is a striking illustration. Ten years after the Great Recession, that debate is at a standstill. On the one hand, austerity has exacerbated inequalities and has not permitted the necessary and efficient recalibration of welfare states (Hemerijck 2013). On the other hand, fiscal stimulus looks like a blunt instrument in a world that has not yet begun its deleveraging process (Buttiglione et al. 2014).

Third, regulators and central bankers have considered certain ad hoc technical solutions (e.g., more stringent capital requirements, and loose and accommodative monetary policies) sufficient to ensure the stability of the global financial system and achieve robust economic growth (see Turner 2016; Bernanke 2011). The problem with such options is that they generally lag behind financial sophistication and are blind to the perverse effects they are likely to have on investors, and the unintended incentives they often create. Shadow banking and in fact the entire rise to dominance of structured finance and securitisation have resulted from original opportunities created by ad hoc regulation *reactively* responding to interim crises.

This also reflects the need for policymakers and politicians to be seen as "doing something" in response to crises, which dissipates once the news cycle has passed (Mayntz 2012, 23). In turn, it shows the relatively weak position of reform activists, who are usually overwhelmed by the technicality of a subject that even regulatory experts struggle with. Politicians feel pressure to promote short-term growth, not long-term reform. As Dobuzinskis' chapter points out, the consequences of regulatory choices are often unclear in advance. Furthermore, in a deep study of banking regulations across European nations and the US, Busch (2009, 240) states in regard to expert-level discussions that "the situation in banking regulation is thus characterized by both empirical and theoretical ignorance: there is neither empirical knowledge about what "works best", nor is there a scholarly consensus about the approach that could be taken." All of this impedes action as well as harmonisation efforts.

Fourth, leading politicians and regulators may have a material interest in adopting and implementing policies that do not adequately address the underlying problems that produce financial instability. For example, politicians have long used government spending as a short-term tool to maximise their chances of being re-elected (see Buchanan and Wagner 1977 for a seminal work); and key regulators are often from the financial industry and return to finance after their stint as regulators.

It is important to note the hypocrisy of the financial industry in regard to regulatory proposals. In the immediate aftermath of the crisis, they pushed for bailouts, including of AIG, the largest insurer of their financial instruments, so as not to suffer the consequences of their own risk taking. However, this never led to an understanding of the need for different regulatory approaches. In fact, belief in deregulation (see Alan Greenspan) has yielded a certain "stickiness" or "path dependency" in terms of attitude, culture, and personal predilections, which tends to institutionalise it beyond the capture discussed in Cohn's chapter (Mayntz 2012, 21).

Our view here is radically different. The authors who have contributed to this volume consider that the financial system is fundamentally flawed, requiring a first-principles rethink and a *proactive* analysis. Although ethical failures and short-term strategies at large firms are major challenges (Santoro and Strauss 2013; Vasudev 2016), we narrow our focus to financial regulatory issues, mainly because they can be addressed directly by legislators, policymakers, and bureaucrats.

WHY POST-CRISIS REFORMS HAVE COME UP SHORT

As of this writing, there is no evidence that the issues we bring up in this volume have been acknowledged, let alone addressed. In fact, the actions of the Trump Administration, major regulators, and the US Congress are quite the reverse. The Administration moved in February 2017 to delay or eliminate the "fiduciary rule," by which financial advisers were required to consider their client's best interests, rather than commissions or fees, which was one of the issues around the 2008 crash when Wall Street investment houses such as Goldman Sachs shorted the financial instruments they were selling. The Administration watered down Dodd-Frank, claiming that liquidity requirements were slowing the recovery, and that reporting rules were unduly affecting small and medium lenders as well. This is despite the fact that commercial and business loans from banks increased from $1.2 trillion in February 2011 to $2.1 trillion in February 2018. The Administration also took over direct control of the Consumer Financial Protection Bureau (CFPB), now run by Mick Mulvaney, the head of the Office of Management and Budget, which promises to slow down if not halt its active advocacy on behalf of consumers given his hostility towards what he called "an out-of-control bureaucracy." The CFPB had collected nearly $12 billion in refunds—involving 29 million victims of fraudulent or illegal financial lending practices as of the end of 2016—and increased the transparency and bargaining power of consumers more generally. Since taking over the CFPB, Mulvaney has halted new investigations, stopped the bureau's collection of certain data from banks, instituted a hiring freeze, and proposed cutting off public access to a database on consumer complaints (Broder 2018; Werner and Paletta 2018; Flitter and Rappeport 2018). These initiatives reflect a rejection of liberal values, especially transparency and competition.

In fact, in the current institutional and political context where "kludgeocracy" has become a dominant pattern,[1] rent-seekers have been increasingly influential and successful (Lindsey and Teles 2017). The financial industry provides a striking illustration. Recent actions by the US Congress demonstrate that the power of the financial lobby continues to loom large. In May 2018, Congress agreed to free thousands of small and middle-sized banks from strict rules such as "stress tests" included in the Dodd-Frank Act. The legislation also allows some large institutions such as American Express and BB&T Corporation to no longer be considered "systemically important" and subject to stricter oversight. The House voted 258–159 to approve this regulatory rollback that the Senate had already passed, with 33 Democrats supporting the measure. The Fed and the Office of the Comptroller of the Currency (OCC), now run largely by Trump appointees, have proposed easing the limits on how much the largest banks can borrow. This change was opposed by Obama administration appointees at the Fed and the FDIC, who believed that it was too soon to reduce capital requirements for the largest banks. The Fed has also proposed to loosen the proprietary trading safeguard under the Volcker Rule, and enable the largest banks to establish their own risk limits. This change could be highly profitable, but also make the banks more vulnerable to major losses. The six largest US banks have all lobbied either directly or through trade groups for changes to the Volcker Rule. The loosening of the Volcker Rule is simply one part of a coordinated effort to relax

---

[1] "Kludgeocracy" consists of "addressing social problems that funnel resources through the private sector and allow rent-seekers to skim off some of the flow" (Lindsey and Teles 2017, 129).

regulations implemented after the 2008 financial crisis (Rappeport and Flitter 2018; Editorial Board 2018).

As Quaglia and Spendzharova (2017) point out, there has not been anything near an adequate response to the 2008 crisis in good part because of diverging interests among the key countries. While the US and the UK are the dominant financial markets, France and Germany are more secondary. The US and UK saw the need for reform, therefore, predominantly from a domestic reform and national competitiveness perspective, rather than one of ensuring shared new global standards. Thus, global regulatory bodies mentioned throughout the volume, such as the Financial Stability Board, have not yet acquired any space to create international capacity or authority behind a shared regulatory regime. Moreover, "Brexit" can at least partly be tied to the rejection of stricter European financial regulations. The challenges to align US and UK standards with those of continental Europe are daunting and stem from differences in the historical development of the sectors. For example, the re-enactment of Volcker rule provisions "ring fencing" investment from retail banking in the US applies to foreign banks operating there. Yet, German and French banks, and their regulatory representatives, strongly oppose such rules because they have a tradition of banks being closely connected to corporations. As Keller (2018) discusses, European banks also engage regularly in successful lobbying efforts to shape policy. As in the US, this has helped to prevent more aggressive regulatory reforms, such as the proposed financial transactions tax by the EU Commission (Kalaitzake 2017). Thus, as Keaney (2017) discusses, resonant with Chaps. 2, 3, and 4 in this volume, the domestic capture of the state by financial groups leads to transnational collusion to avoid serious global financial regulatory reform.

These discrepancies are not just of academic interest; the lack of harmonisation around global regulations has major long-term implications for how the global financial market will grow and evolve. Consider, for example, that before Brexit, the UK exported 23 billion pounds worth of financial services to the EU, leading to a 19 billion pound surplus. Financial services account for 11.8% of its overall economic output, with 23% of financial services revenue coming from services to the EU (European Parliament 2017, 10).

The Financial Stability Board has set out four primary pillars to guide reform: making financial institutions more resilient; ending "too big to fail;" making derivative markets safer; and transforming shadow banking. Duffie (2018) concludes that very little progress has been made in the latter three of these pillars, and even with the first one, the progress (through increasing liquidity requirements) has been insufficient. In fact, increased liquidity requirements may actually lead to further concentration of the banking sector absent efforts in the others. As Dobuzinskis' chapter notes, regulation is bound to create new systems for evasion, and the more complicated the rules, the more likely the evasion. As Herring (2018) points out, even establishing the appropriate capital requirements for "stress tests" has proved very challenging given the multitude of modes in which banks store capital and their varying, and at times opaque, risk profile. More vexing still is that the interconnectedness of financial institutions—exacerbating the collapse of the US housing market in 2008 and leading to the sovereign debt crisis in the Eurozone—continues unabated (Allen et al. 2018). Thus weakness in a specific region that is seemingly limited in nature is very likely to have systemic implications. Moreover, the re-regulation efforts have largely ignored shadow banking, which remains a major source of concern (Bell and Hindmoor 2017).

Another part of the problem as reflected in the previous chapters is the large constellation of actors involved in global financial regulation, ranging from international organisations such as the IMF to looser agreements like Basel and to private sector organisations such as the Group of Thirty. Along with these is a lack of transparency of financial transactions—as reflected in the Busumtwi-Sam's and Hira et al.'s chapters—and in the shadow banking system. The latter consists of financial transactions among private intermediaries that are largely unregulated. There are no reliable estimates, but shadow banking could be larger than traditional banking. In part, this is because it helps to circulate some of the big pools of investment capital controlled by pension funds. These are most likely concentrated among now-global too-big-to-fail institutions, creating the possibility for contagion effects (Avgouleas 2012, 12–13, 51). Shadow banking not only evades regulation, thereby increasing risk taking, but also does not rely on a deposit insurance or lender of last resort. Regulatory harmonisation among the major economies is essential, because anti-regulatory arguments at the domestic level often rest upon the claim that additional financial regulations will cause a loss of competitiveness for both the financial sector and other parts of the economy (Mayntz 2012, 22). Combine these with increasing signs of a resurgence of a housing bubble in major urban centres in the West, from Toronto to London to San Francisco, and we can discern clear flashbacks to the persistence of regulatory issues leading up to the 2008 crash. This has convinced some commentators to promote institutional harmonisation, perhaps even in the form of a World Financial Authority akin to the WTO for trade. At the very least, transparency in shadow banking and derivatives have to be achieved to properly gauge risk. Derivatives are estimated to represent an astounding 30–40% of the assets of the largest US and UK banks (Buckley 2016, 18). Thus, a run on financial instruments is likely to spread across borders and may not be detected until too late to avert a crisis. Global solutions are more challenging given the increasingly vital role of Chinese investment and holdings in the West, the opacity and vulnerability of their domestic financial system, and signs of a global trade war initiated by Trump in 2018 that will likely reverberate throughout financial markets.

We devote considerable time to analysing the US financial landscape because its position remains crucial in at least three respects. US ideological influence in the economic and financial fields is so great that regulatory reforms there can and will constitute a roadmap for reforms elsewhere. Second, the investigation, prosecution, and enforcement power of the US administration can move the lines and thus lead to a new paradigm. For example, after months of intense pressure, Switzerland consented in 2009 to reveal the names of several thousand wealthy American clients of UBS to US authorities, resulting in a historical breach in Swiss banking secrecy. Lastly, since the Washington Consensus (Williamson 1989), many emerging economies have implemented market-based financial measures, which has helped to boost GDP growth but has also increased economic cyclicity (Rancière et al. 2008). As Fig. 7.1 depicts, even major emerging countries with an intermediate level of capital controls (e.g., Brazil and Russia)[2] were affected by the 2008 crash. This reflects global interconnectedness and the strong dependence of most countries on the US business cycle and financial regulatory framework.

Given the traction of the issues discussed above, what is the way forward? As discussed in the Introduction to this volume, we do not subscribe to any particular political or ideological agenda. Our empirical studies demonstrate a variety of political perspectives. US and Western policy on financial regulation has alternated between orthodox liberalism or neoliberalism on the one hand, and interventionist liberalism on the

[2] We use Chinn and Ito's index of financial openness. See http://web.pdx.edu/~ito/Chinn-Ito_website.htm

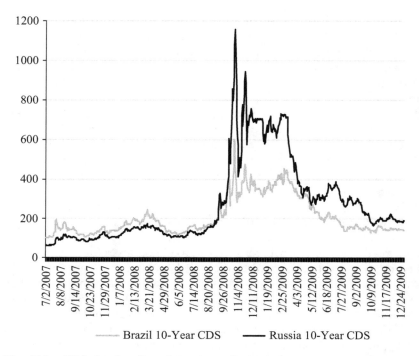

Fig. 7.1 CDS for Brazil and Russia, July 2007–December 2009. (Source: Datastream)

other. After the 2008 financial crisis, there were indications of some revival of interventionist liberalism with the 2010 passage of the Dodd-Frank Act. Today, however, neoliberalism is clearly in the ascendancy again with the moves toward financial deregulation in the Trump administration, US regulatory agencies, and the Congress. Despite the current signs of growth in the US economy, the deregulatory changes implemented soon after the 2008 financial crisis are closely tied with the signs of growing risk in the banking sector discussed above. The ascendancy of neoliberalism is combined with a good dose of neomercantilism in trade and finance in the Trump administration, in its efforts to increase US competitiveness and preserve US hegemony. This combination of neoliberalism and neomercantilism does not bode well for the development of a more effective international regime for financial regulation as it simultaneously erodes trust around global rules and invites tit-for-tat behaviour that will further pose a threat to existing cooperation.

Chapter 2 (by Laurent Dobuzinskis), Chap. 3 (by Theodore H. Cohn), and Chap. 4 (by Norbert Gaillard and Rick Michalek) in this volume focus on the US to better identify the fundamental flaws of *finance* capitalism. The weaknesses identified—i.e., government failure, market failure, regulatory capture, and moral hazard—can affect other developed as well as emerging countries. Paradoxically, they can also affect state capitalist economies. China is an interesting case. We have not studied the Chinese regulatory framework because its idiosyncratic characteristics—e.g., the opacity and extreme politicisation of the decision-making processes—do not fit our willingness to advance solutions in order to restore *liberal* capitalist values. However, the Chinese political economy is equally crippled with government failure, regulatory capture, and moral hazard problems. Party, national, and local government leaders as well as regulators often exert influence to support specific business sectors or firms. In the meantime, the largest well-connected companies take advantage of implicit government guarantees to increase their leverage and risk-taking. The well-reported construction of "ghost towns" based on real estate speculation shows that Chinese companies are in no way immune to asset bubbles, regulatory capture, and moral hazard based on corruption, favouritism, and opaque financial reporting. All these dysfunctions undermine the credibility of policymakers, generate massive contingent liabilities, and weaken the long-term stability of the Chinese financial system (see Elliott and Yan 2013; Collier 2017). What is at stake here undoubtedly echoes the analyses of Dobuzinskis, Cohn, and Gaillard and Michalek of the US.

China and other emerging economies also have institutional constraints and less developed financial markets that limit effective regulation (Kawai and Prasad 2011). However, it is quite unsettling that US *finance* capitalism could have common features with Chinese *state* capitalism.[3] This suggests that the US financial system has been progressively perverted for the benefit of a few business oligarchies (see Lindsey and Teles 2017). Although our chapters do not pretend to be normative, we find that any significant divergence from critical values of *liberal* capitalism creates malinvestment, rent-seeking strategies, and unfair competitive advantages (frequently correlated with the size and the political connections of the

---

[3] See Kurlantzick (2016) for an exhaustive study of state capitalism.

economic players). The other chapters in this volume provide further evidence for this far-reaching conclusion.

Chapter 5 (by James Busumtwi-Sam) and Chap. 6 (by Anil Hira, Brian Murata, and Shea Monson) investigate how inadequate and sometimes non-existent national and international regulations can deprive governments and citizens of financial flows required for the public welfare. For example, the lack of cooperation and well-established rules at the international level prevents policymakers from controlling offshore finance, a cornerstone of tax evasion. This issue is challenging for all countries in the world, except for a few small tax havens (see Vlcek 2008). Tax evasion distorts economic, financial and tax relations between major companies and governments (Overesch and Rincke 2011). More concretely, free competition is biased (generally to the benefit of the unprincipled firms) and governments lose tax revenue.[4] When tax evasion scandals are publicised through the media and other sources (e.g., the Panama Papers and the Paradise Papers in 2016 and 2017, respectively), growing public anger and resentment can endanger democratic governments and nurture populism.

The poor regulation of remittance flows may be considered a limited problem, involving primarily low-income economies. This is an incorrect assumption, as capital flows across the North and the South are inextricably intertwined, including both remittances and capital flight. The challenges posed illustrate the lack of competition in the financial services area experienced by most developing and emerging countries. At a time when mobile finance services are booming (International Finance Corporation 2014), a new set of international rules is indispensable to address this issue. In the specific case of sub-Saharan African countries, redesigned regulations could be a key factor in the materialisation of an "African Renaissance" (Shaw and Nyang'oro 2000).

*   *   *

While observations in the literature about the growing dominance of the financial industry—dubbed the "financialisation" of the economy—are not off base, we lack relevant theories and instruments to create an

---

[4] This problem – especially acute in emerging countries, where it is more difficult to levy taxes – is reflected in the persistently low tax revenue to GDP ratios posted by the BRIC economies. See World Bank data, available at https://data.worldbank.org/indicator/GC.TAX.TOTL.GD.ZS

efficient regulatory landscape beyond the need to reduce the influence of lobbying firms. The decline of manufacturing in the West, the technological advances in production that accelerate labour supply/demand imbalances and the growing concentration of investment funds constitute long-term changes in economies. From globalisation to demographic ageing to the unprecedented migration of populations, any question of returning to the postwar forms of Keynesian-inspired regulation is moot. The development of new giants in the economy—such as Google, Apple, Facebook, and Amazon in the US, Baidu, Alibaba, and Tencent in China, and the disrupting companies such as Tesla, Uber, and AirBnB—mirrors fundamental shifts in technology leading to structural changes in the nature of production and employment.

A research agenda, then, should focus on the development of a third millennium financial regulatory system that embraces these fundamental changes in the financial landscape. This goes beyond creating greater regulatory autonomy, fairness, and ability to act in the interests of not only the financial industry, but all other industries and consumers who rely upon finance to keep transactions flowing throughout the economy. It should embrace the most structural aspects of the economy, such as globalisation. The absence of such an agenda explains the wholesale and largely directionless retreats of Trump, the Brexit vote and the increasing drift towards unilateralism and nationalism. The gaps our chapters reveal are thus only a partial reflection of the work that needs to be done. From government failure, market failure, regulatory capture, and moral hazard to inefficient regulations regarding remittance flows and offshore finance, there are major areas of neglect in the global financial architecture. As our analysis shows, the necessary process of regulatory renovation can only occur when a re-alignment of the political-industrial forces, for too long fixated on maintaining the status quo (essentially based on a light touch regulation and unconditional bailouts), takes place. Political economy research and advocacy are needed, now more than ever!

REFERENCES

Allen, Franklin, Itay Goldstein, and Julapa Jagtiani. 2018. The Interplay among Financial Regulations, Resilience, and Growth. *Journal of Financial Services Research*. 53(2–3): 141–162.

Avgouleas, Emilios. 2012. *Governance of Global Financial Markets: The Law, The Economics, The Politics.* International Corporate Law and Financial Market Regulation. Cambridge and New York City: Cambridge University Press.

Bell, Stephen and Andrew Hindmoor. 2017. Are the major global banks now safer? Structural continuities and change in banking and finance since the 2008 crisis. *Review of International Political Economy.* 25(1): 1–27.

Bernanke, Ben S. 2011. *The Effects of the Great Recession on Central Bank Doctrine and Practice.* Speech by Ben S. Bernanke, Chairman of the Board of Governors of the Federal Reserve System, at the Federal Reserve Bank of Boston 56th Economic Conference, Boston, Massachusetts. October 18.

Broder, Jonathan. 2018. Financial Services Deregulation: Should Congress ease up on Wall Street? *CQ Researcher* Apr. 6, 28:13.

Buchanan, James M. and Richard E. Wagner. 1977. *Democracy in Deficit: The Political Legacy of Lord Keynes.* New York: Academic Press.

Buckley, Ross P. 2016. The Changing Nature of Banking and Why It Matters, 9–27 in Ross P. Buckley, Emilios Avgouleas, and Douglas W. Arner (Eds.). *Reconceptualising Global Finance and Its Regulation.* Cambridge and New York City: Cambridge University Press.

Busch, Andreas. 2009. *Banking Regulation and Globalization.* New York: Oxford University Press.

Buttiglione, Luigi, Philip R. Lane, Lucrezia Reichlin, and Vincent Reinhart. 2014. Deleveraging? What Deleveraging? *Geneva Reports on the World Economy, No. 16.*

Collier, Andrew. 2017. *Shadow Banking and the Rise of Capitalism in China.* Singapore: Palgrave Macmillan.

Duffie, Darrell. 2018. Financial Regulatory Reform After the Crisis: An Assessment. *Management Science.* 64(10): 4835–4857.

Editorial Board. 2018. Fed Makes a Risky Bet on Banks. *New York Times,* June 1.

Elliott, Douglas J. and Kai Yan. 2013. The Chinese Financial System: An Introduction and Overview. *John L. Thornton China Center Monograph Series, No. 6.*

European Parliament. 2017. Implications of Brexit on EU Financial Services. Directorate-General for Internal Policies, Policy Dept. Report IP/A/Econ 2016-22. Brussels: European Parliament.

Flitter, Emily and Alan Rappeport. 2018. Bankers Hate the Volcker Rule. Now, It Could Be Watered Down. *New York Times,* May 21.

Hemerijck, Anton. 2013. *Changing Welfare States.* Oxford: Oxford University Press.

Herring, Richard J. 2018. The Evolving Complexity of Capital Regulation. *Journal of Financial Services Research.* 53(2–3): 183–205.

International Finance Corporation. 2014. Mobile Financial Services: Its Role in Banks and in the Market, available at https://www.ifc.org/wps/wcm/connec

t/5e24430042b925809415bc0dc33b630b/M-Banking_Workshop_ Presentation_Jan28-2014_ENG.pdf?MOD=AJPERES

Kalaitzake, Manolis. 2017. Death by a Thousand Cuts? Financial Political Power and the Case of the European Financial Transaction Tax. *New Political Economy*. 22(6): 709–726.

Kawai, Masahiro and Eswar S. Prasad (Eds.). 2011. *Financial Market Regulation and Reforms in Emerging Markets*. Tokyo and Washington, DC: Asian Development Bank and Brookings Institution Press.

Keaney, Michael. 2017. The Aftermath of the Financial Crisis: Continuity and Little Change. *Political Studies Review*. 15(1): 6–17.

Keller, Eileen. 2018. Noisy business politics: lobbying strategies and business influence after the financial crisis. *Journal of European Public Policy*. 25(3): 287–306.

Kurlantzick, Joshua. 2016. *State Capitalism: How the Return of Statism is Transforming the World*. New York: Oxford University Press.

Lindsey, Brink and Steven M. Teles. 2017. *The Captured Economy*. New York: Oxford University Press.

Lo, Andrew W. 2012. Reading about the Financial Crisis: A Twenty-One-Book Review. *Journal of Economic Literature*. 50(1): 151–178.

Mayntz, Renate. 2012. Institutional Change in the Regulation of Financial Markets: Questions and Answers, 7–28. In Mayntz (Ed.). *Crisis and Control: Institutional Change in Financial Market Regulation*. New York: Campus Verlag.

Overesch, Michael and Johannes Rincke. 2011. What Drives Corporate Tax Rates Down? A Reassessment of Globalization, Tax Competition, and Dynamic Adjustment to Shocks. *Scandinavian Journal of Economics*. 113(3): 579–602.

Quaglia, Lucia and Aneta Spendzharova. 2017. Post-crisis reforms in banking: Regulators at the interface between domestic and international governance. *Regulation & Governance*. 11(4): 422–437.

Rancière, Romain, Aaron Tornell, and Frank Westermann. 2008. Systemic Crises and Growth. *Quarterly Journal of Economics*. 123(1): 359–406.

Rappeport, Alan and Emily Flitter. 2018. Congress Approves First Big Dodd-Frank Rollback. *New York Times*, May 22.

Reinhart, Carmen and Kenneth Rogoff. 2009. *This Time is Different: Eight Centuries of Financial Folly*. Princeton: Princeton University Press.

Santoro, Michael A. and Ronald J. Strauss. 2013. *Wall Street Values: Business Ethics and the Global Financial Crisis*. Cambridge and New York City: Cambridge University Press.

Shaw, Timothy M. and Julius E. Nyang'oro. 2000. African Renaissance in the New Millennium? From Anarchy to Emerging Markets? *African Journal of Political Science/Revue Africaine de Science Politique*. 5(1): 14–28.

Turner, Adair. 2016. *Between Debt and the Devil – Money, Credit, and Fixing Global Finance*. Princeton: Princeton University Press.

Vasudev, P. M. 2016. Financial Misconduct, Ethical Theory, and Regulatory Ethics – Promoting Accountability. *Journal of Business, Entrepreneurship & the Law*. 9(1): 93–128.

Vlcek, William. 2008. *Offshore Finance and Small States: Sovereignty, Size and Money*. International Political Economy Series. Houndmills (UK) and New York: Palgrave Macmillan.

Werner, Erica and Damian Paletta. 2018. 10 years after financial crisis, Senate prepares to roll back banking rules. Mar. 4. Found at: www.washingtonpost.com [accessed May 10, 2018].

Williamson, John. 1989. What Washington Means by Policy Reform. 7–20. In Williamson, John (Ed.). *Latin American Readjustment: How Much Has Happened*. Washington: Institute for International Economics.

INDEX[1]

A

Austerity, 6, 16, 21, 51, 59, 234

Austrian economics approach, 37–42, 37n1, 50, 52, 53, 57, 64

Avi-Yonah, Reuven S., 214

B

Bailout, 3–7, 9, 11, 13, 18, 21, 27, 55, 59, 87, 115, 123, 132, 136, 141, 141n50, 142, 144, 233, 235, 243

Bank for International Settlements (BIS), 93, 132, 171, 180, 185

Banking deregulation, 6, 11, 16, 19, 24, 25, 27, 29, 38, 41, 48, 50, 51, 61, 64, 72, 73, 76–81, 83–87, 90–93, 101, 102, 105, 122, 140, 235, 240

Banking regulation, 29, 71, 72, 93, 99, 101, 103, 234

Base erosion
loss of taxes, 211, 217

Basel Committee on Banking Supervision (BCBS), 93

Basel I Accord, 44, 57n23, 94

Basel II agreement, 62, 94–102, 104

Basel III, 62, 94, 98–100, 102–104

Bernanke, Ben, 42, 129, 137, 137n43, 138, 234

Born, Brooksley, 9, 81

Bretton Woods, 9, 9n3, 111, 115

Brexit, 10, 12, 223, 237, 243

Bubble, 4, 5, 7–9, 11, 13–15, 19, 21, 43, 44, 46, 57, 64, 80–83, 100, 137, 138, 226, 238, 241

Buchanan, James, 53, 55, 56, 234

Bush, George Walker
Bush Administration policies, 44, 59, 77

---

[1] Note: Page numbers followed by 'n' refer to notes.

© The Author(s) 2019

A. Hira et al. (eds.), *The Failure of Financial Regulation*, International Political Economy Series, https://doi.org/10.1007/978-3-030-05680-3

C

Canadian banking system
  vs. US, 49, 49n11, 58n25
Captive insurance
  for tax evasion, 208
Carpenter, Daniel, 73–76, 86, 92, 100
Charities
  for tax evasion, 197, 204, 205
China effect on financial markets, 7, 8,
  22, 23, 26, 196, 239, 241
Clinton, William Jefferson
  Clinton Administration policies, 48,
  77, 84, 87
Cohen, Benjamin J., 7, 9, 10, 220n3
Commodity Futures Trading
  Commission (CFTC), 9, 61, 81,
  92, 125, 145
Common Reporting Standard (CRS)
  for tax harmonisation, 210–211, 219
Conflicts of interest, 2, 18, 27, 29,
  132n36, 133, 192, 222
Constitutionalisation, of banking
  system, *see* Public choice approach
Consumer Financial Protection Bureau
  (CFPB), 83, 85, 130, 235, 236
Continental Illinois, 7, 114–117, 116n9
Credit default swaps, 81, 105, 130,
  131n34, 207
Credit rating agencies, 7, 18, 19, 29,
  44–45, 52, 88–90, 97, 101–103,
  118n11, 119, 123–139, 123n16,
  124n20, 131n35, 135n40, 144,
  145
Crotty, James, 19
Cryptocurrencies, 10, 23, 26, 54, 192,
  194, 216

D

Debt, 6, 7, 13, 15, 16, 19, 21, 29, 31,
  41, 43, 44, 46, 47, 54, 59, 63,
  64, 72, 80, 88, 99, 111–113,

113n2, 115–117, 120–122,
  126n26, 127, 128, 132, 134,
  135, 138, 141–144, 160n5, 176,
  193, 207, 238
Disintermediation, 113, 113n1
Dodd-Frank financial reform Act, 21,
  25, 45, 60, 61n26–28, 83–85,
  87, 90, 102, 105, 127, 127n29,
  127n30, 130, 135, 140, 181,
  222, 235, 236, 240
Drezner, Daniel, 19

E

European banking reforms, 62
European Central Bank (ECB), 56,
  59, 60, 63

F

Fannie Mae and Freddie Mac, 66
  government-backed mortgage
  security companies, 44
FDI, *see* Foreign direct investment
Federal Deposit Insurance
  Corporation (FDIC), 5, 7, 25,
  48, 48n10, 78, 80, 115, 115n6,
  116, 116n9, 124, 125, 129,
  129n32, 236
Federal Reserve, 4, 5, 20, 29, 40, 42,
  43, 46, 48, 49, 52, 53n17,
  57n23, 60, 61, 77–79, 82, 91,
  94–96, 111, 112, 116, 124–139,
  137n42, 137n43, 138n46,
  139n47, 146
Finance capitalism, 2n1, 12, 29, 111,
  113, 121, 233, 241
Financial Action Task Force (FATF),
  171, 172, 172n10, 179n13,
  209–210, 216–218, 222
Financial gatekeepers, 27, 29, 114,
  123, 124, 133, 142, 145

Financial innovation, 6, 7, 10, 15,
    15n5, 19, 23, 29, 77, 83, 95,
    114, 120, 123, 125
Financialisation
  growing dominance of financial
    sector, 5, 17, 113, 117, 242
Financial Stability Board (FSB), 17,
    17n6, 22, 237
Foreign Account Tax Compliance Act
    (FATCA)
  US tax evasion measure, 210, 211,
    218, 219, 225
Foreign direct investment (FDI),
    156–158, 160, 196, 197, 199,
    200
Foundations
  for tax evasion, 146, 202–204, 210,
    212, 213, 223, 225
Free banking, 53–55, 57, 63

G
Gerding, Erik, 57
Glass-Steagall, 5, 25, 29, 48, 61,
    61n28, 78–80, 84, 87, 128, 141,
    142
Global financial contagion, 7, 15, 94
Global financial regulatory institutions,
    9, 10
Goldman Sachs, 84, 87, 92, 123, 128,
    235
Gold Standard
  adoption of, in the US, 3
Government failure, 2, 28, 38–40, 42,
    43, 45, 47, 48, 50, 63–65, 73,
    77, 125n22, 241, 243
Gramm-Leach-Bliley Act, 48, 80, 122,
    128
Great Moderation, 8, 28, 43
Greenspan, Alan, 8, 9, 28, 42, 46,
    77–84, 86, 92, 96, 101, 137,
    137n43, 235

H
Helleiner, Eric, 20, 22, 75, 83, 87, 90,
    99, 102, 140
Housing bubble, 7, 9, 15, 22, 44, 46

I
IMF, see International Monetary
    Fund
Inequality, 17, 19, 26, 142, 163, 165,
    168, 193, 226
Institute for International Finance
    (IIF), 94–100, 102
International Consortium of
    Investigative Journalists (ICIJ),
    191
International Monetary Fund (IMF),
    9n3, 10, 59, 120, 132, 160, 163,
    166, 185, 211, 238
International Swaps and Derivatives
    Association (ISDA), 96, 97, 100,
    130, 131n34
Investment banking, 11, 48, 72, 78,
    80, 85, 118, 123, 129
Irrational exuberance
  effect on financial markets, 4, 5, 22,
    47, 80

J
Japanese regulation, 62
JP Morgan
  financial house, influence on policy,
    11, 79, 84, 92, 102, 114, 128

K
Keynesian
  based on the work of John Maynard
    Keynes, 5, 6, 13, 16, 19, 21,
    24, 25, 38, 43, 47, 58, 59,
    193, 222, 243

Kindleberger, Charles, 5, 23, 80
King, Mervyn, 43, 47, 54, 55, 63,
    125n23
Krugman, Paul, 16, 48

L

Lehman Brothers, 11, 46, 98, 128,
    129, 138n46, 233
Lender of last resort, 23, 55, 60, 115,
    238
Leverage, 7, 13, 19, 20, 26, 30, 43, 54,
    61, 62, 99, 104, 114n5, 124, 129,
    136, 137, 142, 153, 154, 160,
    163, 173, 174, 176, 186, 241
Liberal capitalism, 2, 2n1, 27, 31,
    140, 164n7, 241
Liquidity
    as part of post-crash reforms, 3, 4,
        6, 15, 17n6, 22, 55, 59–61, 99,
        120n13, 123n17, 138, 172,
        235, 238
Long-Term Capital Management
    (LTCM), 8

M

Malinvestment, 28, 43, 44, 46, 50, 241
Mallaby, Sebastian, 77–79, 81
Market failure, 2, 28, 38, 39, 45, 47,
    50, 65, 73, 76, 156, 168, 169,
    169n9, 177, 241, 243
Marshall, Alfred, 39
Menger, Carl, 37n1, 42
Minsky, Hyman, 28, 47, 47n9, 80, 146
Monetary policy, 4, 6, 8, 9, 13, 37–66,
    49n12, 85, 124n19, 136, 137,
    139, 139n47, 146
Money laundering, 154, 155, 161,
    162, 169, 172, 172n10, 173,
    175, 198, 204, 205, 208, 209,
    215–217, 219

Moral hazard, 2–7, 9–11, 20–23, 29,
    31, 48, 60, 72, 80, 87, 111–146,
    113n3, 140n49, 164, 164n7,
    192, 241, 243
Moss, David, 73–76, 86, 92, 100
Mulvaney, Mick, 85

N

Nationally Recognized Statistical
    Rating Organizations (NRSROs),
    see Credit rating agencies
Neoliberalism, 13, 16, 19, 24, 25, 66,
    139, 163, 194, 234, 239, 240
Neomercantilism, 25
1929 crash, 5

O

Obama, Barack Hussein
    Obama Administration policies, 9,
        16, 51, 59, 84, 87, 88, 90, 92,
        127n30, 236
OECD Model Income Tax
    Convention, 194
Office of the Comptroller of the
    Currency (OCC), 125, 130, 131,
    236
Official Development Assistance
    (ODA), 153, 156–158, 162
Offshore banking, 6
Offshore finance
    estimates, 196
Offshore financial havens, 162,
    191–226
Olson, Mancur, 195
Organisation for Economic
    Co-operation and Development
    (OECD), 30, 47, 192, 194–196,
    204, 205, 209–211, 214, 217,
    223
Origins of US banking system, 3

P

Panama Papers, 10, 23, 30, 119,
    191–226, 242
    Mossack Fonseca, 191, 200, 221
Polanyi, Karl, 24, 26
Populist response, 1, 2, 12
Post-Keynesian, 41, 43, 46, 47, 50,
    51, 58, 59, 62, 234
    heterodox, 41
Powell, Jerome, 53n17, 84, 85, 92, 129
Private capital flows (PCF)
    contrast to remittances, 153, 154,
        156, 158, 160
Public choice approach, 37, 38, 50,
    52, 55
Putnam, Robert, 195

Q

Quantitative easing (QE), 9, 60, 137

R

Reagan, Ronald Wilson
    Reagan Administration policies,
        77–79, 84
Regulatory capture, 2, 7, 9–11, 18,
    20, 21, 25, 29, 58, 71–76, 79,
    86, 87, 89, 92, 93, 95–102, 104,
    105, 125, 125n22, 174n11, 192,
    195, 235, 236, 241, 243
    cultural capture, 74, 75, 79, 80, 86,
        90–92, 95, 100, 101, 141
    hard capture, 74, 102
    material capture, 74, 75, 86, 88–91,
        97, 101, 103
    regulatory capture theory, 29, 72,
        79, 87, 98, 99, 101
    soft capture, 74, 103
Reinhart, Carmen and Kenneth
    Rogoff, 4, 10, 14, 43, 72, 91,
    233

Remittances, 10, 22, 23, 27, 28, 30,
    115n7, 153–185, 156n2, 159n3,
    160n5, 179n13, 182n15, 192,
    242, 243
    definition, 156
    diaspora relations to, 155, 156, 160,
        160n5, 161, 161n6, 163, 169,
        172, 174–177, 185
    estimates of, 158, 159, 161
    and financial exclusion, 30, 155,
        169–173, 181–183
    and financial sector development,
        167–169
    and money transfer operators
        (MTOs), 27, 115n7, 172–175,
        174n11, 181, 182, 184
    optimistic view, 163, 165–167
    pessimistic view, 164
    recommendations for reform,
        184–185
Ruggie, John Gerard, 25, 26

S

Savings Taxation Directive
    EU measure for tax transparency,
        211–213
Securities and Exchange Commission
    (SEC), 18, 45, 48, 52, 78, 88,
    90, 92, 93, 125–130, 126n24,
    126n26, 126n27, 127n28,
    127n30, 133, 135, 145
Securitization, 7, 15, 17–19, 22, 44,
    122–123
Shadow banking, 4, 20, 26, 45, 45n7,
    105, 234, 237, 238
Sharman, J.C., 20, 212, 215–217
Shell corporation, 196, 200, 201, 219
Sinclair, Timothy, 19, 88, 131n35
Sovereign wealth funds, 7
Stigler, George, 73, 125, 125n22
Stiglitz, Joseph, 14, 16, 78, 122

Stimulus, 5, 13, 16, 21, 50, 59, 60, 165, 193, 234
Structured finance, xix, 18, 88, 103, 114n5, 119, 121, 122, 126, 127, 130, 131, 133, 133n38, 135, 234
Subprime mortgages, 11, 15, 44, 82, 83, 88, 89, 97, 127, 129, 134, 137
Summers, Larry, 9, 81, 142
Sustainable Development Goals (SDGs), 162, 175, 176
Systemic risk, 17, 29, 43, 46, 52, 60, 83, 99, 113–115, 113n3, 113n4, 123, 136, 140–142, 145, 236, 238

T
Tax evasion, 21, 27, 30, 161, 162, 191–193, 195, 196, 198, 200, 204, 205, 210, 211, 218, 222, 223, 225, 242
  by MNCs, 196, 197, 201
  by terrorists, 197
Tax Information Exchange Agreement (TIEA), 209–210, 218, 221
Tax Justice Network (TJN), 198, 203, 217, 224
Terrorist Finance Tracking Program (TFTP), 215
Too big to fail, 4, 7, 10, 14, 16, 22, 29, 52, 62, 83, 93, 113–124, 114n5, 129, 131, 137, 139–143, 146, 238

Transfer pricing, 162, 205, 206, 208, 211, 214, 217, 221, 224
Trump, Donald John
  Trump Administration policies, 2, 12, 25, 26, 40, 51, 53n17, 61, 64, 83–86, 92, 102, 105, 195, 223, 235, 236, 239, 240, 243
Trusts
  for tax evasion, 4, 202–204, 212, 213, 218, 220, 222
2008 financial crisis, 1, 2, 15, 20, 24, 25, 27, 29–31, 50, 59, 72, 73, 76, 77, 80–83, 86, 88, 90, 92–94, 98, 100–104, 153, 154, 158, 185, 198, 207, 233, 237, 240

V
Volcker, Paul, 78–79, 92, 101, 112
Volcker Rule
  proposed reform, 17, 60–62, 78, 83, 236, 237
von Hayek, Friedrich August, 28, 37n1, 53, 54, 58
von Mises, Ludwig, 37n1, 42

Y
Yellen, Janet, 42, 84, 85, 138, 139
Young, Kevin, 74, 96, 97, 100

CPSIA information can be obtained
at www.ICGtesting.com
Printed in the USA
LVHW081814050519
616713LV00007B/498/P

9 783030 056797